Penguin Critical Studies

A Portrait of the Artist as a

John Blades was educated at Manchester University. He is at present engaged on research in the work of James Joyce, and is a lecturer in English at Cleveland College, Redcar.

Penguin Critical Studies
Advisory Editor: Bryan Loughrey

James Joyce

A Portrait of the Artist as a Young Man

John Blades

Penguin Books

PENGUIN BOOKS

Published by the Penguin Group
Penguin Books Ltd, 27 Wrights Lane, London W8 5TZ, England
Viking Penguin, a division of Penguin Books USA Inc.
375 Hudson Street, New York, New York 10014, USA
Penguin Books Australia Ltd, Ringwood, Victoria, Australia
Penguin Books Canada Ltd, 2801 John Street, Markham, Ontario, Canada L3R 1B4
Penguin Books (NZ) Ltd, 182–190 Wairau Road, Auckland 10, New Zealand

Penguin Books Ltd, Registered Offices: Harmondsworth, Middlesex, England

First published 1991
10 9 8 7 6 5 4 3 2 1

Copyright © John Blades, 1991
All rights reserved

The moral right of the author has been asserted

Filmset in 9/11 pt Monophoto Times
Printed in England by Clays Ltd, St Ives plc

For my mother and father

Contents

Acknowledgements

For permission to use copyright material thanks are due to the following: the executors of the James Joyce Estate and Jonathan Cape for *A Portrait of the Artist as a Young Man*, *Stephen Hero*, and *Dubliners*; the Bodley Head for *Ulysses*; Faber & Faber Limited for *My Brother's Keeper* by Stanislaus Joyce, *Letters of James Joyce* (eds. Gilbert and Ellmann), *The Critical Writings of James Joyce* (eds. Mason and Ellmann) and *Finnegans Wake*; the estate of Virginia Woolf and The Hogarth Press for *Moments of Being* and *Collected Essays*; and Wayne C. Booth and The University of Chicago Press for *The Rhetoric of Fiction*.

A Note on the Text

All page references to *A Portrait* are to the hardback edition published by Jonathan Cape, the Definitive Text corrected from the Dublin Holograph by Chester G. Anderson and edited by Richard Ellmann.

Page references to other works by Joyce are to the following editions: *Dubliners*, Grafton, 1987; *Stephen Hero*, Grafton, 1989; *Ulysses*, (The Corrected Text), Bodley Head, 1986; *Finnegans Wake*, Faber & Faber, 1989.

Letters I, II, III: *Letters of James Joyce*, (3 vols.) edited by Stuart Gilbert and Richard Ellmann, Faber & Faber, 1957 and 1966.

Ellmann: *James Joyce*, Richard Ellmann, Oxford University Press, 1982 (revised edition).

1. James Joyce and Ireland: Backgrounds to *A Portrait*

Anyhow, somehow and somewhere, before the bookflood or after her ebb, somebody mentioned by name in his telephone directory, Coccolanius or Gallotaurus, wrote it, wrote it all, wrote it all down, and there you are, full stop.

(*Finnegans Wake*, p. 118)

Joyce's life and family[1]

Until the last years of his life, and even in the depths of the most profound poverty, James Joyce always took care to preserve a set of oil portraits of his forebears, lugging them from one temporary address to another. Like Stephen in *A Portrait*, he was deeply conscious and deeply proud of his ancestry:

—Come with me now to the office of arms and I will show you the tree of my family . . . (p. 206)

And earlier in the novel, as the Dedalus family is about to make a 'sudden' removal of their furniture, the family portraits are conspicuously in readiness for flight (p. 67). Whether photograph, sketch or painting, the portrait took on a magical significance for Joyce. And the family portraits could be relied upon as a tangible connection with the keenly felt past, a contact with the constant and stable amidst the turmoil of the Joyce family's frequent upheavals.

Like Stephen Dedalus's, James Joyce's immediate predecessors on his father's side were from the city of Cork in the south of Ireland. It was there that they had made a modest fortune as minor but prosperous businessmen and there that they had lived in comfortable, middle-class, suburban tranquillity founded on the profits from their local property. Joyce's father John Stanislaus Joyce, a Cork man, was widely renowned as a student for his tenor voice and outstanding sporting and theatrical performances, pursued to the detriment of his academic studies – until, with the early death of his father, his immediate future was secured and at the age of 21 he became heir to the family's Cork properties. Overnight, he became what he had always desired, a man of leisure, independent, at last free to indulge his fancy. A headstrong and vigorous young thruster, he also dabbled on the edge of Fenian political activities and

1

only his mother's obstinacy prevented him running over to France on an impulse to join in the Franco-Prussian War.

In about 1875 the family moved north to Dublin where John Joyce quickly settled, exercising to the full his interests in sailing and singing. Here too, he became well known for his voice and, as a popular tenor, he appeared regularly in local concerts. Yet, though he had inherited the family properties and income, he had not inherited his predecessors' business acumen and one venture to set up a distillery in Dublin ended in characteristic disaster when a friend and partner absconded with the liquid assets, leaving the company bankrupt.

However short of funds, he was never short of influential friends and, by pulling a few of the right strings, he was appointed secretary of the United Liberal Club, which supported Home Rule for Ireland. Later, as a result of his successful efforts in the General Election of April 1880, John Joyce was awarded a permanent and relatively undemanding post in the office of the Collector of Rates for Dublin.[2] In addition to the prestige of the appointment, it also afforded him the more tangible opportunity to wed Mary Murray, daughter of a wines-and-spirits agent who had formerly had some dealings with John Joyce's ill-starred distillery. So, although John himself could not abide the rest of the Murray family (of whom he was freely contemptuous), and in spite of their disapproval of the match, the marriage took place on 5 May 1880. However, his mother, who had resolutely objected to the marriage (on the grounds that the Murrays were beneath him) refused to attend and promptly returned to Cork, where she died not long after.

The Joyces now set up home in fashionable Kingstown (Dun Laoghaire) on the sea just to the south of Dublin, at a distance calculated to dissuade any of the Murrays from paying them regular visits – though John, a hearty, congenial man, always encouraged his friends to visit, especially at weekends. In time, however, the couple returned to live in Dublin where, on 2 February 1882, Mary Joyce gave birth to James Augustine, their second child (the first did not survive). Over the next eleven years there was hardly a time when she was not pregnant, giving birth to a further three boys and six girls. On the other hand, the antithesis to this fecundity was the spiralling decline of the family fortune as, swiftly, one after another of their properties was mortgaged off and, like the Dedaluses in *A Portrait*, they were continually forced to move addresses in an attempt to keep at least one step ahead of the rent collector and the bailiff.

However, when James Joyce was born his parents' circumstances were still very prosperous and later, at their home in Bray, his father was still able to indulge his twin passions for sailing and generous hospitality, the latter of which his son so vividly captures in the Christmas dinner episode of the first chapter of *A Portrait*. The rapidly expanding family was joined too by James's granduncle, William O'Connell, who had come up from Cork and whose characteristic mildness and paternalism towards James also find their way into the novel in the form of Uncle Charles (with a similar habit of smoking black-twist pipe-tobacco – 'such villainous awful tobacco').

Throughout all of his work Joyce drew closely on his friends and relatives as source material for characters, and two other key figures in Chapter 1 of *A Portrait* are also modelled on people from Joyce's own childhood at this time. One of these, John Kelly, was a very popular and colourful figure, a cunning Fenian rebel with a shady, lawless background who had served a series of prison sentences for political agitation, a direct consequence of which was that three of his fingers were permanently cramped from picking oakum (see p. 28). The counterweight to such an unconventional moral influence was provided by the other prominent figure in the Joyce childhood home, Mrs 'Dante' Conway who came to live with the family as a sort of governess to James. A fiercely religious and embittered woman, she had abandoned her convent training after inheriting her brother's vast fortune, accumulated through exploiting the African 'savages' (p. 36). Soon after her marriage, however, her husband deserted her, taking her considerable fortune with him to South America.

Mrs Conway acted as James's governess only briefly for, in the autumn of 1888, his parents packed him off to one of the best Jesuit colleges in Ireland: Clongowes Wood College at Sallins in County Kildare. An imposing edifice, centred on a rebuilt medieval castle and associated with historic Irish patriots, it was and still is a staunchly conservative, highly regarded institution whose curriculum included 'sums', spelling, writing, geography, history, and the rudiments of Latin. Yet, although it was run on the lines of an English public school the study of the Roman Catholic religion was the most important subject – and the Jesuit influence was to remain with Joyce throughout the rest of his life. On entry, Joyce was six and a half years of age (or 'half past six' as he described himself) much less than the normal age for admissions and being so young he was given a room to himself in the college infirmary rather than the dormitory, so that the nurse could keep an eye on him.

In general his time at the college appears to have been a happy one –

in contrast to Stephen Dedalus's – though he often felt acutely self-conscious about his social inferiority compared to the other boys.[3] Like Stephen though, Joyce was bony, weak of sight and nervous, and as the youngest boy in the school he suffered in his first few months from the ragging of the older boys. A particularly memorable bullying however was not at the hands of fellow pupils but one of the masters, Father James Daly. The incident is described in painful detail in the opening chapter of *A Portrait* in which, like Joyce, Stephen has his glasses broken by another boy and is then unjustly beaten and humiliated by the prefect of studies, Father 'Baldyhead' Dolan of the novel. In *A Portrait* Stephen later reflects on this 'pandying' as the only punishment he had received at the college (p. 159) – another contrast with Joyce's own career since in reality Joyce himself was far less virtuous and received more regular punishment, including on one occasion for his use of 'vulgar language' . . . at the age of seven!

During his time at Clongowes Wood Joyce had also begun to distinguish himself as an exceptional scholar, especially in English and Latin (in one year he came first in all Ireland in English composition), but unlike the serious, stiffly academic Stephen of the novel, he was remembered for his quick sense of fun and, while in the Third Line, he followed in his father's theatrical footsteps by taking the part of an 'imp' in the college's annual farce. Nevertheless, by the spring of 1891 his father could no longer afford to keep him at the college and he withdrew at the end of the term. Joyce always remembered with great affection his time at Clongowes Wood and even after shedding his faith he continued to respect his Jesuit teachers as most accomplished and skilled professionals.

In the following year the Joyce fortunes took a further, steeper plunge when, as a result of reorganization, Dublin Corporation took over the Rates office and John Joyce lost his privileged position as a rate collector. In fact, there had been some doubts in the past about his efficiency in this post and, coupled with a reputation for free drinking, the upshot was that he was made redundant, at first without compensation and then after appeal (and some more string-pulling) he was granted a modest annual pension. Yet, in spite of this, Joyce's father was both unable and unwilling to adjust his style of living to fit his newly reduced circumstances and the family's decline into poverty was inevitably accelerated, paralleled over the next few years by a series of hasty removals. Still, though materially bereft, the old man always liked to maintain the pretence of outward dignity – a point which led Joyce to euphemistically describe this home background as 'shabby genteel'.

Joyce's place at Clongowes Wood had become another victim of this inexorable decline. After a short break in his education he was sent to the Christian Brothers' school on the north side of Dublin. The family had now resettled in the city but, unable to afford a good Jesuit school, his father's pride and snobbery at first refused to send his son to the Christian Brothers and Joyce himself regarded his brief experience at the school as inferior to that with the Jesuits and a time which he preferred to forget – in *A Portrait* Mr Dedalus haughtily scorns the Brothers as 'Paddy Stink and Mickey Mud' (p. 73), and in Chapter 4 considers them as simple and honest but common.

However, nearly two years after leaving Clongowes Wood Joyce was back among the Jesuits when, on 6 April 1893, he was entered as a new boy aged eleven at Belvedere College, Dublin. His acceptance at the school had been the direct result of his father's chance meeting with Father John Conmee, former rector of Clongowes Wood College and now prefect of studies at Belvedere, and Conmee generously allowed both James and his brother Stanislaus to attend without payment of the usual college fees – affirmation of James's academic prowess and his father's skilful eloquence.

At Belvedere, the Jesuit system was based on the same principles as his previous college and Joyce settled quickly. Although he made no close friends here, he was well liked by the other boys who relied on him to cod the teachers and win half-day holidays. His intellect flowered and he was soon famed for his essay-writing in particular, for which he won several monetary prizes, such as in the 1894 all-Ireland Inter-mediate Examinations where Joyce won one of the top prizes, an exhibition of £20 (which he also won again in 1895 and 1897). Like Stephen Dedalus (in Chapter 2), he used the money to treat his parents to theatre trips and to lavish meals in expensive Dublin restaurants, showing that if he had inherited something of his father's eloquence he had also something of his financial profligacy. The prizes reflected his strength in most school subjects, with a special aptitude for English and languages – only chemistry proved a persistent obstacle (and who could blame him?). But, as well as proving himself a boy of exceptional scholastic ability, Joyce also took an active part in other areas of school life, being elected prefect of the Sodality of the Blessed Virgin Mary and taking to the boards in several school plays. In one of the Whit-suntide plays Joyce was cast in the part of 'farcical pedagogue' (p. 75) and he used the occasion to impersonate to great and popular effect the style of the college rector, Father Henry, who warmly appreciated the joke (it is important not to identify Joyce too closely with Stephen

Dedalus, and this readiness to play practical jokes is one aspect which distinguishes him from his more sober creation).

If Joyce's star was in the ascendant then his father's was moving as swiftly as possible in the opposite direction for while Joyce's course at school was one of progress and blossoming, at home his father's was one of unrelenting decline, the last of the Cork properties having now been sold to meet debts. But for Joyce himself changes were imminent. Though he had come to be regarded at Belvedere as a boy of exemplary moral standing, a possible candidate for the priesthood, with the onset of puberty there appeared on the horizon new challenges to his piety. His brother Stanislaus recalls their frequent truancies about this time as well as the occasion of James's first precocious flirtation with a maid servant, in itself an innocent encounter but the prelude to a more significant turning point in his sexual development. Aged fourteen, returning one night from the theatre, Joyce encountered a prostitute on the canal bank and, succumbing to her seductive charms and his own passion, had his first experience of sexual intercourse. A similar episode in *A Portrait* (though in a more conducive setting) leads to agonies of conscience and guilt, exactly as Joyce himself had suffered pangs of remorse and shame, being aroused by a similar religious retreat at Belvedere shortly after. Like Stephen's reformation Joyce's too was temporary, and led eventually to his rejection of the priesthood and ultimately to the loss of his faith itself.

Meanwhile, his maturity as a writer was making promising advances. He continued to win prizes for his essays, wrote for the college magazine and experimented in both prose and verse. He was a fast and voracious reader, his tastes embracing all types of literature, though he became especially interested in the work of the Norwegian dramatist, Henrik Ibsen. His social life, however, was limited to friends of the family and he tended to keep to himself, an extension of his drive towards independence of mind. On the other hand, like his father he had a good singing voice and his talent to entertain was always in demand, especially at the home of his close friends the Sheehys (the convivial atmosphere of their evenings is sketched in the novel, pp. 70 and 223), and Mary Sheehy in particular, the object of James's secret worship and the model for 'E.C.' in the novel.[4] Her sisters called him 'Farouche' – fierce and wild – on account of his energy but also his untidy appearance. His own musical preference was for Irish comic and sentimental pieces but like Stephen Dedalus he had a weakness for the songs of Elizabethan composers such as Dowland. The young James Joyce was also as famed for his lively wit as for his singing at these gatherings and could usually be relied upon to inject ingenious word plays and practical jokes into their games.

As his time at Belvedere College came to an end Joyce found himself more and more in conflict with the disciplines and demands of his teachers and with the ethos on which the college itself was based. His potential 'destiny' was becoming more clearly understood (the novel focuses sharply on this in Chapter 4) and Joyce clearly identified religious servitude as chief among a number of obstacles to achieving it. His career now becomes one of increasing alienation from the doctrines of the Catholic Church.

In 1898 Joyce found himself in a vigorous, new, intellectual milieu as he left Belvedere to enter University College, Dublin. The first Catholic university in Ireland, it had been founded in 1853 by an English convert, John Cardinal Newman, and after struggling for almost thirty years to finance and establish itself it had merged with the Royal University. However, though a Catholic institution, the university was permitted to offer only a secular curriculum and for many years it lived in the shadow of the more prestigious Anglo-Irish Trinity College, which catered almost exclusively for the sons of the Protestant ascendancy. Yet for Joyce it was a far from ideal step – the students did not live in and it was also run by the Jesuits, so he was still having to come to terms with both the Church, to which he was increasingly hostile, and his family, on whom he was still firmly dependent for his upkeep.

After the academic distinctions achieved at Belvedere, Joyce's career at University College was now a distinct anticlimax, though it did allow him some freedom for self-expression. He was growing into a tall and assertive young man, unkempt, with a reputation for abstract idealization in his writings. For a time he studied English but his main interests were devoted to modern languages, Italian and French principally. However, in his first year he made a determined effort to apply himself conscientiously to his studies and he achieved his best result – a second-class honours in Latin. But his enthusiasm for college was on the wane. Restlessness for change was an increasing diversion and he began to seek new outlets to engage his powerfully developing intellectual and creative interests outside of the disciplines of academia. Yet, in spite of this, university was important to him, providing him with his strongest friends (who were to remain so for the rest of his life) as well as a sounding board and ready audience for his ideas and early writing.

Two occasions in his first years at university illustrate these points and reveal Joyce's exceptional interest in mainstream European thought, in contrast with the more insular Celtic culture then resurgent in Dublin.

On one of these Joyce found himself defending Yeats's drama, *The Countess Cathleen*, against the rabid pro-Catholic and nationalist attacks it received from other students on its premiere by the Abbey Theatre Company in May 1899; in addition he refused to sign their petition against it (though he also criticized Yeats for not putting up a sterner fight against them), a point which brought to a head his own strong feelings against the Church (see pp. 199 and 230). On the second occasion, in January 1900, Joyce delivered an important paper, 'Drama and Life', to the university debating society in which he clearly set out his admiration for Ibsen, at that time considered a controversial and immoral influence. The debate is presented in full in Chapters XIX and XX of *Stephen Hero* (the first draft version of *A Portrait*) where Joyce also reveals how the college authorities at first tried to suppress his speech – an early instance of the kind of censorship which was to dog his work for the rest of his life.

At the same time Joyce's literary fortunes took a sudden upward swing when the *Fortnightly Review* agreed to publish his review of Ibsen's play, *When We Dead Awaken*, for which he received an extra fillip when Ibsen himself thanked Joyce for the favourable review of his play.[5]

During his time at university the Joyce family's removals continued with degrading frequency. Yet, in spite of their poverty, Joyce's father continued to support his son's literary aspirations both morally and materially. So in return, with the fee from the *Fortnightly Review*, Joyce treated his father in May 1900 to a trip to London where they were dined by Ibsen's esteemed English translator, William Archer. Back in Ireland, Joyce was inspired to his first serious attempt at playwriting, *A Brilliant Career*, and despatched it to Archer for his comments which, though encouraging, were not nearly as enthusiastic as he had hoped for or expected. However, Joyce now became more actively interested in the field of prose writing, though he continued to write poetry, initially for his own amusement, as well as short prose pieces which he called 'epiphanies': fragments of conversation or narrative by which the soul or essence of a person or event was manifested (see Chapters 4 and 7 below). Then in October 1901, at the beginning of his fourth year at university, there occurred a crucial landmark in Joyce's writing career when he prepared his explosive manifesto 'The Day of the Rabblement' – a vitriolic protest against (among other things) the parochial and sycophantic nature of contemporary Irish theatre. In this he outlined his idea that in order to become an artist a man must first assert his individual freedom, isolating himself from the multitude, a concept which he developed more fully through the figure and ideas of Stephen Dedalus in *A Portrait*. However, the college authorities got wind of his project and on the pretext that the proposed article made references to a banned book it was rejected by the editor of the college magazine. Accordingly Joyce took the unusual step of publishing it himself as a broadsheet, thereby asserting his own individuality and attracting a far wider audience than he could otherwise have expected. The article aroused considerable interest and discussion, not least in the college magazine itself, at the same time bringing its author's name to the attention of Dublin's literati. The publicity eventually culminated in the twenty-year-old Joyce's meeting with W. B. Yeats (in spite of the irony that the article had directly disparaged both him and his circle). Regardless of the differences in their ages, manner and culture, Yeats immediately warmed to him and determined to use his influence to promote Joyce's embryonic career.

In October 1902 Joyce received his Bachelor of Arts degree, the occasion being marked by some flamboyant antics from himself and his friends who protested against the playing of the national anthem and he only narrowly escaped arrest. After graduating, his first idea was to enrol on a medical course in Dublin but, against a background of deepening family poverty and his own disenchantment with Dublin, his initial enthusiasm flagged until at length he resolved to take up his medical course in Paris. Although at first sight this appears to resemble Stephen's predicament at the end of *A Portrait* where he is presented as taking flight from a Dublin not only sterile but also hostile to him, it was not quite the same in Joyce's own case; though he did encounter a lot of narrow-minded philistinism he did not face anything like the same moral dilemma, even if later in life he sometimes liked to portray himself as having been forced into exile. Having through Yeats secured the assistance of contacts in London and Paris, Joyce eventually departed Dublin (though not for the last time) in December 1902.

While many of the facts of Joyce's life coincide with those of Stephen Dedalus's career in *A Portrait*, there remain many conspicuous and significant differences. For one, Joyce was certainly not the lonely figure that Stephen is; he was markedly more popular and decidedly more convivial than his creation. It is true though that before his departure Joyce had acquired the reputation of being a cocky and even arrogant fellow and he amplifies this in Stephen's depiction. The most substantial difference however lies in the relationship of each to his family, Joyce's being considerably more intimate and warmer, especially with his father (and increasingly so during his time abroad) than Stephen Dedalus enjoys with his.

Similarly, the novel ends with Stephen on the brink of departure but his departure (precisely because it is on the brink) comes over as more absolute and final than in reality Joyce's was. In fact only a couple of weeks after arriving in Paris Joyce was back home again briefly for the Christmas holiday. When he returned to Paris early in 1903 he completely abandoned any idea of continuing to study medicine and he was now fired instead with the ambition to support himself through writing. He now prepared himself for his new career in art by first framing the basics of an aesthetic philosophy in his notebook (some of which found their way, reshaped, into Stephen's theory in the novel). However, in April of that year he suddenly received the telegram he had inwardly expected but dreaded: MOTHER DYING COME HOME FATHER. For a prolonged period of time her health had been in decline and her fatal illness was drawn out until August. Shortly before her death she begged James to make his Easter duties and his refusal to acquiesce in this haunted his later years (as *Ulysses* testifies; see pp. 5 and 35). For a while Joyce stayed on in Dublin, using the time to write an essay 'A Portrait of the Artist' which almost immediately he began to expand into an autobiographical novel, *Stephen Hero*, and in the following year at the invitation of the *Irish Homestead* he began to write some of the short stories which were later revised as *Dubliners*.

In another way, 1904 was a fateful year for Joyce, for in June he met Nora Barnacle, a bright young woman from Galway who had left home to work as a chambermaid in a Dublin hotel, and they arranged to walk out together on 16 June. The effect of this meeting on Joyce was so momentous that he immortalized its date as the setting of the day's events in *Ulysses* – the day upon which, as he later confessed to her, 'You made me a man.'[6] He persuaded Nora to run away to Europe with him and, having arranged a teaching post in Zurich, the two of them left Dublin under a cloud of secrecy and a dismal October sky.

Because of its crucial place in Joyce's life as well as its air of adventure this departure from Dublin bears a closer resemblance to Stephen Dedalus's flight into exile in *A Portrait*, though the differences are still evident. Yet the adventure was to receive an early setback. And just how perilous the flight was for Joyce and Nora was made more clear when they reached Zurich to discover that not only was there no teaching post but also the director of the school had never even heard of his supposed appointment. They immediately moved south to settle first in Trieste where Joyce found a post teaching English while he continued writing the short stories of *Dubliners* and almost completed

Stephen Hero. Here, in the following year their first child, Giorgio, was born.

At length however Joyce grew restless with Trieste and, in spite of having persuaded Stanislaus to join them as a fellow English teacher, he left with Nora and their son to take a job as a bank clerk in Rome. They had found it increasingly difficult in Trieste to make a living which would allow Joyce time to write and the job in Rome offered hope of both. But Rome was a disappointment to Joyce and the post in the bank proved monotonous and time-consuming. Then on top of this, *Dubliners* was first accepted by the publisher Grant Richards and then rejected – on the grounds that its material could be objectionable. It marked the beginnings of protracted negotiations and wrangling over the book which was not eventually published in extended form by Richards until 1914.

But all was not gloom for Joyce and he received news that another publisher, Elkin Mathews, had at last agreed to bring out a collection of his verse, *Chamber Music* (1907). Uplifted by this turn in fortune, Joyce then began a short, apparently inauspicious story about a man called Hunter but which, after he had seen its greater symbolic potential, he was eventually to expand into *Ulysses*.

Disillusioned with Rome (he called it a city that lived by exhibiting its 'grandmother's corpse'),[7] Joyce returned in 1907 to Trieste where he continued to teach English and where he began to reshape the long straggling *Stephen Hero* into *A Portrait* and the modest improvement in his income enabled him to make a trip to Ireland where he renewed old friendships. However the visit was marred by a wilful rumour that during their courtship Nora had been unfaithful to Joyce with his university friend Vincent Cosgrave (the model for Lynch in *A Portrait* – Joyce's choice of name capturing that sense of treachery which he had keenly felt). While Nora had not been unfaithful to him, the suspicion fed Joyce's perennial fear of betrayal, a fear which is expressed as a recurrent theme through many of his works – for instance, in *Exiles* and *Ulysses* as well as in *A Portrait*.

Although Joyce had left Ireland in 1904 he made a number of trips back to his homeland over the next few years and in his imagination and his works he returned to it continually. On one visit home he set up the first regular cinema in Dublin, the Volta, and he secured a commission to sell Irish tweeds in Italy – neither of which ventures was successful. However in the literary sphere Joyce's fortunes were beginning to look considerably more rosy. By the outbreak of the First World War his literary activity had reached an unprecedented level:

Dubliners had been published in book form and *A Portrait* had begun to be serialized in an English magazine; he had started both *Ulysses* and his solitary dramatic work, the Ibsenesque *Exiles*. The onset of war now forced Joyce and his family to seek refuge back in Zurich yet, ironically, in spite of the hostilities and the disruption to his life his reputation was beginning to spread widely. Through Yeats and the American poet, Ezra Pound, Joyce was awarded an official pension by the British government and his precarious financial situation was improved still further through the generous patronage of two wealthy benefactresses, Harriet Shaw Weaver and Edith McCormick. Moreover, after initial difficulties *A Portrait* was eventually published, first in the USA in 1916 and then in England in the following year. It immediately attracted favourable reviews, especially in the USA, and its advanced techniques helped to stimulate the interest of other writers and artists. It also helped significantly to establish Joyce's position among the foremost progressive European writers, a prominence which was underlined by the appearance of extracts from *Ulysses* in 1918.

By this time the family had returned to Trieste, following a brief stay in Locarno where Joyce convalesced after the first of countless eye operations to relieve glaucoma, a disease which afflicted him for the rest of his life. Trieste, however, had suffered as a consequence of the war and was now in decline. The family was unable to settle there again, and so in 1920 with the help and persuasion of Ezra Pound a move was made to Paris. It was a happy decision – Paris in the 1920s was the fashionable centre of avant-garde art and thought, a seed-bed of new ideas and experiment and the ideal atmosphere in which to launch *Ulysses*, the culmination of seven years' work and the novel which was to mark Joyce as the most influential twentieth-century writer.

It appeared on Joyce's fortieth birthday, 2 February 1922, and, as with all his previous works it appeared only after a catalogue of difficulties with publishers and printers. Published eventually by the tiny Paris house of Shakespeare and Company in a much corrupted version (whose legacy is still with us today), in the USA the book was banned until 1934 and it did not appear in England in a widely available edition until 1936–7. Although ostensibly recounting a single day in the life of its central character Leopold Bloom, a Jewish advertising agent, his meeting with Stephen Dedalus and the infidelity of his wife Molly, its perspectives, together with Joyce's use of Homeric mythology, projects its vision far beyond the Dublin of 16 June 1904 on which it is set. Although its theme is basically simple the novel employs techniques which were to revolutionize twentieth-century literature (for example, in the use of modulating styles and perspective, and the interior monologue, aspects of which Joyce had begun to explore in *A Portrait*). By paralleling Bloom's wanderings around Dublin with the exploits of Homer's Odysseus, Joyce breaks across the time scale of the novel, making a hero of the Everyman, Bloom, and an Everyman of the hero, Odysseus.

Soon after *Ulysses* was published Joyce began work on *Finnegans Wake*, an enormous undertaking which was to occupy almost the whole of the rest of his life. It is based in part on an Irish ballad which tells of the miraculous resurrection of its hero after he is given whiskey at his own wake. The book is infinitely more than this, however, and it defies synopsis. Its subject matter is encyclopaedic in range and yet it appears to be focused through the dreaming mind of a single sleeping persona. It is written in what has been described as a 'non-language' (in which onomatopoeia, compound words and puns are among its central devices), a dream language which embraces or at least refers to all languages. Its technique explores symbol and myth in radical ways (based on a cyclical theory of personal and racial history) and exploits them at least to breaking point. This cyclical approach is also, as we might expect of Joyce, paralleled in its techniques – for instance, the final sentence is left in the air, to be completed by returning to the opening of the book. The work constantly strives to reconcile and balance a vast range of opposing conditions, holding them in uncertain and comic tension – it is about Everyman (one character's nickname is 'Here Comes Everybody') and yet about no identifiable character; it is both general and particular, nonsense and all sense.

Finnegans Wake appeared in sections over the following years and they were received with at best polite reservation and puzzlement, at worst open hostility, as it still is (Stanislaus called it 'drivelling rigmarole'). It was written against a background of severely chronic eye trouble in spite of the series of operations which Joyce had undergone. Relationships with old friends such as Ezra Pound, T. S. Eliot and Wyndham Lewis had become strained, partly as a direct result of their expressed reservations about the new direction which Joyce's work was now taking. But in their places were new admirers and colleagues, more receptive and encouraging of new ideas, including Samuel Beckett whose own work shows the distinct marks of his close contact with Joyce.

There were problems too with his own family. The death of his father in 1931 had filled Joyce with grief and remorse – his short poem 'Ecce Puer' is an elegant expression both of his deep sorrow, as well as of his joy at the birth of his grandson two months later to his son, Giorgio. But there was also the persistent decline in the mental health of his daughter, Lucia. Born in 1907, she had suffered mental disorder in increasing severity from her teenage years and Joyce felt a great personal responsibility for her condition. She spent long periods in institutions and underwent a wide variety of experimental but ultimately futile treatments. Eventually, exasperated, Joyce himself hoped that by developing her artistic talents she might improve though this was without prolonged success and the rest of her life was spent in a series of mental hospitals.

If the 1920s marked for Joyce a period of sustained success, both material and artistic and of relative stability, issuing from the almost universal acclaim of *Ulysses*, then the 1930s was a decade of more equivocal fortunes, characterized by a scenario of personal disruptions, of persistent artistic scepticism and, on the broader scale, of national and political upheaval across a Europe on the brink of devastation.

Finnegans Wake was at last published in 1939, shortly before the outbreak of the Second World War, and Joyce, having lived since 1920 for the most part in Paris, was again forced by war to seek refuge, again in Zurich. But his general health had deteriorated greatly since his last exile in this city. Troubled by stomach pains as he had been for much of his adult life, little attention was given to their reappearance soon after his return to Switzerland and his condition worsened. Peritonitis developed as a result of an undiagnosed perforated duodenal ulcer and, four weeks after leaving Paris, Joyce died on 13 January 1941.

Political, religious and cultural background

In Chapter 5 of *A Portrait*, Stephen declares resolutely that the overriding prerequisite to becoming an artist is freedom – specifically freedom from the three nets: 'nationality, language, religion' (p. 207). And by the end of the novel he avowedly refuses to serve any of these ideas in whatever form they may appear: '... home, ... fatherland or ... church' (p. 251). He abandons his study of Irish language, mocks another student's enthusiasm for Gaelic sports, and scorns the nationalists as hypocrites while at the same time he is paradoxically proud of his own ancestry among the ancient Irish tribes (pp. 206–7). In the same breath he also acknowledges that nationality and religion are among the strongest influences of the Irish life that has formed him:

—This race and this country and this life produced me, he said. I shall express myself as I am.   (p. 207)

The novel can be seen as Stephen's struggle to come to terms with and resolve the tensions, hostilities and open conflict of these forces with the artistic vision, particularly in the violent context of revolutionary, reactionary Ireland. By the end of the novel he has come to understand his destiny as artist as the duty of expressing the 'conscience' of his race. Joyce himself, though a socialist, did not take an active part in politics and gave up his Roman Catholic faith during his early youth, and in the novel Stephen assiduously avoids all discussion of any of these themes, at least in themselves. However, the novel does explore in detail the way in which these themes inevitably impinge on Stephen's life through their powerful pervasive influence. As the Christmas dinner episode (Chapter 1) underlines, religion and politics are inextricably woven into Irish public life. They are the source too of some of Joyce's most ironic touches in the novel.

To examine the political and religious backgrounds to the novel we can usefully take the year 1800 as a convenient starting point. In that year, after centuries of English colonization and exploitation, Ireland was made part of the United Kingdom by the Irish Act of Union. This annexation dissolved the 500-year-old Irish parliament (in the novel Mr Dedalus refers to the building, now a bank, on p. 99) and replaced it with direct rule from London. Ironically, the chief opposition to the Act came from the Protestant population, partly because it removed political power from their hands but also because there were plans for Catholic emancipation. Accordingly, as a result of these plans and of the promise of subsidies to Catholic foundations, the Catholic Church made a deal and gave its support to the Act. An important result of this configuration was that nineteenth-century Irish politics tended to emphasize demands for Home Rule, with power devolved from London, rather than for outright independence itself. While the Protestant Ascendancy resorted chiefly to parliamentary and financial muscle to express its dissatisfaction with the new *status quo*, some of the disenfranchised and dispossessed Catholic peasantry hoped for direct action and rebellion. At about the same time the series of failures of the potato crop, culminating in the disastrous famines of the 1840s, hardened already passionate enmities and strengthened the need for action – though this often became channelled into escape and mass emigration, mainly to the USA. One direct result of the famine was a dramatic decline in the widespread use of the Irish language (from 4 million speakers in 1841 to 1.7 million in 1851). While this was due in part also to the exodus of the population, it was chiefly the result of official policy to replace Irish with English as the first language, since Irish was associated with a backward peasant life while English was the language for social elevation.

By the middle of the nineteenth century, the Catholic Church was co-operating more and more with the British government. In 1802 the Christian Brothers had opened their first school for mass education, and seminaries for priests too now began to be set up. Successive governments had made grants to Catholic institutions in Ireland such as the highly influential Royal College of St Patrick at Maynooth for training priests, a condition of these being that staff and students took an oath of loyalty to the Crown. The Church too regularly and officially denounced revolutionary acts and organizations and was thus regarded favourably by the government who permitted the further establishment of schools and colleges. Stephen Dedalus's own college in *A Portrait*, Clongowes Wood, had been founded in 1814 by the Jesuits in a former castle – ironically the centre of local Irish rebellion against the English in the seventeenth century (as Stephen hints on pp. 9 and 10) – yet as a college it was run on firm English public-school lines. His second school, Belvedere College, was founded in 1841 and University College Dublin in 1853, again both by Jesuits.

The Catholic Church saw that the way to progress lay through parliamentary means and the Catholic Relief Act of 1829 sought to encourage this by granting middle- and upper-class Catholics the right to vote and take seats in Parliament. But some, finding support in the Irish peasantry and industrial poor (who had no vote), favoured more direct and even violent policies. One such was Michael Davitt (1846–1906) (see *A Portrait*, p. 7). A member of the Irish Republican Brotherhood and the Fenians, both of which groups advocated violent rebellion, he had taken part in a disastrous uprising in 1867 and was the man responsible for obtaining weapons for the Fenians. In broad terms, he favoured ownership of the land by the peasant tenants who worked it; though he later modified this to a policy of land nationalization, it was a policy which quickly attracted mass support. In 1879 he founded the Irish National Land League, with Charles Stewart Parnell (1846–91) as its president. Parnell, Stephen Dedalus's hero in the novel, was in fact an Anglo-Irish Protestant landlord who had inherited his family's estates at the age of thirteen. He had become a Member of Parliament at only twenty-nine – a charismatic orator and brilliant tactician beloved of his Irish followers, Catholic and Protestant alike, but despised and feared by British politicians. Together with Davitt, Parnell's Land League promoted an aggressive policy of civil disobedience chiefly through peasant farmers withholding their rents, with the ultimate aim of redistributing land to tenants but at the same time compensating their former landowners. Eventually, on 12 October 1881, as the increasing agitation reached crisis point, Parnell was arrested. As a consequence, the 'Chief' (or the 'king' as Mr Dedalus calls him) was immediately transfigured into a martyr and the level of agrarian outrages increased sharply. He was released seven months later, after giving certain assurances in exchange for government concessions, but four days after his release, in 1882, there occurred the 'Phoenix Park murders' in which two high-ranking British officials were brutally killed. Although the perpetrators were arrested and executed, *The Times* accused Parnell of being implicated in this and other crimes, printing letters which purported to prove his involvement. Not until eight years later, in 1890, was he finally cleared when a commission was able to show that the letters were the work of a forger named Richard Pigott (his hand was revealed by his persistent misspelling 'hesitency', a feature which Joyce exploits to comic effect in *Finnegans Wake* (pp. 16, 35, 97 *et seq.*).

Parnell's downfall in 1890 however occurred at the height of his popularity, with the realistic prospect of Irish Home Rule in sight, and was the result not of *The Times* scandal but of a divorce case sensation. The relationship (subject of the violent clash between Dante Riordan and John Casey in Chapter 1 of *A Portrait*) concerned an affair between Parnell and Katherine O'Shea (wife of one of Parnell's fellow MPs) which had begun in 1880, apparently with the full knowledge of her husband. However, when O'Shea sued for divorce Parnell was disgraced as an adulterer, thereby offending supporters both in his own and in other sympathetic parties, who subsequently withdrew their support on moral grounds. The Christmas dinner clash in the novel captures the controversy precisely. Moreover, as Mr Casey remembers, the Catholic clergy now turned against him:

... the priests and the priests' pawns broke Parnell's heart and hounded him into his grave. (pp. 34–5)

In the fierce argument at the Christmas dinner, Joyce also conveys dramatically the intense conflict which the divorce scandal aroused, with Dante's uncompromising support of the clergy's denunciation of Parnell set against the unwavering loyalty of Mr Dedalus and John Casey to their, by then, dead hero.

In addition to the twin heroic roles of martyr and Messiah, focused on vividly by the novel's opening chapter, Stephen also draws out, and later develops in full, the crucial theme of betrayal which figured so powerfully in Parnell's downfall. When he refused to stand down as leader of the Irish Party he was shamelessly deserted by a large majority of his colleagues and forced to resign; in Chapter 5 Stephen pinpoints the 'Bantry Gang' as the paradigm of such betrayal (p. 233) – referring to a group led by Timothy Healy who, although originally loyal supporters of Parnell, later rejoiced in his downfall. (At the age of nine, Joyce himself composed a poetic attack on this treachery in 'Et tu, Healy?', which his father, a staunch Parnellite, published privately; see also Joyce's short story 'Ivy Day in the Committe Room'.) In succeeding elections Parnell failed to regain political support and after marrying Kitty O'Shea in June 1891 he retired to Brighton where four months later he died. He was brought home to Ireland to be buried in a spectacular funeral and Stephen's dream in Chapter 1 vividly depicts the return of the dead hero's body.

Of course, in the novel Parnell is more than just a physical or historical figure (and he takes on a powerful symbolic presence in Stephen's consciousness). Joyce brilliantly exploits his heroic stature to draw out and unite the novel's religious and political themes with the theme of Irish history, the ever-present spectre. It also helps Stephen to characterize and stress the perils of loyalty in public life and, by extension, the threat posed to the free artistic spirit from the all-pervasive moral dominance of the Church in Ireland.

Like Joyce, Stephen too turns his back on the contemporary Irish cultural scene, as well as on its religious heritage. But in this Joyce was swimming against the tide in Ireland. During his youth, at about the turn of the century, increasing nationalist fervour was beginning to rediscover an outlet outside of, yet at the same time an extension to, direct political activity in a resurgence of popular interest in all aspects of traditional Celtic life and culture. One aspect of this was traditional sports, through the Gaelic Athletic Association which had been founded by Michael Cusack in 1884 to promote their widespread adoption (and which Joyce satirizes on p. 184). The peasant ways of life, for long associated with failure and decay, received renewed attention as the potential wellspring of Irish cultural regeneration and native identity. Writers such as Yeats, Synge and Lady Gregory began to study the neglected language and folklore of peasant life chiefly in the west and south of Ireland, where the Irish language had survived British attempts at its eradication. Although neither Yeats nor Synge wrote in Irish they used its idiom and rhythms, as well as the mythology and settings of the ancient or peasant ways, adapted to address a modern audience. This renewed interest was also expressed by an increase in the demand for modern translations of old Irish texts – one such translator, who had a marked influence on Joyce's own verse, was James Clarence Mangan, and Joyce recognized in the exiled Mangan a figure of heroic suffering similar to that of Parnell. Eventually, Joyce too turned to this cultural reservoir in his latter days to make use of Irish lore, particularly in the legendary character of Finn MacCool in *Finnegans Wake*, though often with ironic overtones.

It was not therefore a decadent cultural life on which Joyce turned his back but an energetic and popular one. Its chief and abiding legacy, however, was not poetry or folk literature but, after a very stormy inception, a thriving national theatre, represented physically in the building of the Abbey Theatre (eventual home of the Irish Literary Theatre), and the works of Synge, Yeats and, later, Sean O'Casey. On the other hand, Joyce considered the movement to be insular and its attitude introverted rather than progressive. It had an inclination towards symbolic abstraction and esotericism, a tendency epitomized in the poetry and writings of George Russell (A.E.) and his circle.

But not all contemporary Irish writers followed the trend into the past. Some Anglo-Irish writers such as George Moore, Oscar Wilde and George Bernard Shaw looked beyond Ireland for their inspiration and their audience. Moore and Shaw especially were influenced by broader cultural movements in European literature and theatre. Moore, a novelist from a landed Irish background, at first exiled himself in Paris where he embraced the influence of both French Symbolist poetry and the novelists of the Naturalist movement, before rediscovering his native culture late in life (his autobiographical *Confessions of a Young Man* makes an enlightening comparison with Joyce's *A Portrait*). George Bernard Shaw, on the other hand, after an early career as a novelist, came under the influence (like Joyce) of Henrik Ibsen and as a playwright worked to exploit Ibsen's revolutionary dramatic method as a vehicle for his own sociological and socialist ideas. However, the work of both these Irishmen has a distinct English character, Irish with an English accent, which for Joyce could not be authentic.

Although Joyce turned his back on both English and Irish literary scenes he did not reject them out of hand. As always in his work he absorbed what he found important, useful or interesting and assimilated it into his own artistic designs. Because his work taps into the Irish scene which forms the basis of it, it is inevitable that it should partake, at least in ironic terms, of its cultural interests. At the same time, his attitude and approach are firmly within a more distinctly Modernist, European and international tradition. In addition to the influence of Ibsen, Joyce also acknowledged the influence or at least an understanding of a vast range of other European writers, most of whom he had read in their own language, including Dante, D'Annunzio, Hauptmann, Flaubert, Balzac, Rabelais, Gorky, Tolstoy and Turgenev, as well as writers in English, chiefly Swift, Sterne and Blake. In *Dubliners* Joyce sketched a range of characters trapped by their city in varying degrees of spiritual paralysis, 'outcast from life's feast' as he called them. But as he also admitted, they represent different aspects of himself as he might have become had he remained in Dublin. By escaping he was able to avoid its nets and thereby open up his writing to a richer variety of cultural forces through which to discover his own voice and its conscience.

The conception of *A Portrait*

Dublin 1904
Trieste 1914

Although these dates at the end of *A Portrait* are intended to indicate the ten years of its composition, the novel's origins go back still further – initially to Joyce's practice as a young man of writing and collecting his random 'epiphanies'. Some of these early fragments have survived; just how important they were in providing the basis of significant moments and as the foundation of the structure becomes clear if they are compared with the novel, especially in the early chapters where Joyce often transplanted them word for word; for instance the 'Apologise' episode (p. 8) and the tramcar encounter (pp. 72 and 226) are both closely extracted from Joyce's notebook of his own personal experiences.[8]

The next, more explicit, step came on 7 January 1904 when in a single day Joyce wrote the essay 'A Portrait of the Artist' and submitted it to *Dana*, an Irish literary magazine. Although it was subsequently rejected on the grounds that it was incomprehensible, the editor did admire the writer's style. However, in his diary, Joyce's brother Stanislaus confided his own suspicion that the essay had really been rejected, at least in part, because of the sexual experiences described in it. It is a hectic, garrulous manifesto with a great amount crammed into its eight pages. At its centre is an abstract though unmistakably Joycean artist-figure whose growth is (like that of Dedalus in the novel) traced through a sequence of developmental stages, pointing out among other things that even the characteristics of a man's childhood are evident in the finished artist – a Freudian element which is implicit in the novel too. In spite of its exhortation to writers to concentrate on the psychology and personality of a character rather than on externals, its own central character is vague and elusive, wrapped in lofty idealized imagery and often archaic diction. Yet despite his self-consciousness the artist-figure is typically defiant, asserting the independence of the artistic will against the hostile rabble.

A month later Joyce began his novel in earnest. Turning away from writing verse, for the time being anyway, and fragmentary pieces, he made brisk progress on his first extended prose work, using for it the working title of *Stephen Hero* (after the ballad 'Turpin Hero') which had been suggested by Stanislaus – and Joyce often turned to his brother for advice and information on this and other works.[9] Pleased with this progress Joyce began showing the completed draft to friends, not all of whom showed the same enthusiasm. Some recognized themselves as characters in the work and objected while others expressed reservations about its narrative. One important person to whom he showed it was the poet George Russell (A.E.), editor of the *Irish Homestead*, who was so impressed by Joyce's style and wanted to encourage this new talent that he invited him to write short stories for the journal. As a result the first of Joyce's stories, 'The Sisters', was published in August 1904 and was followed by others which were eventually to be reshaped into the *Dubliners* collection.

Meanwhile, over the next two years, Joyce persevered with *Stephen Hero*. But by the time it was completed he had become disheartened with it; by comparison with *A Portrait*, it is densely written in a pedestrian style almost completely lacking in the vigour and subtle irony which animates the revised version. Then, in September 1907, Joyce told his brother of his intention to rewrite the whole novel, concentrating the action more closely on the central figure of Stephen Dedalus (who was to have been renamed Daly – the same name as the real priest at Clongowes who had strapped him) and reducing *Stephen Hero*'s vastly detailed thirty or forty chapters to five concise sections. However, after countless rejections from publishers Joyce became so dejected that (so the story goes) he flung the manuscript on to the fire – from which it was rescued by his sister Eileen.

The following years were marked by further disappointment, dominated by the failure of *Dubliners* to find a publisher. Then, in December 1913, Joyce received a very promising letter from Ezra Pound who, prompted by Yeats, invited him to send examples of his work which

21

could be published in British or American journals. Pound himself was closely involved with the *Egoist* magazine and was at this time very active on the London literary scene. So, having by now completed the first three chapters of the novel, Joyce eagerly complied by sending off what was ready; an admiring Pound arranged for serialization in the *Egoist* itself – in twenty-five instalments, beginning on Joyce's thirty-second birthday, 2 February 1914, and finishing on 1 September 1915.

Pound's intervention had been crucial to the appearance of the novel in print, nor did his efforts now cease, as he continued energetically to seek a publisher willing to bring the work out in book form. In general, its reception among *Egoist* readers, especially other writers, had been warm and encouraging but this did not facilitate finding a publisher – for example, the reader's report for Duckworth (who had published D. H. Lawrence and Virginia Woolf), while admiring the craftsmanship and originality of it, thought that it was 'a little sordid', too realistic for public taste and in need of further pruning. Although at this distance it is difficult to appreciate how any such offence to public sensitivities could have been aroused by the book, the general publishing climate in 1916 was not considered favourable to the appearance of *A Portrait* – D. H. Lawrence's *The Rainbow* had recently been prosecuted for its 'realism' and British printers refused to consider Joyce's novel unless changes were made or passages cut from it. None could be found to print it as it stood and therefore, turning to the USA, Pound together with Harriet Shaw Weaver persuaded the New York publisher Huebsch to bring it out. The first edition appeared in America on 29 December 1916, and in England on 12 February 1917.

Early sales of the book were promising and on the whole early reviews were favourable. Most reviewers made reference to the 'sordid reality' of some sections of the novel (describing it for example as 'offensive', 'foul-smelling', or 'coarse'), and some denounced what they considered to be obscenities – though without giving details.[10] H. G. Wells's comments were typical of this particular complaint in accusing Joyce of a 'cloacal obsession', though his review was otherwise sympathetic:

The value of Mr Joyce's book has little to do with its incidental insanitary condition. Like some of the best novels in the world it is the story of an education . . . The technique is startling, but on the whole it succeeds . . .

(*Nation*, 24 February 1917)

Another feature which many reviewers picked up was the psychological realism of it, especially Joyce's method of communicating this obliquely, without addressing the reader directly. On the other hand, among less favourable reviewers, Virginia Woolf in the *Times Literary Supplement*, 10 April 1919, referred to the 'comparative poverty of the writer's mind', while another concluded with hasty pessimism, 'It is doubtful if he will make a novelist' (*New Statesman*, 14 April 1917). Probably the warmest reception came from the French critic, Valéry Larbaud, who described the novel as a 'great advance' whose technique took the reader to the essence of the character's thoughts and in which the reader played an active role in the creation of character. In general though, reviewers regarded *A Portrait* as a work promising genius even if not every page of the novel testified to this. Joyce himself, though naturally pleased by the fact that his novel had at last seen the light of day, had mixed feelings. He considered that some reviewers had been unfair particularly in misunderstanding the moral effect of the 'dirt' and he was also dismayed at the large number of misprints – nearly 400 he calculated – which he had not had the opportunity to correct.

After a promising start sales for the book fell off rapidly; in view of his poverty, Joyce surprisingly took this philosophically. Although he continued to keep a close eye on the fortunes of his first published novel – especially through translations and its reviews (to which he paid particular regard) – it was out of the way and his attention had now become engaged in the pursuit of more demanding projects: the struggle to stage his play, *Exiles*, and the challenge of the opening pages of *Ulysses*.

2. A Commentary on the Novel and Joyce's Themes

> *But would anyone, short of a madhouse, believe it? Neither of those clean little cherubim, Nero or Nobookisonester himself, ever nursed such a spoiled opinion of his monstrous marvellosity as did this mental and moral defective (here perhaps at the vanessance of his lownest)* ...
>
> (*Finnegans Wake*, p. 177)

Chapter 1

'Once upon a time ...' begins Joyce's novel – and also begins Mr Dedalus's story about baby tuckoo, who is Stephen. The novel opens with a storybook convention, a cliché even; yet as soon as it opens the reader's repose is quickly disrupted when the normal storybook convention is followed by a sequence of apparently disconnected fragments without commentary (the novel begins and ends in fragments). However, in relation to the work as a whole the first two pages (up to Dante's verse) can be considered as a sort of overture, setting down in the microcosm of Stephen's infancy most of the themes and encounters which occur throughout the novel: the 'nets' of family and politics; sexuality hinted at through Eileen Vance; art in the form of his father's story-telling and Stephen's song; Stephen's cunning in the need to hide; the threat of admonition which by Chapter 2 will have become most familiar; and throughout there is the all-pervasiveness of the senses.

We also become quickly aware of the tone of irony in the opening as we try to fix in our minds the various narrators. Addressed at first to a small boy in a simple indulgent style, it suddenly disintegrates without warning into parataxis: who is telling the story? whose are the fragments and whose consciousness connects them? is someone pulling our legs? There is no reply.

Faced with this silence, one of the chief difficulties of penetrating *A Portrait* lies in understanding just what is happening in the novel. This is principally because Joyce's oblique technique of presenting a disjointed story-line as though it were being recollected at random – in imitation of the haphazard, fragmentary process by which the mind recalls events, people, snatches of conversation and names – produces a narrative that is seldom neat and well organized, with events in chronological order and with equal passages of writing allocated to equal parcels of time. Instead, the mind which Joyce imitates recalls these things in the order in which they are associated with each other, connected by similar settings or by the repetition of important details; the memory switches back and forth over time, selecting fragments and tying them together with other fragments (a feature which early critics equated with montage technique in cinema).

This 'stream-of-consciousness' approach allocates order and prominence to events, features and characters not according to their chronology but in proportion to their importance; therefore, we should not be surprised that the Christmas dinner scene in Chapter 1 has over twelve pages devoted to it even though it covers less than one hour of time (in Chapter 5, Joyce covers at most only three days in the first seventy-odd pages but six weeks in the last five pages). So even from the beginning, with its deceptive 'Once upon a time', the reader is shaken out of his passivity and manipulated through sudden disruptions in time and place, back and forth, by the association of ideas and thoughts whose connection, at this stage anyway, is not readily obvious.

It becomes clear, however, that the first section of the novel consists of an accumulation of Stephen's fragmentary memories of childhood. The story of the moocow is linked in Stephen's imagination to the Byrnes' sweetshop; then a memory of his father leads to that of his mother and through the sound of her piano to Uncle Charles (in fact Stephen's granduncle); and finally to Dante Riordan who disapproves of Protestants (see p. 36) and of Stephen having a crush on one, Eileen Vance.

Although the first section opens with a rich store of associations and introduces many of the novel's important features and themes, their significance does not become fully clear until much later, leaving a sort of myopic haze with no immediate sign of remedy. However, one of the most important keys to Joyce's approach, both here and in the novel as a whole, lies in the part played by the senses. In this opening section we can already see how important they are to Joyce's method – for example, the smells of Stephen's father and mother; the warmth and cold of the bed; the colours red and green which are reflected in Dante's choice of maroon and green for the backs of her brushes. Similarly, the way one sense sets off another, to be recalled by the memory, represents an important formalizing function for Joyce (as it does for Stephen), giving the fragments form and significance.

The technique can be seen again and again in this chapter: in Stephen's sensitivity to heat and cold (p. 11; later manifested in the fever/

chill, pp. 17 and 21); the smell of turf and the peasants' clothes at Mass (p. 18); the rhythmic sounds of the train and the refectory (p. 17); the noise of the sea, rising and falling (p. 27). The senses are vividly expressed too in the masterpiece of the Christmas dinner with its opulence and generosity – which also serves to establish Mr Dedalus's wealthy situation at this time ('. . . and a very good time it was . . .') from which the novel charts his steady decline.

At the same time, Stephen's general responsiveness to these stimuli is symptomatic of his more specific artistic sensitivity, which derives much of its energy from the vigour of his imagination. In the opening chapter this is expressed in a variety of ways: in his speculations on the possibility of a green rose (pp. 7 and 12), in the vivid dream of his own death which links his position as victim with that of Parnell, and finally in his fear of the Rector. And yet it comes as a revelation to Stephen to discover that Fleming has painted the clouds maroon in his geography book (p. 15) – it is a quantum leap, suddenly opening up imaginative possibilities for him, no longer compelled by the constraints of the real world. He has a flash of insight into the freedom of art, a freedom which makes possible a green rose and maroon clouds and it is the prospect of this freedom which Stephen will actively pursue in Chapters 4 and 5.

Linked with this sensitivity to external stimuli (sounds, smells, etc.) is Stephen's sensitivity to words and to the relationships between different words, between words and reality, and between sounds and semantics. Simon Moonan is described as 'McGlade's suck' (p. 11) and this sparks off a train of thoughts in Stephen's mind, first linking 'suck' to the idea of Moonan as McGlade's toady and then reflecting on the ugliness of the sound. He then pursues its associations, visualizing water drawn down a plug hole, taking him back to the time he stayed at the Wicklow Hotel and finally he notes how the word imitates its sound: suck! He does the same later with the words 'kiss' (p. 15) and 'cancer/canker' (p. 22), and the puns on belt (p. 9) and Athy (p. 26). Then there is a fascination with schoolboy argot: 'fecked', 'scut', 'smugging' – all typical preoccupations of Joyce's own writing as a whole.

Sensitivity for Stephen however is both a blessing – his imagination allowing him to savour the promise of home life and enriching his perception (such as the mild calm evening at the end of the chapter) – and a curse; for example, it is the source of his suffering, literally, at the hands of Father Dolan later in the chapter. Ironically, this punishment immediately follows Stephen's own speculations on what it would be like to be pandied and when a classmate warns that the whole school is to be thrashed for what the older boys have done he tries hard to imagine the pain, almost as if he seeks the experience (p. 46).

The two prevailing senses in the first chapter are touch and sight, and the imagery which the two generate, of the hands and eyes, set up currents which eventually converge on the episode in which Stephen is pandied. The importance of the hands imagery is clear but the eyes also figure here – Stephen's glasses have been broken and without them he is severely handicapped – and Father Dolan's brutal punishment unites this with Stephen's highly sensitive touch (as Father Dolan steadies his hands Stephen notices the prefect's soft touch and for a moment expects him to shake hands (pp. 52–3). Further, as if to underline this convergence, Joyce matches the pain in Stephen's hands to his stinging tears together with the prefect's claim that he detects guilt in Stephen's eyes. Nor is this dichotomy of the senses limited to the first chapter – throughout the novel they continue to be for Stephen a source of pleasure, in Chapters 2 and 4 especially, but also the source of his harrowing, in Chapter 3.

However, in the first chapter, Stephen's experience is characterized chiefly by striving to escape the reality of school life through the cosy images in his imagination, particularly of going home to his family (he keeps a count of the days of term remaining, p. 10). It is also a striving, punctuated by intense moments of realistic suffering, during which the reader's attention is brought into acute focus through the eyes of Stephen. These moments include the intimidations by Dante (p. 8) and Wells (p. 14); they also provide the basis of the central crises in each of the three major sections of the chapter: Stephen pushed into the square ditch by Wells, the terror of the Christmas dinner quarrel, and the pain and humiliation of the pandying.

The square ditch incident is typically gratuitous schoolboy bullying, but the incident serves also to remind us obliquely and facetiously of the fate of the mythical birdman, a point which takes on greater significance in later chapters. On the realistic level, it serves here principally to heighten our awareness of Stephen's vulnerability and weakness, his feeling of inferiority (especially social inferiority, because his father is not a magistrate, pp. 13 and 26). At the same time, it brings into sharp relief the advice from his parents, given as they leave him at school on his first day, 'not to speak with the rough boys' and 'never to peach on a fellow' (p. 9). Significantly, the incident presents Stephen with the role of victim, a role which he comes to terms with and even embraces through the heroic figure of Parnell, archetypal victim; when Stephen feverishly imagines his own death, it is with the death of Parnell that he identifies. His parents' advice and his related sense of honour prevent him from informing on Wells, and further reinforce this role by imposing on him a duty of silence. So, in comparison with the trauma that the Christmas gathering generates, the square ditch incident is easier for Stephen to resolve, not only because of this role-playing, but also because he has the support of his school fellows in condemning Wells as 'mean' (p. 14) – the same apparent support which follows the pandying later.

However, at the Christmas dinner, the great set piece of the chapter, Stephen is a helpless spectator of a violent confrontation, with the two chief guardians of his youth, Dante and his father, as the main antagonists. The scene is a triumph, not only in Joyce's dramatic presentation of the clash with its finely woven ironies, but also in the manner in which it draws out the themes and currents lurking just beneath the surface of this and later chapters. Critics have justly hailed the dinner scene for its realism, from the detailed evocation of the setting and the atmosphere to the precision with which Joyce constructs the conflict and delineates character.[1]

Another of Joyce's central techniques in *A Portrait*, and clearly discernible in this chapter, is the use of contrast and polarity – the juxtaposition of two opposing ideas to set off and to draw out the essence of each as well as to increase tension and to spur the novel's forward momentum (a technique which Joyce exploited and refined more fully in his later works). So, in the first chapter we soon observe Stephen's urge to differentiate and to contrast: his mother has a nicer smell than his father; all the boys have different clothes and voices, and different ways of walking (pp. 13–14). and there are two further related points: first, Stephen's recognition that in his as yet stable world the order is both centralized and hierarchical (the lines at school, the ranks of the Jesuit order) – Stephen literally locates himself within the order of his universe (p. 16); and, second, both his and Joyce's concern with opposites – hot/cold, wet/dry, red/green, Catholic/Protestant, noise/silence, open/closed – implies the precariousness of that stability, underlined by a serious blow inflicted upon it at the Christmas dinner table at which he is permitted to sit with his elders for the first time.

With undisguised ironies the Christmas section ruthlessly polarizes the characters in both their politics and temperaments through underlying discords which are drawn swiftly to the surface. One such irony lies in Stephen's protracted anticipation of Christmas as a relief from the tribulations of school life; the richness of the description with which it opens is itself a contrast to the disease and darkness of Stephen's illness in the previous section. Nevertheless, the first sentence already hints at the conflict to come, with the imagery of the red and green (holly and ivy) reminding us of the rivalry on the Irish political scene between the supporters of Davitt and Parnell, now complicated by the moral controversy over Parnell's private life (as well as the conflict between imperial and republican, England and Ireland).

In addition to foregrounding the current political tensions, the scene also has critical moral implications for Stephen since his father adopts a consistently humane and compassionate position in contrast to Dante's rigorously doctrinaire stance, mirroring for Stephen that of the Church itself – the first of many knocks against the Church. On the one hand, when Mr Dedalus returns after his stroll with John Casey, he appears cordial and congenial, greeting Dante, pouring the drinks and joking about the hotel-keeper (compare this image with the one of him, brief and unseen, in poverty in Chapter 5, p. 178); on the other, Mrs Riordan, a tenacious, bigoted harridan, appears sullen and uncompromising from the outset, going straight for the throat of her host.

Although the conflict of duties between religion and politics – church versus state – is not a new one, it was a particularly relevant and sensitive question in the Ireland of the late 1880s. However, the particular political issue at stake here is not as important in itself for Stephen as is the moral effect of political conflict in general. But the issue is more than just that of 'church versus state'. Since the novel is primarily concerned with development – the development of the artist – the more crucial point for Stephen lies not in who is correct, his father or Dante, but in the memory of the terrible conflict itself which the question sparks off.

The full effect on Stephen of the Parnell issue in general and of this Christmas strife in particular is twofold and not fully realized until Chapter 5. The first of these, as we have seen above, involves the theme of betrayal, represented by the lingering spectre of Parnell but which Stephen also encounters at first hand – in Chapter 5 he ridicules the predisposition of Irish politics to treachery and betrayal (p. 207), and recalls the Bantry Gang's betrayal of Parnell (p. 233). It is also one of the reasons for Stephen's reluctance to form close friendships, though not the only one.

The second effect of the traumatic experience at the Christmas dinner is ultimately for Stephen to completely reject any feelings of loyalty to either religion or politics, eventually regarding them as paralysing, constantly threatening to compromise his intellect and freedom. The effect can be seen in Chapter 5 when he points out to Davin:

Critical Studies: A Portrait of the Artist as a Young Man

... When the soul of a man is born in this country there are nets flung at it to hold it back from flight. You talk to me of nationality, language, religion. I shall try to fly by those nets.   (p. 207)

and in a later discussion with Cranly:

... I will not serve that in which I no longer believe whether it call itself my home, my fatherland, or my church: ...   (p. 251)

The Christmas section brings to a head all those ghosts, the theme of time and the nightmare of history (personal and political memory), which lurk in the back of Stephen's period at Clongowes Wood including: the reference to Hamilton Rowan, the English influence at the college (Wars of the Roses, cricket and magistrates), Cardinal Wolsey (church v. state again), as well as Parnell himself. It also brings to a head other hints of conflict or rivalry which have been brooding: sports matches, Stephen's rivalry with Jack Lawton, and the matter of his snuff box (for which Wells shoves him in the ditch).

At the close of the Christmas section, the fury of the conflict is unresolved and remains resonating in the air. The tension subsides and the focus of the novel returns to Clongowes Wood. However, the morality theme is prolonged further as we overhear the schoolboy gossip about what the older boys did. In Stephen's mind the sin of stealing altar wine for pleasure takes on enormous gravity, highlighting his youthful naivety. And similarly his awe at the word 'smugging' underlines both his isolation from the others as well as his dormant sexuality, not to be awakened until the next chapter. Once again the actual crime is less important than its role of preparing us for the impact of Stephen's own punishment, and the outrage following the rumour that the whole school is to be thrashed is a foretaste of that indignation which follows Stephen's pandying.

As the first episode begins, Stephen Dedalus is alone again, physically now as well as spiritually. Although he listens to the other boys, he does not speak and they do not involve him. He now appears as he has in the previous two sections of the chapter, withdrawn and passive, yet the significant difference here is that Stephen's decisive step to complain to the Rector dramatically demonstrates to us the enormous leap in his development, and brings the chapter to its thematic climax in the confrontation between Stephen and the Catholic Church, working through the morality of its teachers and the image of the victim. This is Stephen's moral vindication.

As we have observed him elsewhere, he is a solitary and on the edge of his line, isolated by intimidation and his own physical frailty, his solitude highlighting his own inwardness which is further reinforced by the narrative point of view, working as it does through Stephen's consciousness. He hears rumours at second or even third hand, has trouble with school slang and takes no part in the dialogue (although 'he wanted to ask somebody about it', (p. 43). The reader also learns early on that his glasses have been broken and that without them Stephen sees everyone as small and distant; he is of course set apart by this too, a point which is physically underlined in Mr Harford's writing class as he sits idly musing to himself while the other boys scratch away with their pens. As he does so his thoughts turn immediately to morality and we see in one moment both the hypocrisy of the Jesuit teachers and also Stephen's mental acuity in drawing attention to it. Mr Harford is 'very decent' but all the other teachers could be fiercely angry, like Father Arnall. And Stephen wonders if it is a sin for a priest to be 'in a wax' as it should be or whether the priests are above the Church's law (these are typical of the sort of theological wrangling in which he indulges and which erode his faith by degrees; see also the openings to Chapters 3 and 4).

Stephen's response to the pandying itself is complex but it is clear that the physical pain is not as wounding as either the emotional pain or the affront to his pride. Again and again he kicks against the cruelty and injustice of it, the humiliation of the prefect's accusation of 'schemer', the injury to his innocence, the ignominy of being ranked alongside Fleming. As if to give another nightmare twist to Stephen's suffering, the prefect threatens further visits, with the ominous tones of Macbeth's 'Tomorrow, and tomorrow, and tomorrow . . .' (p. 50). Further, the section also hints at betrayals, real and potential, not least that by Father Arnall, who makes only a perfunctory attempt to support Stephen even though it was he who had exempted him from the work, Then, although Stephen receives the verbal support of his classmates over the injustice ('It was cruel and unfair . . .', p. 53) and they urge him to complain to the rector, he is wary of their loyalty, a first whiff of betrayal:

The fellows had told him to go but they would not go themselves. (p. 56)

and there is the risk of future humiliation, too, if his complaint to the rector fails – with the likelihood of an additional pandying from Father Dolan.

It is Stephen's pride or ego which is at stake here – an abiding feature

31

of his character throughout – and in due course it is this which triumphs over fear. At first humiliated, Stephen then struggles with his pride in deciding whether or not to see the rector, vainly comparing his own name (like that of the great men in history) with Father Dolan's (which sounds like a washerwoman's). Briefly he is tempted to withdraw, escape and hide out of the way but, instead of following a passive course as in the past, he now asserts himself and his integrity; the triumph which follows marks the vindication and restoration of his pride as much as it trumpets a popular victory over Father Dolan. However, to Stephen this acclaim is less important for public approval than for the personal moral rectitude he has secured, demonstrated by his struggle to be free of the other boys – his physical independence reflecting his moral individualism.

By the end of the chapter he is alone again, and happy to be so. He has engaged with the world, changed it and, having done so, withdrawn from it. By the end of the novel as a whole he will refuse to serve those things which he cannot believe in and will defend this hard-won freedom:

... using for my defence the only arms I will allow myself to use – silence, exile, and cunning.   (p. 251)

Already by the end of Chapter 1 we can see these 'arms' in action, though they appear more often as natural aspects of his own character than as arms taken up. His detachment or isolation from others is a form of exile, a form which implies silence, and there have been many hints already of his cunning: feigning involvement in the rugby (p. 8), pretending not to see that his mother was about to cry (p. 9), and silently pretending to watch a game of dominoes, alone in a corner of the playroom (p. 14).

After a series of trials and some suffering, the chapter finishes on a high note of success, Stephen having matured from 'baby tuckoo' into a figure filled with self-esteem. Having been placed by his father at the centre of the moocow story, he has now placed himself at the centre of his own story.

Chapter 2

The fragmentation and disruption in Joyce's narrative technique, which we saw in the opening chapter of the novel, now intensifies, reflecting the break up and disruption in Stephen's life. The pace of change now increases and, though we naturally see Stephen continue to develop, his progress is less distinct and less singular than it was in the previous chapter. Also, whereas in Chapter 1 his progress was often the result of his response to external stimuli, here it is usually the result of both maturation and obscure internal promptings. In spite of the fragmentation and the diversity in this chapter of his experiences, we can discuss Stephen's development under three principal headings: (a) his relationship with authority, (b) his artistic progress and (c) sexuality.

RELATIONSHIP WITH AUTHORITY

Stephen is now back at home on holiday from Clongowes Wood at the family's new home in Blackrock. After the heady momentum which closes the previous chapter, the opening to this one is a quiescence (what Joyce would later call a *ricorso*). After making his way among the adults in Chapter 1 he how finds himself subject to his adult relatives and under their close supervision. We first see him under the patronage of Uncle Charles ('Stephen's constant companion', p. 61) who urges him to eat fruit for the sake of his bowels, then Mike Flynn instructs him in athletics; he also accompanies his father and Uncle Charles on their walks. His freedom is strictly limited within the dusty regime of adults whose urgings represent old ways and the past, and significantly their walks are always circular (like Patrick Morkan's horse in 'The Dead'), signifying habit and paralysis. After the surge and thrust of Chapter 1, Stephen is now continually caught in a series of people traps.

However, his restive spirit anticipates changes and we begin to see Stephen left more to his own devices. In the evenings, his imagination is indulged in reading *The Count of Monte Cristo*, and escaping through fantasy and a variety of romantic postures and heroic adventures, first through a toy theatre, then alone in the neighbourhood of Blackrock. Later, Stephen himself becomes an authority figure when he leads a gang of boys, modelling himself on Napoleon, until he wearies of child's play and the gang eventually disbands. He becomes restless, aware of approaching adolescence, uncertain of his future but vaguely aware that he has been singled out for some special fate, a predestined career to be heralded by a mysterious figure whose anticipation comes to dominate his outlook (not unlike his distorted image of the heroine, Mercedes, from *Monte Cristo*). Yet he has no idea what exact form this figure may take – it would be female, faintly seductive although, like the biblical Annunciation, she embodies religious rather than sexual symbolism, at least for the time being. However as we see continually in *A Portrait*, reality insistently intrudes on Stephen's dreamworld in the most uncompromising manner, dragging him back to its shabbiness, and filling him with despondency. He roams the docks and red-light districts restlessly, in search of a revelation of his destiny, until disappointment makes him impatient and frustrated with his life, its enigma and lack of direction.

Yet, against this background of stagnation and frustration, we see Stephen move more decisively away from his family. This is so, partly because of his freedom to explore alone, inwardly and spiritually, in addition to his physical roaming of the city and its docks, but also due partly to a decline in his father's authority and solicitude, both correlatives of the decline in the family's prosperity. In the second section they move home yet again and each move, as well as bringing them closer to the city, also places them in increasingly drabber circumstances. Although he spends so much of his time exploring Dublin's streets, Stephen is disheartened by the move, and Joyce's portrait of the city here and in the next chapter is the nearest he comes to a social comment, though much less directly than that in *Dubliners*. Its labyrinthine ways have clear Daedalian affinities but, in ironic contrast to his recently discovered freedom, Stephen now feels trapped by its squalor and sordid dreariness. The ache in his soul, exacerbated by the strange encounters with relatives and other children (p. 69), together with his failure to realize the dream of Mercedes amid this 'dear dead dirty Dumplin', finds no relief – nor will it until it finds eventual expression in Stephen's drive for escape at the end of the novel.

Further disappointments follow. After his long holiday Stephen learns that because of his father's financial predicament he is not to return to Clongowes Wood College – yet another downward spiral – though Mr Dedalus has been able to pull some strings to get Stephen into another Jesuit college, Belvedere, rather than send him to the Christian Brothers.

At the same time he learns that what he thought had been a confidence with Father Conmee (over the pandying) has not only been divulged to his father but also broadcast to the staff of his previous college, making him a laughing stock. It is one more betrayal, one more erosion of authority and particularly that of the Catholic clergy. With unwitting irony, Mr Dedalus concludes: 'O, a jesuit for your life, for diplomacy!' (p. 74).

As another betrayal, it is one of a series of such soul-destroying encounters with authority figures; for example, the admonition theme which is introduced through Dante (p. 8) reappears here when Mr Tate forces him to retract the alleged heresy in his essay (a theme which reaches its climax in Chapter 3 when Father Arnall forces Stephen's repentance). He is also mugged by Heron, his jealous rival, and then he is humiliated by his father on the trip to Cork. At the same time, we also see him adopting roles of authority himself both in terms of his own self-assurance and in relation to other people – leader of the gang, secretary of the college gymnasium and, after winning a literary prize, he takes over the paternal role (defaulted by his father) by treating the family to dinner. In one of the confrontations with Heron and his lieutenants, his literary tastes are subjected to an inquisition and he speaks with authority and passion on his favourite authors (pp. 82–3). Further, because of his sobriety, Stephen is cast in the leading role in the college play, ironically that of a 'farcical pedagogue' (the part which Joyce himself took at school in Anstey's *Vice Versa*, in a send-up of the college rector). We see now a Stephen more on top of his environment, less in awe of it, though the family's continual removals send regular disrupting shocks through it.

It is clear that, after the victory scored in Chapter 1, Stephen now avoids confrontations at all costs where possible. At the time of his pandying at Clongowes he had resisted his own impulse to hide and keep out of the way, choosing instead to put his trust in Father Conmee but, having come now to repudiate that trust in the light of its betrayal, he actively adopts the tactics of escape and evasion. We learn that in situations of potential conflict he has been making vows to silence (p. 82), and Chapter 2 throws up several examples of such conflict. Stephen is confronted twice by Heron – on the first occasion (pp. 82–4) he resists and is beaten by him and his two friends; but on the second, although he becomes briefly angry at his adversary's impertinent remarks about Emma, Stephen stops himself rising to the bait, submitting himself with stifled indignation to their taunts (pp. 77–80 and 84). They are among the first clear threats to his freedom and dignity, empty gestures threatening to humble his youthful spirit:

... he had heard about him the constant voices of his father and of his masters, urging him to be a gentleman above all things and urging him to be a good catholic above all things. These voices had now come to be hollow sounding in his ears.   (p. 86)

This freedom is not won without a price though, and the price for Stephen is solitude, as we see him turn aside without regret into a figure of lonely brooding, withdrawing from conflict but also from contact as a whole. He is set now on a loveless career and, on one occasion at a children's party, having shunned the company of the other children, we are told that '. . . he began to taste the joy of his loneliness' (p. 70).

It is this drive towards independence, combined with his vanity and a romantic imagination, which accounts for Stephen's notion that he is set apart for a unique destiny, an extension of his image of Parnell as Messianic hero. His budding individualism makes him dimly aware of (and at the same time prepares him for) a calling so exceptional that it is incomprehensible to him, at least for the present, until the annunciation in Chapter 4 when he apprehends the vision of the estuary girl as his call to art; until then it is but vaguely understood as the promise of a tryst,

. . . a premonition which led him on told him that this image would, without any overt act of his, encounter him. (p. 67)

Clearly the imagination is as significant in Stephen's interpretation of this phenomenon as it is in the artistic faculty itself, his strong imagination, working in isolation, enabling him to contemplate such possibilities just as it enables him to indulge in dreamplays of the Count of Monte Cristo.

At Cork, however, reality forces itself in and he receives several shocks to his self-complacency as he accompanies his father to the university. We have seen how Stephen, trying to avoid unpleasant conflicts through cunning, also frequently tries to withdraw from the reality of the outside world into an inner refuge (p. 65) – yet the visit to Cork to sell off the remains of his father's property there, like so many other intimations of the family's financial social decline, is yet another reminder of an ever-present rude reality, lying on the fringe of the imagination.

As Mr Dedalus revisits his old haunts, jawing with old friends and harping on their salad days, he uses his pride in his Cork roots to isolate and humiliate Stephen, through an alcoholic haze, treating his son like a rival (pp. 97–8). As a result Stephen too begins uncomfortably to feel his own past grow dim and his childhood dead and the coldness of his new ways (pp. 98–9). The reminiscences of his father and his cronies force him to see his own life from the point of view of others and, as he moves outside of himself and begins to share their ordinariness, he has the harrowing fear that his destiny may after all be a delusion.

It is a point which had been demonstrated to him earlier when, at the university, Stephen is horrified by the word 'foetus' carved into a desk.

But, as the epiphany which follows it reveals, he is horrified not by the morality of the word but by the realization that he shares the same vulgarity of mind as the student who had carved it. Whereas formerly he had seen this as a symptom of his own unique depravity, he is now shocked to discover how ordinary his sexuality really is. He is forced inexorably to reflect on the coldness of his life, the draining away of his youth, and the sterility of his loneliness in contrast to those around him.

ARTISTIC DEVELOPMENT

On the other hand, Chapter 2 also contains important pointers to Stephen's steady artistic development, the second of this chapter's major themes. Chief among these is the poem which he composes, inspired by his farewell to E.C., Emma Clery, after the party at Harold's Cross (the initials are explained in *Stephen Hero* – in *A Portrait* she is never referred to except as E.C. or Emma). Although he sits in smug isolation after his song recital at the party, he later escorts Emma to the tram. As they talk he yearns to kiss her but, in spite of his conviction that she wishes it, he fails to bring the moment to its fruition. For him it is a moment of enduring crisis whose vividness and gravity remain with him for the rest of the time in the novel, inspiring not only that poem which he stutteringly composes at home the next day but also, indirectly, the one which he writes 'after ten years', set out in full in Chapter 5 (p. 227). Although we are not shown the earlier effort it seems to have been strongly influenced by Shelley and by Stephen's love of Byron (p. 72). As he begins to write he recalls too the occasion of the Christmas dinner in Chapter 1 after which he had tried to compose verses to the memory of Parnell (as a nine-year-old Joyce had done in his poem 'Et tu, Healy'). Where earlier he had failed, now by dogged persistence he is successful – though he is motivated as much by the simple romantic idea of writing a poem as inspired by any genuinely creative impulse, elaborating his work in ostentatious imitation of the Byron poems in his collection.[2]

His poem omits the details of the scene and its two characters are generalized (in fact it anticipates the villanelle in Chapter 5 which is even more of an abstraction), but significantly, whereas in real life he had failed to kiss Emma, in the poem he is successful: art improves on nature, compensating for the inadequacies of reality. On the whole Stephen finds art easier to cope with than real life and realizes his desires through art as yet another of many forms of escape in the novel. It confirms a point made earlier by the narrator: that words are the primary means by which Stephen understands the real world (p. 64); in Modernist terms the world of art and literature precedes the world of real life. To a large extent it also explains why, for much of the early part of the novel, Stephen recoils from fully engaging with that 'real life', favouring instead the inner life of the imagination or living through literature, as he does, for instance, with *The Count of Monte Cristo*. It is taken up later too in Chapter 4 when, as Stephen stands on the estuary, he selects a phrase to describe the skyscape before him. Though he reflects on the relationship between words, feelings and reality, he prefers the beauty of the words to that of the real scene to which they relate.

– A day of dappled seaborne clouds.

The phrase and the day and the scene harmonised in a chord. Words. Was it their colours? He allowed them to glow and fade, hue after hue ... No, it was not their colours: it was the poise and balance of the period itself. (pp. 170–71)

In spite of his insistence at the end of the novel that he will go forward to encounter the reality of life, for most of the book we observe him trying to avoid it.

Chapter 2 is a chapter of upheavals and frustrations in Stephen's life – physically, in the family's moving house, as well as emotionally – and Joyce reflects this in the frequent disruptions. Against these, however, the world of art offers Stephen equilibrium and a fixed point and he seizes them even though it is significant that he should have found these in art rather than, conventionally, in his religion, though for the time being the religious influence endures – a point demonstrated, for example, by heading his poem with a Jesuit motto, A.M.D.G. (*Ad Majorem Dei Gloriam*: for the greater glory of God), and concluding it with another, L.D.S. (*Laus Deo Semper*: praise be to God always).

But there are other signs of the increasing importance of art, especially in literature, in Stephen's life. As well as his greater interest in reading (he relieves his unrest by steeping himself in the work of subversive writers, p. 80), we are told more about his own writing. The weekly essay is his central concern now and a major challenge. On one occasion he suffers the humiliation of Mr Tate's charge of heresy (p. 81) but, towards the end of the chapter, his talents are endorsed by being awarded an essay prize and exhibition money which he sets about squandering in a riot of spending. As said before, he appears to have inherited his father's profligacy with money, though his own spending is motivated less by generosity than by vanity and an urge to indulge himself. At the end, when the funds are exhausted, he is ashamed by the failure of his munificence to bring him any closer to his mother and the rest of the family. A sudden memory of the lost days of Clongowes Wood innocence, together with the romanticized image of Mercedes, points up the sordidness and futility which he feels keenly about his life, its lack of firm direction and true feeling. The prize is his first real public commendation of literary talent, but a talent which he now turns to lewd and erotic scribblings, the 'improper arts', as he describes them in Chapter 5.

Another expression of his increasing interest in literature is literary criticism, with his raw theorizings – anticipating the aesthetic philosophy of Chapter 5 – shown now in his quarrel with Heron and friends. We are alerted by his bird-name (birds in *A Portrait* have a threefold significance: as figures of admonition as well as of flight and of beauty, pp. 8, 175 and 230). His interrogation recalls for Stephen a similar confrontation with Mr Tate over the heresy allegation. But against Heron he now stands defiant and asserts his choice of writers: for prose, Newman (whom Joyce also loved for his exquisite style) and for verse, Byron (though Joyce preferred Blake). Clearly, Stephen's *risqué* endorsement of this libertine and social outcast is a provocative assertion of his own free-thinking, a point which inverts the moral effect of Heron's claim that Stephen is a 'heretic'.

SEXUALITY

At root here is simple rivalry, of course, and a rivalry essentially sexual in origin. Sexuality is by far the most powerful theme of the chapter, manifested in the general but pervasive atmosphere of brooding unrest, frustration, and of movement as a whole. This is paralleled by the background changes of the family's fortunes, of instability, material decline and upheaval. In the foreground are Stephen's own unrest, his disillusionment with family and dissatisfaction with life, all of which lead to his restless wanderings on the Dublin night streets. His encounters with girls are difficult and unsatisfactory (pp. 69–71) and he later submits to crude and brutish sexual fantasies.

This latter feature is the product of a combination of a powerful imagination and an overpowering sensuality (signalled in the first chapter by Stephen's preoccupation with Eileen's smooth white hands), together with his frustrated sexual yearning. His sensuality and imagination maintain their high potency, but in the latter half of the chapter they focus on a more definite object – the opposite sex. His sexuality is projected first through a vaguely idealized notion of a tryst represented by the sentimental fantasy over Mercedes (pp. 66–7) and then physically transfigured into the idea of Emma and the 'kiss denied', reaching ultimate consummation in the carnal embrace of the prostitute at the end of the chapter. However, although the narrator generally presents Stephen as suffering here the same range and intensity of emotions as in Chapter 1 (fear, anger, frustration, humiliation and joy) his fantasies are essentially loveless. But it is a lovelessness which does not evoke our sympathy since it stems principally from Stephen's own selfish will, impelled by sexual desire. While there may be something of a search for love in this agitated, agonized yearning, when it reaches its climax in the brothel it is primarily lust, not love, which is gratified.

Throughout the chapter, sexuality continues to surface directly as well as indirectly, usually to emphasize Stephen's anxious predicament of uncertain expectation. After the Mercedes–Monte Cristo episode, three epiphanies follow involving girls which epitomize this – each is introduced with the phrase: 'He was sitting'[3] – and in one of which Stephen himself is actually mistaken for a girl (as in the college play, Bertie Tallon is similarly mistaken, p. 76). In the one involving E.C., what we learn is on the whole limited to her physical appearance, located not in the point of view of the narrator but of Stephen, who in watching her searches for particular signs in her body and clothing, her 'vanities' (p. 71), and we learn nothing of Emma herself. She is referred to only through the pronouns 'her' and 'she', and Stephen's enigmatic use of her initials for his poem (in which she remains a vague, distant figure) helps to stress her elusiveness (by adhering to this narrative viewpoint the narrator collaborates with Stephen's perspective: sticking exclusively to her physical details makes us, too, see her not as neutrals but as Stephen does).

In this chapter she becomes for him an idea rather than a real person, the poem an expression of his blunted sexuality (in immediate relation to himself, not to others, p. 218) and he is made to confront this more explicitly during the school play when Heron jealously probes his feelings for her, exposing Stephen's raw and vulnerable sensitivity. His taunt about seeing her makes Stephen burn with momentary fury and after the play, when he discovers that she had not been there, Stephen is overwhelmed both by the shameful realization of his vanity and by his weakness before his own fierce desire for her. In spite of his powerful fixation on her she remains for us only the shadowy object of his frenzy.

Where the early part of the chapter is concerned with the Call –
represented symbolically in the form of Mercedes – the final section of
it deals with the Fall, again symbolized in the form of a woman, the
prostitute. The external scene is typically evoked through imagery of
darkness, secrecy and squalor but, in implied contrast with the innocence of Chapter 1, Stephen's response is now depicted in terms of
lascivious sensuality. Although it is Stephen who has gone out to the
brothels and actively sought out the girls, it is the girl herself who
brings the moment to its crisis. She is the seducer in the final act and he
falls, succumbing to the seductive allure of her body and to the charm
of the brothel's colours and fragrance. It is she who embraces him, an
embrace ironically more maternal than carnal.

The narrator now stresses Stephen's passiveness – he is paralysed by
the moment, unable to kiss her until as she does so he swoons in her
arms. He surrenders his conscious, rational nature to an overwhelming
physical passion (one of the rare occasions in the novel when he does
become fully immersed in the emotional action instead of living it at a
cerebral distance), and, to stress Stephen's passiveness, the narrator
stresses the elements of ritual and initiation which the occasion is for
Stephen. Yet the style is not lax but rigorous and highly controlled, set
as a foil to Stephen's swooning emotion, suggesting a further analogy
with the Daedalus myth (Stephen sets his mind to the unknown)[4] – the
passionate nature of man as Minotaur is held in check by the maze of
man's reason, and Joyce's strictly organized prose containing Stephen's
fierce emotion in the same way.

As in many other areas of his experience, Stephen has already
explored in his mind what he will test in reality. The absence of love
here also underlines the coldness of his formalized contact with the girl
and is a hint of his future course. Just as, by the end of Chapter 5, his
literary work is dominated by form (villanelle and diaries) so his sexual
venture is a formal relation, devoid of the lyricism of his earlier romantic
idealism (although, in fact, the aura of their embrace is very much in
the same manner as Stephen's previous fantasies and just as illusory).
In *Ulysses* too he is bewildered by the word 'love' ('the word known to
all men'), and his visits to the Nighttown brothels have become commonplace.

The whore is the end of his searching, promising rest as well as
release, certainty and, above all, knowledge. Accordingly the thematic
strands and emotional frustrations of the chapter find their resolution
and relief at this moment but, whereas in previous moments reality has
an acutely sharpening impact on the focus, here it is softening and

yielding. At the same time, the chapter's finely woven rhythms are focused tightly on to this moment, for instance, in the interplay of dark and light settings and the rhythm of Stephen's hopes and disappointments – as they did in Chapter 1. But the triumph towards which they draw, like the intermediate successes along the way, are here less public and less concerned with the assertion of the ego than simply with its survival.

Chapter 3

The structure of this chapter is largely determined by the three-day structure of the retreat: Father Arnall's sermons, with a section on either side, prologue and epilogue, resemble the structure of Dante's *The Divine Comedy*, as Stephen travels like Virgil from Inferno (becoming aware of sin and guilt), through Purgatorio (fear of the death of his soul, despair and contrition), to a glimpse of Paradiso (expiation, Mass and Communion). The retreat itself is based on a model set out in *The Spiritual Exercises* (1548) by St Ignatius Loyola (founder of the Jesuits and of whom St Francis Xavier was a disciple), and the sermons themselves are developed from a seventeenth-century Italian text translated as *Hell Opened to Christians, to Caution Them from Entering into It*. It is a chapter of excesses, in Father Arnall's terrorizing sermons and in Stephen's responses to them, both of which features are the source of its humour, Joyce's own divine comedy.

The chapter as a whole covers five days:

Day 1	Rector interrupts the maths lesson to announce the retreat dedicated to St Francis Xavier, a great missionary and saver of souls
Wednesday	Afternoon: Father Arnall's sermons begin. Purpose of the retreat is to withdraw, reflect, understand. Subject is the 'four last things': death, judgement, hell, heaven.
Thursday	Death and Judgement (a) Particular judgement (b) General judgement (Doomsday)
Friday	Sin and Hell Morning: physical torment of senses – darkness, fire, filth and stench; noxious company, division, no friends or family Lunchtime: English lesson Evening: Spiritual torment 1. Pain of loss of God, light and goodness

2. Pain of conscience (stings: memory, futile sorrow, remorse)
3. Pain of extension
4. Pain of intensity
5. Pain of eternity of hell

Saturday   Feast of St Francis Xavier – 9 o'clock Mass

Stephen's moral state is summed up in the opening paragraph by pointing up the needs of his belly – the intellect is still subsumed by the bodily appetite – and the horrors to come are dimly prefigured in the opening atmosphere: it is a dull December dusk, threatening a 'gloomy secret night', devious and weary. The words 'dull' and 'dark' plod ponderously over the opening pages like a routine, as the narrative style settles to a sluggish catalogue of statements. At this stage there is no hint of remorse, and Stephen's familiarity with the ways of the brothel district implies that his visits have become commonplace. Now aged sixteen, he idly contemplates the night's activities during the course of his maths lesson, to which he shows complete indifference (compare this with his enthusiasm for that lesson at Clongowes, p. 12). He is equally indifferent to the state of sin in which his soul languishes, and even to the hypocrisy implied in his being a prefect of the sodality of the Blessed Virgin Mary, though at the same time he is prevented from resigning this office by the possible embarrassment which it would cause. Ironically, he considers that his being in such a state of sin actually brings him closer to Mary, the refuge of sinners. Yet fornication, having laid open his soul to eternal damnation, has also opened it to other deadly sins, particularly pride. However, in spite of this declared indifference, his thoughts continue to dwell on sin and, by the very act of identifying and naming his sin, he comes to acknowledge his own guilt, at least within the terms of his religion. He also derives a wilful pleasure from exploring theological niceties and contradictions to their conclusion which, while perverse, serves to prolong Stephen's attention within the context of Catholic morality, preparing the way for his eventual repentance.

Pride, which has featured strongly in the opening chapters, now surfaces again and begins to predominate. Stephen takes pride in wrangling, arrogantly scorning his religion (another of those voices threatening to 'humble the pride of his youth', p. 179) and disparaging the faithful at Mass. Pride plays a large part too in both his original and later visits to the prostitutes. It is pride which prevents him from

43

acknowledging the superiority of God and making a confession, but it is also pride which eventually makes him repent and then delight in his state of grace.

Yet even as the Rector announces the retreat, we see Stephen's conscience begin to prick him faintly with fear. The retreat is to be in honour of St Francis Xavier, whose prowess the rector proudly extols in terms both of mathematics (ten thousand baptized in one month!) and of might, both of which are the key parameters of the sermon itself.

In spite of the fierce intent behind Father Arnall's fearful set piece and in spite of Stephen's timorous reaction to it, Joyce's comedy repeatedly makes itself felt and also makes clear how we are to respond to it. Ironies abound even in the priest's introduction to the retreat, chief among them being the very reappearance of Father Arnall, Stephen's former Latin master at Clongowes Wood. Old-looking now, he makes Stephen recall his earlier school, the playground, the ditch and the infirmary where he dreamed of his own death, but most of all of his lost innocence (as the epiphany on p. 112 indicates).

Ironically he asks the boys what changes they *cannot* remember, misattributes his opening quotation (to Ecclesiastes when it really is Ecclesiasticus, 7:40), and then urges the moral stalwarts of the sodality of the Virgin Mary (namely, Stephen Dedalus) to set a good example to the other boys. Later, a contrite Stephen feels that every word of this sermon is intended for himself but already, at the start, he begins to feel this especially after Father Arnall hopes that the retreat may help to lead any sinners back to grace again.

Throughout the novel both we and Stephen are given frequent sudden shocks of reality working through the narrator's earthy prose, often as a foil to Stephen's idealism, and usually to sharpen up the real world as a comment on Stephen's thinking. In Chapter 3 Joyce puts this to excellent moral purpose. For instance, when Stephen returns home after the first day of the retreat he finds it difficult to stomach his dinner, in spite of his earlier expectations, and the congealed-food images combine with the references to the appetite to stress both his current brutish preoccupation with the body as well as incipient stirrings of guilt:

So he had sunk to the state of a beast that licks his chaps after meat. (p. 115)

The main thrust of Father Arnall's sermon, however, is not morality but intimidation. The hell he describes is a medieval vision (compare those of the painters Bosch and Brueghel) but undoubtedly one which the boys can comprehend on their own level. Although it is the soul which suffers its horrors, it suffers them on a bodily rather than a spiritual dimension. Through intimidation and chiefly by the scale and intensity of his depictions, he actively seeks to harrow and terrify the boys, especially those undergoing the temptations and confusions of puberty. They create their effect on Stephen (and on the reader) by the way in which they take up themes and images from earlier in the novel and, working again through Stephen's acute imagination, force him to interpret the burden of the sermons as directed personally at himself, in fact exclusively at himself. Because the 'action' of the novel has become more verbal and internal and because Joyce occasionally omits the speech marks (see p. 115 on) the sermon actually appears to come less from the preacher than directly through Stephen's own mind. This has two chief effects. One is that it allows us to hear the preacher's words and Stephen's response to them more or less simultaneously, and the other is that it brilliantly sets up the intensely claustrophobic atmosphere of this part of the chapter, sharpening Stephen's (and the reader's) fixation on the words, words which are Stephen's gateway to reality. We see hardly anything else of Stephen's activities over the next few days even though, in reality, he still has free time most evenings at home. The impression we get though is that his thoughts are firmly focused on the wages of sin and very little else, adding further to the claustrophobia and to his conviction that every word was meant for him.

Among the earlier themes and images which the sermon touches on, that of division strikes a very familiar note. Father Arnall mentions this as a fact of death and then includes it as one of the torments of hell: that the sinner is separated from family and friends with no possibility of ties to relieve the suffering, no hope of family relationships or friends or country (pp. 117–26) – but we have seen already that Stephen is actively adopting this course in the form of detachment, alienation and exile. And the retreat itself takes place in isolation of the 'busy bustle of the outer world' (p. 112), as Father Arnall insists, to enable them to leave behind any possible relief from distraction or worldly pleasure. Then another theme we see taken up from earlier chapters is that of the senses and their importance in Stephen's development, since from the very opening section we have seen how the narrator, working through Stephen, has established the fundamental link between raw physical sensations and language. For Stephen they have been, in Chapter 1, a source of curiosity and differentiation (smells and temperature, etc.), and in Chapter 2 a source of pleasure and sin, in the feel of clothing and the delights of the flesh. Now Father Arnall turns them about by reminding him that in hell these are the perfect source of torment since they were also the origin of the sin itself: 'Every sense of the flesh is tortured ...' (p. 125). Vividly he catalogues their horrors: unceasing darkness, the howling of the damned, scum and a lake fire, and the foul stench (curiously Father Arnall becomes preoccupied with this foul stench but in the next chapter, when Stephen mortifies the senses he finds that of smell the most difficult to torture).

Finally there is one theme which concerns Stephen's own character most directly. Towards the end of his diatribe on physical torments, Father Arnall explains that the sinner's shame will be deepened by the stark realization that he has been discovered by God: 'Time was to sin in secrecy, ...' (p. 127). This too hits home with Stephen as it has long been part of his strategy of silence and cunning to conceal from everyone what he has been up to (for instance, the darkness under which Stephen operated in Chapter 2 is a correlative of this secrecy and deviousness, and he was embittered to learn that Heron had penetrated his tentative relationship with Emma). Further, his duplicitous position as a sodality prefect is also a form of deception – self-deception. (In Chapter 5 Stephen claims that the only arms he will use to defend himself with are silence, exile and cunning, and it is important to note that these characteristics are already part of his armoury as early as Chapter 3.)

Thus Father Arnall's sermon makes Stephen interpret what is said as a dire warning exclusively to himself. Ironically, his own pride and the strength of his imagination account for this conclusion to a great extent, and his egoism draws into himself all that is said.

On Thursday, Stephen again visualizes his own death – as he had in Chapter 1 (p. 24) – only this time his body is less an object of heroic worship than one of revulsion. His imagination conjures up a comic tableau in which Emma is at his side, and they are standing before the benign motherly figure of the Virgin Mary, forgiving the two of them (that Emma should be implicated is another fiction on Stephen's part and probably a lingering hangover from his desire for her). The three of them together – piously reconciling the twin medieval aspects of woman, carnal and maternal – is naturally an idealized image of virtue contrasting expressively with his earlier erotic fantasies set out in sordid letters ingeniously composed to horrify young girls. The contrast not only points up his wickedness of course but, more important, his awareness of it and his timorous shame, and these in turn point up the success of Father Arnall's words on his fertile imagination.

It is the imagination, likewise, which passes judgement on Stephen's soul, already on the brink of destruction; he construes a row of raincoats as ominous, headless corpses of 'gibbeted malefactors' (p. 128). For once, he is relieved to hear the voices of his classmates during lunch, as we return to reality (Father Arnall and the narrator shrewdly interpolate these pauses for Stephen to stew in his guilt and for us to watch him squirm). Mr Tate's quip (p. 128) is intended to restore perspective to the narrative, but Stephen is now so intensely absorbed with fear that he misses it and spends his break in a nightmare trance while all around him the other boys munch indifferently away at their food.

According to his original scheme, Father Arnall was to have reached heaven in the concluding part of his sermon. However, he forgets and never leaves hell, dwelling for too long on the infernal and lingering until the end of the third day, with more of his harrowing portrait and a detailed inventory of the pains of hell. Clearly, this aptly suits the overall moral effect on Stephen as well as providing the narrative climax to the chapter, rather than discharging the accumulated moral energy with a rosy prospect of heaven's delights. Instead, the climax is carried over from the sermons into the Mass and Stephen's communion, which functions as the Paradiso intended by Father Arnall.

So far we have considered the effect of the sermons on Stephen's intimate nature and the way in which his background and upbringing combine together with Father Arnall's words to create that effect. But how do we evaluate the sermons in themselves? Seriously, or as a great joke? And against whom? Certainly Joyce's achievement in them is masterly. They are a vividly horrifying and uncompromising depiction, and the narrator's technique of using Stephen's own consciousness as a window makes the reader more intimate with the experience and the experience more unified. Equally, their rhetorical energy is overwhelming and their powerful intimidating effect is clear to see. Even without close analysis we can see that many of the speaker's effects rely heavily on rhetoric and there are some extraordinarily vivid and striking images, such as the analogy between eternity and the small bird moving a mountain of sand grain by grain (p. 135), and the hellish clock ticking '. . . ever, never; ever, never.' (p. 136 – another of the cluster of alternating sound rhythms in the novel, see also pp. 17 and 90). At the same time, although Father Arnall claims that this punishment is the work of a just God, the sermons are clearly preoccupied with a portrait of a ruthless regime (like Dante's admonitory eagles), vindictive and intolerant, devoid of mercy and compassion.

In fact, Joyce's joke is on and against the Church. The comedy is another indictment of the Roman Catholic obsession with an avenging God and his absolute authority, bereft of the very virtues expected of mankind in the first place. Their effectiveness relies heavily on Father

Arnall's own powerful imagination, too. His obsession with the vividly exaggerated details of hell and its suffering begins itself to sound perverse; for example, in his depiction of the heaped and bound decomposing bodies of the damned, with their boiling blood and of 'tender eyes flaming like molten balls' (p. 125). His preoccupation with the small print of hell, classifying punishment first into 'pains' and then the pains into 'stings' in addition to the assortment of tortures and torments makes hell sound more bureaucratic than demonic. Also, after having one's corpse 'decomposing ... a jellylike mass of liquid corruption' (p. 124) and then the brain 'boiling' and the bowels 'a redhot mass of burning pulp' (p. 125), the sting of memory would hardly seem to matter (p. 132).

Stephen's response is frequently comic, too. Not only is he spiritually stunned by the sermons but also physically convulsed. By the end of the third day he can barely walk from the chapel and he is convinced that his personal destruction is imminent as he wobbles back to his room. His response to the excesses of the sermons is itself excessive (as Chapter 4 confirms) and it reinforces Joyce's comic purpose, starting with his own vision of bestial horror and a bout of vomiting, followed by repentant self-abasement before the Holy Ghost. Gradually however his disposition for theatricality displaces his fear and he indulges in postures of meek piety and awestruck humility (resembling the sort of swooning movement experienced by Stephen at the end of Chapters 2 and 4, see pp. 104 and 177). At length the expansive glow of jubilation reaches its climax of brilliant radiance in which even the pudding and his sausages participate (p. 149).

At first sight Father Arnall's set pieces appear as plain yet forceful religious sermons but, at the same time, we can recognize that their symbolic effect on Stephen resembles that of other familiar figures of intimidation already met in the novel: Dante, Wells, Dolan, Heron – all threatening to humble his youthful spirit. Like later appeals to Stephen in terms of political, religious and family allegiances, this is a crucial confrontation with authority, both secular and religious. However, whereas in the previous chapter we had observed Stephen at last beginning to cope with such figures (mainly through silence and evasion, stirred on by pride), we now see him reduced by terror to a trembling submissive. So, in terms of Stephen's progress towards artistic freedom and intellectual autonomy, this chapter marks a figurative as well as literal retreat towards conformity. He is forced to concede to not only the demands, but also the morality and the credo of the Church, partly because it is so all-pervasive and exclusive – at home and at school – but even more because he is forever meeting it in his conscience. Every word of the sermon seems to be 'for him' simply because the Church has drummed the same words and the same morality into him since childhood. So, in effect, the sermons are an externalization of Stephen's conscience at this stage, and of the morality imposed upon it – even when Stephen visits the prostitutes he still describes it as 'sin' (pp. 101 and 102). It is not so much that he has been constructing a new moral code for himself, as just trying to break the received one and, in doing so he is constantly being reminded of it. In due course, the long-term effect of this conflict on Stephen will be to make him first analyse and then ultimately reject his religion and its code but, for the time being, his progress is arrested and reverted by it.

We see that the effect of the sermons begins to be marked in the final section of the chapter where, seeking refuge at home, Stephen's fertile imagination now populates his bedroom with silent furies and grotesque beasts, projections of his guilt and an insight into his private hell. He undergoes Father Arnall's hell in microcosm. But it is neither guilt nor even remorse at his sin which lies at the heart of his change. The cause is not even moral. It is primarily fear – he is cowed by a vision of hell, by the threat of his soul's eternal torture. And in this lies the possibility of future rejection. Eventually he is cowed into seeking salvation in religion though it takes an immense effort of courage to visit the chapel in order to make his confession. (Each of the first four chapters finishes with Stephen plucking up courage to make a visit which will lead to knowledge and elation – all of them prologues to that departure in the final chapter, uncertain and restrained.)

Ironically, we see him making his way to the chapel along the same labyrinth of dirty ill-lit streets, and under the same kind of darkness as that in which his 'fall' had occurred. He is directed to a chapel by an old woman, and there his confessor is an old priest, both of them symbolizing the old ways to which Stephen now retreats. Darkness pervades both the church where he makes his atonement and the streets on his way back home. And then, at the end of the chapter, his ecstasy of grace bursts out in rapturous imagery of light and whiteness. At Mass, in both literal and metaphorical communion, he is described as 'happy and shy' fulfilling his prayer to be so, yet at the same time reversing his previous movement towards alienation (in Chapter 2, happiness was equated with solitude), and merging himself, for the present at least, in the common tide of other lives.

The boys were all there, kneeling in their places. He knelt among them, happy and shy.   (p. 149)

Chapter 4

Towards the end of this chapter we are told that Stephen 'could wait no longer' (p. 168) and he strides off 'abruptly' to discover his destiny, leaving behind both his father, who is trying to arrange a place for Stephen at university, and the Church which has just tempted him with a lifetime of order and obedience. Both are hollowsounding guardians of his youth now and he strides purposely off to seek his own clues to his future in a mysterious tryst. The chapter marks a crucial watershed in Stephen's development, in his relationships with the tandem themes of family and religion and also with what he comes to recognize as his artistic destiny. It opens with images of constraint and discipline and closes with freedom, while among its chief concerns are order, power and the Daedalus myth. We can examine it by considering its three principal thrusts: Stephen's rejection of the priesthood, his attitude towards his family, the epiphany of the estuary.

The chapter begins with a list of Stephen's daily devotions, in a prosaic businesslike style, reflecting Stephen's new systematic routine. The opening prolongs the momentum if not the ecstasy of the previous chapter, intensifying Stephen's swelling piety while at the same time defusing the accumulated emotional force. After the joyous vision of salvation comes the day-to-day business of penance. Monk-like (he later describes himself as a monk, p. 224), Stephen dogmatically imposes on himself a strict religious regime, dedicating the days of the week to different devotional areas. Again we see the eminence of mathematical principles in his approach to this, dividing his time with a rigour reminiscent of Father Arnall's sermons. Not only days of the week, but parts of the day, are carved up too. He is scrupulous as well as meticulous, allowing no relief and no compromise in his discipline and prayers. These are explicitly dedicated for the relief of souls in purgatory, though his zeal is blunted a little by not knowing exactly how many days or years, he had stored in their account (like a 'great cash register', p. 151). He perseveres however and, recognizing the risks of spiritual exaltation (that he might actually come to enjoy or take pride in his devotion), he sets out to mortify each of the senses.

However, the narrator's voice is unmistakably ironic as we observe Stephen going scrupulously about the various processes of his devotion.

In fact, he is over-scrupulous in this, resembling the priest in Joyce's short story 'The Sisters', Father James Flynn, who dies as a result of spiritual paralysis, described by one of his sisters as 'too scrupulous always' (– an obsessiveness in moral questions and a tendency to exaggerate minor sins and guilt to an unreasonable level. Ironically, Stephen's scrupulousness is accounted for in part by his pride, just as it is complemented by vanity through the various postures which he adopts (in the same way that Joyce's ironic narrator appropriates and exploits the language of the Church, its vocabulary and tonalities, in mock reverence).

The narrator goes further though, telling us that by his dedication Stephen even approaches such a degree of selflessness that he momentarily catches a rare glimpse of the undeniable possibility of love:

... and only then for the first time since he had brooded on the great mystery of love did he feel within him a warm movement like that of some newly born life or virtue of the soul itself.   (p. 153)

But it is only a glimpse and the chance is gone. In the following sentence he resumes his posture:

The attitude of rapture in sacred art, the raised and parted hands, the parted lips and eyes as of one about to swoon, became for him an image of the soul in prayer, humiliated and faint before her Creator.   (p. 153)

At first sight, Stephen's posture and role-play may suggest to us that after all he does have the capacity for selflessness which comes about by denying his own identity – for example, he pictures himself praying in the catacombs (among the dead, p. 150), and he sees himself fading out of existence (p. 153; see also pp. 24 and 98). But all they really show is Stephen's anxiety about himself; on the one hand, they enable him to cope with his ego and, on the other, they are a way of locating himself in the world by temporarily ceasing to be himself.

At the same time, he does (however briefly) recognize the possibility of love and understands the love of God but, as he admits to Cranly in Chapter 5 (p. 245), he is unable to love other people or God and feels remorse that he cannot approach them more closely. And this failure of love is one reason for the failure too of his religious devotion at the start of the chapter, as he himself acknowledges:

To merge his life in the common tide of other lives was harder for him than any fasting or prayer ... (p. 155)

It recalls a similar failure in Chapter 2 when his prize money does not bring him any closer to his family. He fails to find companionship and he is unwilling and unable to sacrifice himself or his aspirations in the service of others.

Another reason for the failure of his devotion is the extreme zeal ('scrupulousness') itself, impossible to sustain and whose aims are too absolute to achieve. His inability to punish the senses to his own satisfaction also contributes further to his failure, and yet another factor is Stephen's own suspicion that his prayers are ineffectual either in achieving relief for the souls in purgatory or in quenching his deep pangs of guilt. He becomes convinced by this feeling, and by the continual presence of temptation, that his original confession had failed because it was not sincere (p. 156). But then he has second thoughts and gradually persuades himself that after all because he had amended his life his confession must have been valid and true.

A more important reason for failure though, uniting all these points, lies in the tremendous feeling of power with which Stephen's renewed state of grace endows him: the possibility of yielding to temptation reveals to him, in a flash, the profound power to undo all his efforts. Although at first this appears capricious, it becomes translated by the second section of the chapter into a more rational position following Stephen's interview with the director. The meeting recalls previous encounters with figures of authority; as Stephen gazes at the curves on the director's skull, we are suddenly taken back to the end of Chapter 1 and the skull lying on Father Conmee's desk, and so induced to compare Stephen's performance on the two occasions (pp. 57 and 157).

Stephen is now undoubtedly more objective and more discreet in his attitude towards authority. As he awaits the director he is much less in awe of the occasion, impatient even, and his exchanges with the director are cautious, polite, at times indulgent and, above all, non-committal. He listens in 'reverent silence', relaxed though puzzled at the reason for the director's summons. But as he listens, his mind instinctively translates and subverts the priest's awesome appeal, via his own eccentric perspective, setting up a comic contrast between the two and highlighting the folly of the director's appeal; for instance, in the preamble to the interview when the director uses the French '*les jupes*'; these words immediately trigger in Stephen's mind not thoughts of religion but, by different association, the irreverent realms of sexuality and women's clothing, exposing his delicate susceptibilities. However, when the director turns more directly to the possibility of a vocation in the priesthood, the idea appeals at once to Stephen's pride, especially with thoughts of power and eminence; he is proud, too, that the director has singled him out like this.

Firstly, the idea coheres with Stephen's own partiality for role-play – he had occasionally pictured himself as a Jesuit priest or acolyte, silent, anonymous, devout but aloof, selflessly administering the ritualistic functions and offices of the Church before his pious flock. Again the theatrical element proves irresistible to his imagination and eventually the daydream reaches its climax later in the prospect of:

Reverend Stephen Dedalus, S.J.   (p. 164)

Secondly, he contemplates the priesthood in terms of its power: the privileged status of the Jesuits with their secret knowledge and secret powers. But typical of Stephen's frailty is that this becomes translated into the salacious prospect of hearing the intimate confessions of women and girls (a simoniacal temptation closely following his reference to the sin of Simon Magus, (p. 162).

To strengthen his overture, the director then tries different strategies on Stephen, including a reminder that his Christian name is that of the first martyr (stoned to death in about AD 35)[5] and by doing so he makes explicit all the many earlier elements which have elaborated the role of victim for Stephen. But it is an error, and the last time (as well as the first) that this Christian element surfaces explicitly; from this point Stephen never again contemplates this role. Instead, the focus switches to the significance of his surname, from Christian to Daedalian mythology.

In spite of these inducements, Stephen eventually rejects the offer of the priesthood. But why? It cannot simply be that he has lost his faith. Clearly, although his faith does indeed fade at this moment, there is no crisis of conscience for Stephen – and even if there were such a crisis, then a career in the Church could hold out the hope of a revival of dead faith. There are, however, several reasons for his refusal. One is in the harsh realistic prospect of the coldness and rigour of the Jesuit order – often mentioned in Chapter 1 and called to mind again now (p. 164) – threatening to swallow his pride and individuality. Another, more important, reason is the commitment involved, that he would have to remain a priest for ever. In either case, there would be no freedom to choose. Moreover, the interview acts as a catalyst, compelling Stephen to face up to wider questions of religion too. He reflects that, while he has always respected the Jesuits, some of their judgements are now beginning to sound childish (p. 159). They are also becoming a liability, threatening to compromise his free spirit – he remembers one priest who disparaged Victor Hugo in favour of an obscure Catholic bigot, Louis Veuillot, not on intrinsic aesthetic grounds but on the basis of religious dogma (p. 160). The question of the priesthood has broadened in Stephen's thoughts to include the question of his very commitment to religion itself.

Though not yet aware of any artistic 'destiny', Stephen shrinks from the choking order and discipline of the Church in preference to his own view of life as a fluid surface of disorder. Indeed, returning home after the interview, Stephen passes a Jesuit house where he becomes persuaded of the folly of the priesthood; instead, he embraces the concepts of sin and the Fall both as inevitable and as proof of his essential humanity. He becomes convinced even more of this when he arrives home and sees again the squalor of the Dedalus house. He now warms to its lack of order, finding in it a ready endorsement of his decision, as yet unvoiced, to reject the sterile life of the priesthood. In one of the novel's few touching moments, Stephen joins his ragged brothers and sisters in mournful song and he is filled with remorse for their straitened circumstances having been denied the opportunities freely bestowed on himself.

In addition to negative reasons for his rejection of the priesthood, there is also the positive one that in the disorder of life he discovers a gratifying expression of ordinary humanity, which he acknowledges in the recognition that he is bound to fall. It is a crucial moment in his development, the recognition of human fallibility and the inevitability of sin (contrast this with his scrupulous extremism at the start of the chapter), and it is the key to the possible future redemption of his artistic spirit. (However, in the next chapter he rejects or neglects this key.) Ironically, the idea of disorder consoles his confused mind as he learns that, whereas in the Church the failure of his impossible ideal means death of the soul, in art it is the life's blood, the stuff of everyday living out of which he can make order. He finds promise in this idea which is then made starkly real in the chaos of his own home life, with its poverty and squalor and repeated removals:

He smiled to think that it was this disorder, the misrule and confusion of his father's house and the stagnation of vegetable life, which was to win the day in his soul.   (pp. 165–6)

The withering picture of a cursed home life, with its air of rotting cabbage and mean fare, harks back to the sordid world at the end of Chapter 2 and the beginning of Chapter 3 with the same implicit moral undertones. Furthermore, the similarity also underlines the paralysing emotional trap of domestic life for Stephen, as well as reiterating the relentless decline of Simon Dedalus, with yet another removal imminent to deny the bailiff as well as to seek cheaper accommodation. The poverty and weary resignation of the children soften up the reader for the poignancy of their singing rounding off the second section – a rare glimpse of Stephen with his brothers and sisters, in which he seems genuinely moved by both these aspects of their situation.

The singing brings to a close the first two sections of this chapter; then there follows a slight hiatus in which Stephen's separation from the Church is made complete. His caution and discreetness with the director and his ability to see through the lure of his proposal vividly portray him as a mature single-minded individual on the threshold of adulthood (compared with the boy at the beginning of the chapter). As we have seen in previous chapters, he imposes his individuality through the ability to make autonomous decisions with increasing foresight. Having to some extent shaken off the net of religion, he moves forward to what is, in effect, the central climax of the novel, in the last section of the chapter.

This begins with Stephen's physical as well as symbolic departure from his father, after becoming impatient of waiting and spurred by ambition, and our attention is turned more explicitly towards the Daedalus/Icarus myth for the first time. We are reminded of this in a number of its aspects – including the one in which, as the archetypal inventor in Greek mythology (Stephen's 'artificer', pp. 173 and 257), Daedalus was responsible to the king of Crete for designing the maze in which the Minotaur was confined. That Joyce placed considerable personal importance on this aspect is clear from the fact that he signed some of his early stories as 'Stephen Daedalus'; he hints at this aspect metaphorically throughout *A Portrait* – for example, in the tense struggle between Stephen's intellectual and emotional leanings (reason and lust, as Father Arnall's sermons make clear), with the eventual outcome that Stephen overbalances in favour of reason. Daedalus is, of course, more renowned for the wings by which he and Icarus escaped the island, though Joyce develops only the Icarus aspect of this. The fabulous artificer is paralleled with Stephen's own inept father by silent and ironic contrast – the unformulated figure of the artificer haunting the novel only as an inspirational presence for Stephen. Hints of the Icarus element abound, but most strongly in the association of Stephen with overreaching ambition.

So Stephen leaves his father, setting off for the sea, buoyant with pride, convinced of the wisdom of his decision to reject the priesthood, excited at the prospect of university. After the darkness and claustration of previous chapters and of the opening to this one, the prose now takes off with a sudden flight of elation, paralleling the freedom in Stephen's heart as he strips away the past. It is a flight of the spirit, in expectation of the flight at the end of the novel – with music, flames, a midnight wood and wild stampeding to underline exhilaration, and the imminent revelation of his fate, dimly anticipated since Chapter 2. An encounter with a group of Christian Brothers briefly halts the rush, recalling the period of Stephen's shame in Chapter 3, but their piety is beyond him now.

As he approaches the sea, 'obeying a wayward instinct' (p. 169), he is, Icarus-like, wary of its claim upon him but at the same time lured on to escape across it. Characteristically, he searches for words to capture the sensations felt and speaks them softly, 'A day of dappled seaborne clouds', allowing the music of the words to interplay with the feelings themselves (from the beginning we have seen how, for Stephen, words are the window on reality – for example, pp. 11 and 64, and the sermons of Chapter 3). The music of his reverie begins again to rise but as it does Stephen is suddenly shaken by another call, the real shouts of college friends, anonymous and crudely naked as they rise from the sea:

—Hello, Stephanos!

—Here comes The Dedalus! . . .

—Come along, Dedalus! Bous Stephanoumenos! Bous Stephaneforos! (p. 172)

Ironic and antipathetic, they break rudely into Stephen's daydream, their scornful insults tying his name with the sacrificial ox.

Many critics regard these as Joyce's own ironic treatment of Stephen's fanciful aspirations, and some have seen them as partial proof that Stephen is misguided and therefore doomed to failure as a writer. However, Joyce himself makes no explicit comment. Stephen is clearly roused by the shouts, at first angered by the shock to his airborne spirits, and he (as well as the reader) is compelled to reflect on their sobering effect.

Yet he comes to terms with them, first philosophically through deference, then by seeing that, on the one hand, they typify the sort of philistinism ('nets') he seeks to escape but that, on the other, they also represent the everyday experience of life, the very stuff of art as he sees it. Instead of deflating his spirit their ironic comments are, in fact, translated into strong presages of his future, the 'call of life to his soul', suddenly evoking the legend of the winged Daedalus, and he moves from them towards the sea. He is immersed in a general air of uncertainty, dimness and trancery; reality melts into excitement and myth, while the narrator's words become misty, subjective, unanswered and connotative rather than explicit. The chapter as a whole is much possessed with secrets and mysterious revelation, with the unfolding of Stephen's future, and it is out of this haze that Stephen becomes convinced of his fate, by dint of brooding on his surname and the 'fabulous artificer' of the myth.

Alone again, Stephen's gaze is caught by the figure of the girl also standing alone in one of the rivulets of the Liffey's estuary, and he becomes enraptured by the beauty of her figure, its poise and its softness. Her beauty is girlish, mortal and sensuous – it combines with his mood and with the aspect of the day. As they gaze long at each other, Stephen is overwhelmed by the sacramental timelessness of the moment, then, unable to contain his exuberance, he turns away and races across the sands. She is transfigured by his soul into both the angel of annunciation of his vocation as artist and, at the same time, the embodiment of that beauty which in art he would strive to capture – she is the word made flesh.

At first, this momentous annunciation is characterized only as a faintly audible voice, but after he begins to wade into the sea Stephen recognizes his destiny, in the figure of the girl, beckoning to his soul. She comes to him as that harbinger promised in Chapter 2 (p. 67). She is the essence of beauty too, the end of art as Stephen defines it in the next chapter, the word of beauty made flesh. However, the perspective is exclusively Stephen's, subjective and intuitive, raising uncertainties about the reliability of his epiphany – like Macbeth's witches she has a catalytic effect on him. But does she awaken Stephen to a calling he is truly equipped for and dimly aware of, or does she merely trap a dreamer weary for escape and carried along by the accident of his surname?

Yet the impact of the estuary is unmistakable and forms the focal point of the climax. Stephen once again alone and in silence, the moment draws together themes and motifs which have quietly simmered throughout and which now culminate in a sort of religious ecstasy for him. The three major themes of religion, nation and family have all been evident in the chapter – he has left behind his family, rejected the call of religion, and now he contemplates the prospect of quitting his country. Also recurrent has been the idea of alienation which underpins each of these major themes – for example, in the Christmas dinner section, the children's party in Chapter 2 and the hell sermon of Chapter 3. Now Stephen becomes gradually aware of the most difficult split looming ahead: that with his mother who is hostile to his intention of going to university. He describes it as a 'first noiseless sundering of their lives'

(p. 169), and it is the sternest obstacle to his ambition (it reappears in Chapter 5 and continues to haunt Stephen even in *Ulysses*, after her death and his return to Dublin).

As the epiphany subsides, Stephen is certain of his way forward. His solitude is represented now not in terms of loneliness but, like the end of Chapters 1 and 2, in terms of freedom, assertiveness and joy. After the reverses of Chapter 3 there is now a firm conviction that Stephen has come through, stronger, wiser, more mature, his vision clearer and himself more equipped to begin to test it. In this way, Chapter 4 is a more complete and resurgent denouement, thematically as well as emotionally, than Chapter 5. A phase of Stephen's life has become complete – perhaps what biographers used to call 'The Formative Years' – since after this chapter Stephen is already fixed and the emphasis moves away from his development.

But if Joyce had ended the novel here, how would it have been different, with Stephen triumphant? It would, of course, have finished with a happier ending on a more optimistic note filled with youthful idealism, with Stephen's aspirations in the ascendant and with an air of certainty. But the stress would have been less on art than on freedom. And the novel would not have confronted the reality which Stephen (as Joyce before him) will have to face: the imminent prospect of loneliness as the consequence of exile and pride.

After the estuary scene, the mood collapses into anticlimax at the beginning of Chapter 5 and only gradually recovers as we see Stephen expose his vision to the ordeal of the reality of life – of poverty at home, of reconciling his egoism and ambitions with his family and friends, of the still persistent hollowsounding voices of Church and politics. Overall, the effect of the last chapter, including as it does his aesthetic theory, the composition of the villanelle and his preparation to leave Ireland, is to make Stephen's vision more realistic and therefore more convincing.

Chapter 5

Following the flight of spirit on the estuary, the narrator now returns the reader with a familiar shock to the reality of the squalor at the Dedalus's home in Lower Drumcondra, on the north side of Dublin. The pawn tickets reveal that Mr Dedalus has disposed of, among other things, the dress coat seen in more affluent times, such as the Christmas dinner in Chapter 1 (p. 28); moreover, he has been using false names as a pledger, to avoid embarrassment. The narrative returns to a domestic setting and ironically to Stephen being washed by his mother at the kitchen sink, even as she continues to disapprove of the university. Together with the succeeding scenes it shows how much Stephen's ordinary life is ruled now by disorder: he does not wash himself; the clock is an hour and twenty-five minutes fast (which no one bothers to correct); he wakes late, missing his lectures; and, as if to objectify the decaying disorder around him, his ears are assailed by the screaming of a mad nun in the nearby asylum as he leaves home. He struggles stoically against it all, resisting these challenges to his will.

In spite of this chaos there are still demonstrations of Stephen's attempts to impose order on the intellectual life – for instance, in the strict discipline of the aesthetics theory and of the villanelle which he composes in the middle of the chapter. For relaxation he escapes into the world of the Elizabethans – particularly their music – or into daydreams, and takes part in occasional recitals such as the one in which he serenades Emma one evening (p. 223).

That Stephen is engaged in a theory of art is first intimated on page 180, and there is also a hint here of the solitude into which his intellectual life is drawing him; this is borne out by other areas of the chapter. His preoccupation with the intellect makes him a lonely figure, introspective, shunning the company of friends, except in one-to-one situations, where he tends to dominate his listener. Now that he has rejected his religion, he frequently uses his listener as a confessor – for example, with Davin and Cranly. In one such situation, Davin's tale about the peasant wife who tried to seduce him highlights both his own naïvety and Stephen's cold and impersonal attitude towards women. As Stephen himself later acknowledges:

A woman had waited in the doorway as Davin had passed by at night ... But him [Stephen] no woman's eyes had wooed.   (p. 242)

A vivid instance occurs, too, on his way to university, when the flower girl touches Stephen on the arm. Suddenly startled, he feels sorry for her poverty but also irritated by her sexuality which he is compelled to confront. To him she is the embodiment of what he regards as typical peasant ingenuousness. She also reminds him, painfully, that he does not have his 'own girl'.

Throughout *A Portrait* we have seen Stephen in a series of major direct confrontations with priests – archetypal figures of authority – with the object of revealing to the reader the levels of Stephen's development. In Chapter 1 he complains to Father Conmee and is later betrayed; in Chapter 3 he is harrowed by Father Arnall into confessing to another, anonymous, priest; but then, in Chapter 4, he faces up to the director of Belvedere on very nearly equal terms. Finally, in Chapter

5, his chat with the dean reveals Stephen himself deferred to as an authority figure. The dean, as an English convert, is more adept in the 'useful arts' such as lighting the fire (recalling Prometheus, another defiant Icarus-like figure) but Stephen takes pride in explaining to him the word 'tundish' – which turns out anyway to be an English word (p. 256). The dean also approaches him for some thoughts on the 'aesthetic question'. Ironically, in *Stephen Hero* when Stephen has prepared his paper to present to the college society ('Art and Life'), it is the Church, in the form of the college president, which at first bans him from speaking – on the grounds that his ideas contradict those of the Church. However, in *A Portrait* it is the Church, now in the figure of the dean, which actively encourages Stephen to complete the paper, making him appear prudent and coy. The episode serves other purposes too – for example, the dean's loveless eyes are a sharp reminder of the chill order of the priesthood which Stephen rejected and of the toll which years of service have exacted. In addition, their discussion of semantics and morals operates as a prelude to Stephen's aesthetics theory later in the chapter, revealing to us the advances in his intellect.

Moreover, when he does formally expound his theory to Lynch (pp. 208–14, 216–19) we see that his ideas are already at a mature stage and cogently articulated. They are unfolded as the two of them walk from the university to the National Library (walking is one of this chapter's chief activities, perhaps suggesting unrest – compare with Chapter 2). It is less a discussion than a lecture using Lynch as a sounding board and, unlike his talk with the dean, Stephen holds forth authoritatively, often superciliously, and occasionally testing and chiding his listener. But, although his theory is rigorous and his arguments generally sound, Stephen appears stuffy and his theory cold and impersonal. Whereas in *Stephen Hero* the narrator makes the point that aesthetics is an unpopular discipline, in *A Portrait* this is made dramatically clear through the figure of Lynch, who is bored and punctuates Stephen's lecture by chipping in with sarcastic remarks; and even the row made by a passing dray, loaded with scrap, seems to make ironic comment.[6]

His theory can be divided into two aspects: on the one hand the definition of beauty and its operations, and on the other the role and position of the artist in relation to the work of art. The first aspect is based expressly on the ideas of Aristotle (*Poetics* and *De Anima*) and Aquinas (chiefly *Summa Theologia*), while the second is inspired by ideas of Lessing and Goethe, with the additional, unacknowledged, influence of Shelley and Pater, Flaubert, Wilde and Ibsen (see Chapter 4 on Joyce's idea of the artist).

The climax of Stephen's intellectual development in the novel, the aesthetic theory, is an attempt to form an objective definition of artistic beauty, by placing the criteria for artistic beauty in the object or work perceived rather than, as the Romantics before him, by placing them in the observer. In other words, whether or not a work of art is beautiful depends not on the mood, tastes, feelings or backgrounds of the observer but on whether the work embodies the prescribed qualities. He starts by defining pity and terror: pity is the feeling which connects the observer with the sufferer, while terror connects the observer with the cause of the suffering. Next, he sets out to define tragedy, distinguishing between the popular or 'marketplace' use of the term and the narrower philosophical use. The tragic emotion involves terror and pity, but it also creates static emotion and is therefore wholesome. Alternatively, such pornographic and didactic or 'improper' arts are kinetic in that they create desire or loathing; improper arts appeal to the baser physical drives of the observer while artistic beauty addresses only on an intellectual plane working through the rhythm of beauty in a work of art (with rhythm defined as the aesthetic relationships between the parts of the work). Further, since art is the attempt to express an interpretation of the world through such things as sound, shape and colour in the form of beauty, Stephen now attempts to define 'beauty', using as his starting point an idea from Thomas Aquinas, 'that is beautiful the apprehension of which pleases' (p. 212). He explains that the concepts of truth and beauty are similar in that they both produce static emotion: truth appeals to or pleases the intellect while beauty appeals to the aesthetic imagination. However, before we can understand beauty, we must be able to understand the stages by which the observer's imagination apprehends beauty.

An encounter with another student brings momentary respite from the lecture for Lynch, and jokes about turnips and pancakes act as mild relief to Stephen's lofty ideas, which he then continues. The three conditions required for artistic beauty are set out (pp. 216–17):

(i) wholeness (*integritas*) – the object must first be recognized as a single complete entity;

(ii) harmony (*consonantia*) – there must be a balance seen between its parts which are united by the rhythm of its structure;

(iii) radiance (*claritas*) – the supreme quality, giving the object its uniqueness and revealing its essence (truth).

The moment that the observer apprehends a work of art, his mind will have been arrested by its wholeness, fascinated by its harmony and enraptured by its clear radiance in a moment of silent luminous stasis. While Stephen's definitions are generally lucid, his explanation of the

61

third condition, *claritas*, the most elusive, is weak and yet although it resembles Joyce's own concept of 'epiphany' (see Chapter 7 below) which is discussed in *Stephen Hero*, it is omitted altogether from *A Portrait*.

Though he struggles to remain objective, Stephen eventually reverts to Shelley's comparison of the mind, in that instant of apprehension, to a 'fading coal' – the epiphany blazes fiercely on the mind and fades only gradually. It is a perfectly apt and analogous image (especially reminding us of Prometheus, by way of Shelley), but while his theory begins with the disciplined rational empiricism of Aristotle and Aquinas, it fizzles out at this point of the 'supreme quality' into a transcendent haze.

However, more important and more successful for a discussion of the aesthetics of the novel itself is Stephen's conception (and probably Joyce's too) of the relationship of the artist to the aesthetic 'image'.[7] He distinguishes three forms: the lyrical, the epical and the dramatic, of which the highest form is the dramatic, a mode in which the author excludes any direct moral comment on his characters; the author thus remains apparently impartial and absent:

The artist, like the God of creation, remains within or behind or beyond or above his handiwork, invisible, refined out of existence, indifferent, paring his fingernails. (p. 219)

Although the novel itself is written in the 'dramatic' form favoured also by Joyce, *A Portrait* has examples of all three. The lyrical form is that of Stephen's own thoughts ('stream of consciousness') in Chapter 1 and in the diaries at the end, (utterances placed in immediate relation to himself). The epical form is typified by the episode in Chapter 3 when Stephen 'prolongs and broods upon himself' until he passes out of himself into that moment when he stands with Emma before the Virgin Mary. The dramatic form is evident in the 'farcical pedagogue' of Chapter 2 and the numerous instances in which Stephen role-plays. Indeed, looking at the novel as a whole, the three forms are configured as distinct phases of the artist-biography – Chapters 1 and 2 embodying the predominantly lyrical phase in which the artistic impulse is almost totally internalized within a subjective identity, then emerging through the 'deaths' of soul and of received faith as epical events (Chapters 3 and 4) on to the brink of a mature, fully dramatic phase, no longer exclusively egocentric but within and beyond the vital human life. However, as we will see, Stephen does not reach this final phase within the scope of *A Portrait*; the key is the predominance of his pride – not until *Ulysses* is the 'proper and intangible aesthetic life' approximated.

A Commentary on the Novel and Joyce's Themes

Just as the aesthetics theory is the climax of Stephen's intellectual development, the villanelle which follows it is the climax of his artistic development (at least within the scope of the novel). At the start of the villanelle section, the narrator's now heightened prose style perfectly mirrors Stephen's tremulous physical and emotional stirring in early morning, with its shadowings of sexual fantasy. As he half awakes, inspiration is aroused in Stephen's soul, enchanted by dreams and nocturnal memories of Emma, until 'In the virgin womb of the imagination the word was made flesh' (p. 221).

As the verses flow, at first fitfully, Stephen recalls the poetry written for E.C. ten years previously; she is also the inspiration of his present attempt. Memory, personal and political, represents for him a sort of paralysis, a sort of neurosis in which he continually returns to the past, a point he makes more explicit in *Ulysses*:

—History, Stephen said, is a nightmare from which I am trying to awake.   (*Ulysses*, p. 28)

He recalls vividly the scene by the tram after the children's party (p. 72) when he had wanted to catch hold of and kiss her but in reality did neither. The verses of that time had picked out only detailed impressions and now the villanelle goes even further, becoming a highly abstracted work.

There is no central recognizable persona; the vague, archetypal figure of the temptress in the complete poem draws together and unites again within herself the shades of Emma and the Virgin Mary (with Stephen as *poète maudit*) – as in Stephen's dumbshow of Chapter 3 (p. 120) – now combined with echoes of the estuary girl and the prostitute. In mood and aspect it shows the influence not of Stephen's former favourite, Byron (pp. 72 and 82), but of Shelley, mystical and elusive, an enchantment of the heart recalling especially that fragment from Shelley's 'Ode to the Moon' quoted by Stephen (p. 99). Evident too is the influence of the French Symbolist poets particularly in its suggestive use of intense image and the interplay of sound for musical effect, though there is nothing reminiscent of Joyce's own early verse except an air of vagueness and a feeling of wistful melancholy.

Critics are divided in their response to the villanelle, though none goes out of his way to praise it intrinsically as verse. Some judge it in the light of Stephen's aesthetic theory which precedes it, arguing that the juxtaposition of the two is a deliberate device by Joyce to highlight Stephen's lack of success, especially as the reader has been led to expect better things from him. Others point to Joyce's own collection of poetry,

Chamber Music (written and published before *A Portrait*), and argue that, since at Stephen's age Joyce was producing far superior work (which is debatable!),[8] if he had wished to present a more promising Stephen he was well able to have given him a more capable, accomplished piece to reflect this. More severe critics have interpreted the villanelle's inadequacies as a signal from Joyce that Stephen's perception of his vocation is misguided and that he is destined, like Icarus, to ignominious failure.

As a lyric it lacks both theme and development other than the purely formal ones imposed by the verse structure. It is devoid of genuine feeling and, for its interest, relies heavily on this formal aspect, on the intricate interplay of words and rhythm. The choice of the villanelle, with its difficult formal demands in a tight rhyme scheme (using only two rhymes throughout), imposes a strict discipline on the composer; the result here is verse which displays virtuosity and firm control but is distant and cold, web-like, as a net. The mesmeric repetition of the key sounds is implicitly masturbatory – the section opens in a highly sensitized atmosphere of sexual fantasy and eventually subsides back into it. Stephen's imagination conjures an Emma who, though in real life has become irreproachable, in dream is compliant (as in Chapter 2), and the overall effects are of inertia and onanism.

Nevertheless, it remains a source of private satisfaction to Stephen, animated as it is by his own private thoughts of E.C. (rather than from within the substance of the poem itself). He lies back and reflects, happy with a sense of accomplishment at having mastered the discipline of the form and excited by the music of its recurring sounds.

However, we should not dismiss it, nor should we conclude from its weaknesses alone that Stephen will necessarily fail in his aspiration. As verse, it certainly disappoints our expectations yet shows the promise of literary endeavour and an acute sensitivity for words and their musical effect. It is important to remember too that it is only a first scribbling down of lines which might later be revised or rejected as juvenilia.

So the villanelle is an indication that Stephen at least takes himself seriously, that his perception of his destiny has some impulse and direction, that is is not petrified exclusively in that mystical annunciation at the end of Chapter 4. However, he must mature if he is to succeed and in the hiatus the artistic impulse urges forward for expression.

Having abandoned Roman Catholicism (p. 248), he now appropriates its terminology for his own ironic use, to define his life's mission as:

... a priest of eternal imagination, transmuting the daily bread of experience into the radiant body of everliving life.   (p. 225)

In a real sense he does regard his calling as a mission: to express the 'uncreated conscience of my race' (p. 257), to expose the moral paralysis of the lives of his countrymen. But first, in order to become a true artist, Stephen is convinced he must become free of any irrelevant extraneous demands on his attention and on his ideal of art for its own sake, free of the 'nets' outlined to Davin (p. 207). For this reason too, as he makes clear to Lynch, art which excites desire or loathing or moralizes about issues is impure because in these forms art is not an end in itself but is exploited as a means to an end. To secure the freedom of pure art he must, ironically, adopt a rigorous self-discipline – 'ironically' because having rejected the rigour of the Jesuits he now seeks a rigour in the order of the artist (typified by the strict control of the villanelle, the logical procedure of the aesthetic theory and, to a lesser extent, by Stephen's arguments with Davin and Cranly, as well as formally in the diaries at the end). Identifying the chief obstacles to his freedom as 'my home, my fatherland or my church' (p. 251), he sets out to overcome their influence using (as we have seen him do already) the tactics of 'silence, exile, and cunning' (p. 251) though (as we will also see) in his ruthless drive for this freedom he blindly sacrifices his humanity.

After the row at the Christmas dinner, politics is sublimated by and large – that is, until the final chapter. Consistent with his declared weapons of silence, exile and cunning, acquired through previous confrontations, Stephen himself rejects any particular political line; in fact, he transcends political debate altogether. An example occurs early on when Stephen, leaving the physics theatre with other students, is invited to sign MacCann's petition supporting the Russian Tsar, international peace, and disarmament – and as the exchange intensifies, it recalls previous intimidating confrontations with Wells, Heron and others. Stephen's smugly facetious response is to inquire how much they will pay him for signing – to which the idealistic MacCann recoils by dismissing Stephen as a 'minor poet' (p. 202). However, Stephen does not rise to this bait and simply transcends the conflict by ignoring it. In addition, the conflict reminds us of Stephen's earlier epiphany of the Abbey riots following Yeats's *The Countless Cathleen*, and in this way Joyce vividly equates MacCann's stifling political dogmatism with the sort of pervasive Irish philistinism which Stephen eventually strives to escape.

On the narrower particular issue of Irish independence *per se*, Stephen expresses no opinion (Joyce himself, although he supported Arthur Griffith's forthright position on Irish independence and professed to being a socialist, took no active part in politics). It is irrelevant to Stephen's aspirations. But it does inevitably impinge on his discussions and consciousness. He is dismissive of Davin, whose grass-roots type of nationalism is associated with the revival of native athletics and the Irish language. Stephen considers him an honest and virtuous friend but one whose dogmatic commitment to the cause enslaves him in a bog-peasant mentality (pp. 183–4). Then, during the banter which follows Stephen's refusal to sign the petition, Davin urges Stephen to join the nationalist cause itself and to resume his Irish lectures. Stephen now begins to revel in their attacks and like a stag he flashes back at them defiantly with his antlers (an image which Joyce used in *Ulysses* and of himself in 'The Holy Office'). He rejects Davin's demand that the individual should sacrifice himself for his nation, on the grounds that Ireland has always destroyed the soul of its people through such empty rhetoric. However, the question of resuming Irish classes is a thorny one for Stephen because he is sour about the friendship between Father Moran and Emma. But on the general nature of Irish politics he is quite firm – he does not grapple with the issues, only with the treachery of its followers whose ancestors allowed the language to be ousted in the first place. He accuses the nationalists of being always ready to betray each other: he cites the example of Parnell which, as well as personifying this fear, also focuses the many references to him throughout the novel (p. 207). Faced by this, Davin can reply only by lamely talking in terms of heroic self-sacrifice, at which point Stephen leaves to expound on aesthetics with Lynch as the conflict dissolves.

The chapter has many such departures and, like the departure from the Dedalus home at the start, it underlines in dramatic terms the thematic stripping away of another of Stephen's 'nets'. Each departure is a falling-off and Stephen is left more and more alone until at the end, as the diaries imply, he can speak only with himself. He leaves these hostile petitioners to join the congenial Lynch, who languishes in the ball alley like a Celtic giant. To Stephen's theory he is a complaisant listener, encouraged more by the prospect of free cigarettes than by illumination but his rugged facetiousness and simplicity work as a chorus, setting off Stephen's humourless gravity.

Although he engages with Lynch now and Cranly later, Stephen's ultimate aim is really to withdraw. Throughout the novel he appears to be involved in a continual process of stripping away, not only of 'nets' but also of people until, near the end of the novel, he is seen talking with Cranly for the last time; then the diaries take over the narrative as he is left to 'talk' with himself. Yet although the students are aggressive and Stephen regards them as intimidating they are life itself in this part of the novel, with their jokes and banter – they are ironically its real vitality too. Accordingly, he appears more and more lonely as he leaves behind what has been pared away. Davin describes him as 'always alone' (p. 206), and Cranly too spells this out to him before vainly offering him the possibility of companionship instead (p. 251) – but his search for intellectual honesty and independence is paramount for him and there is no place for friends in it.

At first it appears that because Cranly has some special relationship with Stephen, being closer to him than anyone else is in the novel, their friendship at least may endure. In their final conversation, Cranly as a friend explicitly confronts Stephen's attitude to the two remaining nets against his freedom: religion and family or home, the two themes inextricably related through Stephen's mother as we can see from his 'confession' about their unpleasant quarrel over religion. He also needs Cranly as his *fidus Achates* in whom he can confide this (p. 243). Although after the first section we do not see Stephen's mother again, her forceful presence is felt almost as a third character in Stephen's exchange with Cranly. Her anxiety started as far back as her disapproval of the university, in Chapter 4, and now his refusal to make his Easter duty as a Catholic precipitates a crisis for her because of his shrinking faith, and for Stephen because of the unacceptable demands of family and Church. Now Cranly's questions draw him out, making it clear that the issue is not really his faith at all – this has already been settled – but whether Stephen will compromise his principle of honesty to himself in order to satisfy his mother. He admits that it would cost him little to make her happy but adds that he could not compromise his honesty to himself by making a duty he did not sincerely believe in. He is as dogmatic in his rejection of his faith as the Jesuits are in their adherence. He is in fact a 'fearful jesuit', as Buck Mulligan labels him in *Ulysses*:

... You wouldn't kneel down to pray for your mother on her deathbed when she asked you. Why? Because you have the cursed jesuit strain in you, only it's injected the wrong way. (*Ulysses*, p. 7)

As he sees it, it really comes down to a question of his duty to his mother. He denies her and is damned in our eyes for it. Moreover, his culpability is further compounded by the fact that he does so immediately after Cranly spells out exactly what he owes his mother (p. 246).

Although Cranly comes at the head of a long series of claims and appeals against Stephen we are not meant to dismiss him as just another of those 'hollowsounding voices' as Stephen himself does. For one thing he is a disinterested intermediary, an honest broker, whose role throughout the discussion is vital: to continually urge the voice of humanity against Stephen's single-minded preoccupations with freedom and self, a voice which is ultimately rejected through dogmatism and pride. Like James Duffy in Joyce's short story 'A Painful Case', whose life is an 'adventureless tale' ('every bond . . . is a bond to sorrow'), Stephen is damned for his translation of love into merely another form of net or trap. He protests that he cannot understand the word in either its spiritual or human senses but as Cranly reminds him:

—Whatever else is unsure in this stinking dunghill of a world a mother's love is not.   (p. 246)

All that Stephen can counter with are some rather lame and unsubstantial precedents, such as the claim that Christ himself had treated his mother with scant regard. Yet without Cranly's idea of humanity and love in particular, Stephen's artistic development will not advance beyond the lacklustre effort of the villanelle, and Cranly scorns him for it: 'You poor poet, you!' (p. 251).

At the end Stephen proclaims that he will go out to find experience, to 'embrace life'; yet the emphasis in the novel as a whole, as we have seen, is on rejection and on what he strips away. By doing this he appears more and more to be isolating himself from other people (whom he treats with suspicion) and actually alienating himself from the life which ought to be the material of his art and which he promises to embrace.

In spite of his words, there is no real sense of adventure in this ending. Cranly offers him a special friendship and Stephen's final momentous silence is the refusal of this offer. The reasons for this are varied. One is that he likes to suspect that Cranly and Emma are lovers and that the old nightmare of betrayal threatens again – he searches for the proof of it in a faint blush on Cranly's cheek when Emma passes them outside the library (p. 236). Curiously, as *Ulysses* makes clearer, Stephen may also be rejecting Cranly's friendship as a proposal of homosexual love.

—And not to have any one person, Cranly said, who would be more than friend, more even than the noblest and truest friend a man ever had.   (p. 251)

. . . Staunch friend, a brother soul: Wilde's love that dare not speak its name. His arm: Cranly's arm . . . (*Ulysses*, p. 41)

And Duffy in 'A Painful Case' dismally asserts: 'Love between man and man is impossible because there must not be sexual intercourse ...' (*Dubliners*, p. 103)

But at root is Stephen's pride – the uncompromising pride which has helped him to survive and at times made him unbearable. Cranly's importuning reinforces Stephen's stag-like obstinacy, and it is ironic that he phrases his defiance in the words of Lucifer, another defiant falling angel, another Icarus: 'I will not serve' (pp. 243 and 251), at the same time recalling Father Arnall's warning of damnation in Chapter 3.

However, the hell which threatens Stephen and which he defiantly disparages is that of loveless solitude. While he turns his back both on Cranly and on his frustrated desire for Emma, and prepares to leave Ireland, solitude now looms as the greatest challenge to his sanity, the fragmentariness of the diaries at the end paralleling precisely the nihilistic threats against his reason posed by loneliness: the nightmare-void on which he teeters precariously. His diaries too are literally introspective and retrospective, with Stephen detached like his ideal artist from the events which they cover – and though their fragmentary form gives them a lively, dynamic flow, the events in them (in contrast with the rest of the novel) are described coldly and at a distance rather than directly through Stephen's mind (though his mind is of course foregrounded in them). Even the possibility of love offered by his encounter with Emma is eventually rejected (p. 256), suffering the same fate as those loves offered by his mother and by Cranly.

In the wake of the dreamy villanelle section, reality acutely returns with the clamour of birds on a late March evening. Stephen waits alone on the steps of the National Library, happy but uncertain. Convinced that the birds are significant, he is troubled that he cannot read their portent: '... augury of good or evil? ... Symbol of departure or of loneliness?' Their shrill cries more likely recall his 'batlike soul' and in order to elucidate them Stephen anxiously invokes the birdmen of ancient mythology: Egyptian Thoth, bird-headed god of writers, and his own eponymous archetype, the hawklike Daedalus, as he does at the conclusion of the book.

Yet, in spite of his bravura and his uncompromising pride, it is not until the end that Stephen explicitly resolves to depart, the fragmentation of the diaries betraying his anxiety and uncertainty through their disjointedness as well as their subject matter.

However, the end, though not quite a whimper, seems inevitable. Despite Stephen's brief second thoughts on 15 April, the motion is irreversible; despite any anxieties, he finally steps forward to encounter the unknown with defiance: 'Welcome, O life!' His prayer in the last diary entry looks out beyond the novel to the future as well as back through those threads of the Daedalus myth woven through the novel, which have sustained Stephen's ambition, back to the motto on the title page:

Et ignotas animum dimittit in artes

words taken from Ovid's *Metamorphoses*, whose Book VIII narrates the tale of Daedalus and Icarus, at the point where the father realizes that their only chance of escape from the king of Crete lies in emulating the birds: 'And he set his mind to work upon unknown sciences', and he sets about making the wings to take flight. Invoked by Stephen's prayer to his 'Old father, old artificer . . .', they highlight not only the uncertainty of his future and its solitude, but also the louring penalty of overreaching ambition.

3. Icarus Allsorts: Characterization

Of course our low hero was a self valeter by choice of need so up he got . . .

(*Finnegans Wake*, p. 184)

In his memoir, *My Brother's Keeper*, Stanislaus Joyce makes the crucial point that '*A Portrait of the Artist* is not an autobiography; it is an artistic creation'. Although there are similarities between the lives of Stephen Dedalus and his creator we should not closely identify the two with each other: 'Stephen Dedalus is an imaginary, not a real, self-portrait and freely treated.'[1]

There is little of the 'Sunny Jim', as the young Joyce was known, about the silent, brooding Stephen; and Joyce himself, even as a young man, was well known for his sense of fun and convivial wit, enjoyed athletics and sport, especially cricket, and compared with Dedalus had a greater love for his father and for his brothers and sisters. Although biographies and the reminiscences of Joyce's friends reveal that there are close parallels in the details of the two lives, and that Joyce invariably used the material of his own experiences, it is clear that he exaggerated and added to these experiences as it suited his fictive intentions.

These intentions have two clear thrusts: to present the development of an 'artist' from early childhood, and to analyse the relationship between formative influences and Stephen's inner states.

Stephen Dedalus

A Portrait is both a *Bildungsroman*, the story of a young man's growing up, and a *Künstlerroman*, the early life of an artist. Naturally, the novel traces the two aspects together but also deals implicitly with the relationship between the two, and the tensions which their different demands on Stephen give rise to, and charts the continuing conflicts between Stephen's drive towards adulthood and his drive towards becoming an artist, and his resolution of the struggle between the demands of both – for they rarely appear to be in harmony, at least according to Stephen's point of view. The 'finished artist' is not a natural phenomenon alone: the artist may be born but his talents and his persona must be nurtured if they are to reach fruition.

Before we examine the artist, we must first examine the young man. Since the stress of the novel is on growth, we will need to examine the changes that occur to and are made by Stephen during its course by exploring its development in terms of three crucial areas: freedom, the emotions and the intellect.

FREEDOM

Given that Stephen eventually foresees his future as an artist, the most significant drive in the novel, in terms of Stephen's character and moral action, is his struggle for freedom. In the light of this struggle, we also need to consider the relationship between Stephen's intellectual and emotional developments and how it is affected by this drive, looking at them all before and then after the crisis which arises in Chapter 3. The three areas are of course essentially integral to the process which converges on the theme of Stephen as artist but, initially, we can consider them as ways in which he deals with the world in general.

There is a sense, though, in which we cannot really talk reductively about Stephen Dedalus's character at any single moment, as though it were fixed. What we have in *A Portrait* is actually an analogue of varying perspectives – because Joyce uses Stephen's point of view to narrate the novel, then the image we have of Stephen inevitably embodies the varying personality of Stephen and is influenced by it, a point which is reflected in the modulation of the novel's styles, which we discuss later. The narrator's presentation of Stephen alters as Stephen himself changes; we do not always have Stephen fixed in our eye or even the same aspect of him, in spite of the fact that he is ever present. For example, what do we actually learn of his character at the Christmas dinner? Anything? Are we looking at him from the same angle when he ambles on his way to university in Chapter 5 as when he is confronted by Cranly at the end?[2]

So, in approaching Stephen Dedalus just as we would approach a living person, we cannot justifiably reduce him to a bundle of convenient labels implying a single uniform person, or even a series of static uniform studies removed from the whole. Our emphasis here must be on change, movement and growth, with dynamic and fluctuating moments close together, then sometimes apart – co-ordinates merging into a poetic unity in the reader's imagination.

The novel charts Stephen's odyssey through a world within himself as well as outside, travelling from those situations in which he is subject to his environment to a stage in which he dominates, controls and understands it, constructing it through his will and imagination and expressing his understanding of it through the intellect and through art. From beginning to end he is at its centre – from the fragments at the opening to the fragments at the conclusion he is, progressively, the object of his father's narrative through to the subject and author of his own.

At first he is awestruck by his world and frightened by its shocks. Cunningly he keeps to the edges of situations, boxing his corner, pretending to be involved but really hiding out of the way – as he does when Dante comes after him in the opening section. The world has a nasty habit of making him its victim, at first through the pricks of its reality – being shoved into a ditch by a school bully and catching a worrying fever, being beaten by a school master, and then the fierce argument at the Christmas dinner. There are a few social surprises too, giving new perspectives – the discovery that his own father is not a magistrate like the other boys' fathers, and that kissing your mother at night is not the done thing, not if you want to fit in, anyway. He learns that there are other ways of doing things, which are challenges to the authority of his home and family.

These shocks are the first in a continual series throughout the novel: they presage the unnerving capacity of external reality to impinge on his dreams and flights of imagination. Thus, Stephen in the early chapters comes over to the reader very much as a victim figure; Stephen himself is aware of this as he comes to terms with it through the heroic victim figure of Parnell, especially in the infirmary when he dreams of his death as a form of revenge against Wells, in the same way that he has already seen (and will see again) the ability of the memory of Parnell to sting the Irish conscience.

Even though he finally breaks out of this passive role of victim during the climax to Chapter 1, when he makes his complaint to the Rector, Stephen never completely abandons this aspect but instead cunningly works it to his advantage, for example in his confrontations with Heron and MacCann and also in translating the artist/society conflict through the same role. Later he tells Cranly that he will use the three weapons available to him: silence, exile and cunning; again we see all three of them at work in Chapter 1.

Of course, Stephen's 'cunning' is the very charge made by Father Dolan as the pretext for the pandying in Chapter 1, though on this occasion Stephen is innocent. But he does keep out of the way, often pretending. In the whole of the first chapter he says hardly anything, silently taking it all in and interpreting what he sees, yet removed from it at a distance. For much of the chapter he appears small, passive and vulnerable, on the receiving end of knocks and, for most of the time, either too small or frightened to knock back.

At this stage Stephen is, for the most part, obedient to this world, typified by his silent fear at the Christmas dinner crisis. But this prepares us for the impact of the final section of the chapter. One of Joyce's important techniques for showing the development of Stephen's moral independence is to show him taking on and making crucial decisions – and the most crucial decision for Stephen in Chapter 1 arises after the pandying. His general moral sense is received from above, from Church and home in the main, and he respects the Rector as the ultimate moral arbiter (though Father Conmee's later betrayal of this confidence deals a severe blow to this respect and to his faith in the clergy in general).

The visit to the Rector, the climax to the first chapter, reveals his acute sense of justice[3] as well as courage and determination to clear his name. His pride also plays an important and early part here since he needs to prove to himself that he has the nerve to carry the visit through but, equally importantly, to clear his name of its association with Fleming, the 'idle loafer'. Although the other boys hustle Stephen by urging him to go, he knows that they themselves wouldn't in spite of what they urge – the spectral image of Parnell rises again with an early whiff of treachery (in the final chapter Stephen defends himself in a similar situation by offering to find the 'indispensable informer' and refers to Tim Healy).[4] The episode reveals his courage and single-mindedness as much by his facing the decision ('He had to decide.', p. 56) as by that long fearful walk along the forbidding corridors, Theseus-like, to face the uncertain figure of the Rector. However, he also notes later, ironically, how cunning and guile are distinguishing characteristics too of the Jesuits themselves[5] – and Stephen's personal champion, Daedalus the 'old artificer', was renowned for his cunning.

Although we admire Stephen's courage ('Manly little chap') there is still something obnoxious about his precocious modesty at the end of the first chapter. In the second chapter we see him back under the tutelage of the adults at home, especially Uncle Charles. Leaving the order of Clongowes he is not free but under the supervision of another dusty regime, the ancient Uncle Charles and Mike Flynn who is way past his best, teaching him to run in the old-fashioned style. Significantly, their Sunday walks are usually in the direction of Stillorgan, a village described as the 'parting of the ways' (p. 64). Throughout the novel Stephen is forever meeting the parting of the ways and, though unaware yet of any so-called 'destiny', he is already making decisions and beginning to assert himself – for example, he is briefly leader of a gang, casting himself in the mould of Napoleon. Whereas in Chapter 1 Stephen's energy was aimed at keeping out of the way and disengagement, in Chapter 2 we now feel it is directed towards getting on and making his own way, to a limited extent at least.

At the same time, Stephen is continually disappointed by his surroundings, which let him down. As the gang collapses and he does not return to Clongowes he feels occasional flickers of ambition, but these are soon damped by the squalor of his home life and his father's financial failure (p. 67). He is eventually alone as the family move home again, this time to the cheerless slums of Dublin. He tires now of children's games and of their company, and at a children's party we see him for the first time begin to savour the joy of his solitude. Throughout the rest of the novel we see this repeated – he finds the fixed point of his much-turning world within himself, against a background of desire and loathing, shifting family life, uncertainty and turbulent sexuality, to the eventual conviction of his destiny.

To some extent his independence is at first thrust upon him by circumstances, but then he actually grasps the freedom defaulted to him. We have seen before how he resembles another of Joyce's characters in this respect, James Duffy (in 'A Painful Case', who tried to live as far away from life as he could in order to objectify his emotions and therefore his ideas, avoiding involvement and contact). Stephen does not explicitly profess the same policy as Duffy does, and Stephen's isolation comes across as more involuntary and at least forced upon him in part by his acute sensitivity (on the other hand, if we compare him here with Mr Bloom in *Ulysses*, it is clear that Stephen's isolation does not arouse anything like the same degree of sympathy which Bloom's alienation does there). But although Stephen strives for freedom the emphasis is on freedom *from* (family, Church, etc.) rather than freedom *to* (create, embrace, etc.). Not until much later in the novel does it become translated into the conscious will to become an artist. He says that he has been marked out by his fate as an artist, his concept being that an artist's sensitivity sets him apart from the rest of mankind, a point which is emphasized in Chapter 5 in his art theory, where the artist is not only objective by disposition but must be by conscious strategy – from his work, its audience, its inspiration and even himself.

On the one hand, we can sympathize perhaps with Stephen's isolation in the novel when we consider that most of his contacts are painful – clashes with Dante, Wells, Father Dolan, Heron and his father at Cork all leave their mark – so that by the end he has become wary of human contact and its claim on him, fearing betrayal. But on the other, if we feel in part some sympathy for this predicament our feelings are very much tempered by the degree to which Stephen himself indulges in his exile; as we are told, 'He began to taste the joy of his loneliness' (p. 70).[6] Yet by the end of the second chapter he also begins to construe this as 'his own futile isolation' (p. 101), in the wake of his failure to use the essay prize money as a means to reforming his relationship with his family. However, this leads not to remorse and reform as we might have hoped but instead to a sterner determination to go his own way, to deal with loneliness by entrenching and hardening it into another role.

His move towards autonomy is spontaneous, surprisingly, at least in the opening chapters – part of a defensive movement into his own inner resources away from harsh, torpid and unstimulating outer reality. Only later is it converted into the conscious drive for the freedom ('unfettered freedom') to express himself as artist.

In terms of his struggle for independence, the climax of the second chapter is the meeting with Heron, mirroring as it does the encounter with Messrs Dolan and Conmee in the first. Each encounter is in two parts, thus inviting comparison, and each involves a beating for Stephen, first by Father Dolan, then by Heron and his attendant creeps. We compare the ways in which Stephen deals with each, and see that his non-violent recourse is the more effective action – in Chapter 1 Stephen chose confrontation with Father Conmee, but in Chapter 2 he chooses evasion.

Although Stephen is becoming increasingly more cunning, in order to cope with reality, his strategy here is a more direct consequence of his proud nature. The encounter with Heron reveals to us not only Stephen's growing intellectual independence, advocating proscribed or *risqué* authors (Mr Tate too accuses him of heresy; see also p. 159), but also his integrity in rejecting the contest and the bait thrown to him by his rival:

He mistrusted the turbulence and doubted the sincerity of such comradeship which seemed to him a sorry anticipation of manhood. The question of honour here raised was, like all such questions, trivial to him.   (p. 86)

This dispelling of childish things and his ability to expose philistinism clearly reveal, more than anything else, the level of his intellectual maturity. Yet this strategy relies less on Stephen's intellect than on his pride and vanity, to protect him against such assaults – the matter is trivial to him, beneath his dignity as much as it is illegitimate.

This is a crucial and successful stage in Stephen's artistic progress – by now we see him independent and self-assured, but sensitive and conscientious, ascetic. Yet at the same time we see a boy who is silent yet articulate, monklike, withdrawn and cautious, growing in resentment towards the guardians of his youth in their many forms, with increasing tension between this resentment and the 'voices of his youth', between his obedience and increasing impatience, turning inwards towards the life of the soul and the imagination. The tension finds brief release in the arms of the prostitute and then reaches a climax in the searching inquisition of Father Arnall's sermons and their aftermath.

EMOTIONS

The main characteristic about Stephen's emotional set-up is its simplism, which is surprising. We note that his sensitivity and imagination, both important factors in his artistic development, are at different times both curse and blessing in their potency; his emotional requirements are seen to originate in them and to animate both. At school he has no friends and his mother forms the emotional centre of his childhood (she has a nicer smell!); and in her absence, the priests at school substitute an uneasy and ambivalent paternalism. Both at home and at school, she forms the centre of his emotional universe, the antidote to the terrors of Dante and school and the figure of conciliation at the Christmas table. In fact, in the first three chapters Stephen has very little in the way of any specific or strong emotional need between missing his mother in the early days at school and his later desire to 'sin with another' which is urged more by the flesh than by feeling. This is surprising too especially in view of his natural impulse to meet almost every situation with an emotional response (typified by his repeated use of the two moral adjectives 'nice' and 'mean', each used emotively) – for example, in the pandying episode in Chapter 1, it is Stephen's deep humiliation which initiates his feeling of injustice.

After the Christmas dinner Stephen's mother loses her explicitly central position in his consciousness in the novel. The reason for this is by no means obvious since it is clear that she continues to exert a strong and inhibitive, if submerged, influence. This has Oedipal overtones and contributes to Stephen's difficulties in his troublesome relationship with Emma (though Joyce makes this less obvious than, say, D. H. Lawrence does in *Sons and Lovers*). At the same time, his father's presence assumes an increasingly larger profile (especially his mythological 'old father' Daedalus), and his love of his mother is first transmuted into the cult of the Virgin Mary before resurfacing in Chapter 5. Here, after we observe her washing him (while his father significantly threatens him from above) Stephen sets out to deny this love by his rejection of her church and its 'love' before quitting his mother herself at the end (though she still packs his clothes to enable him to do this).[7]

The decline of his mother's central position coincides with the general decline of the family's grip on Stephen and the emergence of his powerful sexual drive. Appearing first in the vague, dreamy fantasy of Mercedes (though there are earlier hints – Eileen Vance on pp. 7, 36 and 44, and 'smugging' on p. 43) his libido struggles to express itself amid Stephen's almost exclusively male environment of schoolboys, uncles and friends. Eventually, after his failure to kiss Emma during the tram episode, Stephen's sexual drive becomes thwarted and translated into a symbolic ache, expressed as the turmoil of his role-playing and the frustrated roamings around the docks and slums of Dublin.

Apart from a brief friendship with fellow gang-leader Aubrey Mills, Stephen is unable to form a deep relationship with anyone of either sex. After Heron's taunts about Emma at the college play, he is filled with shame at her absence and at his own vanity. As a result of these experiences and his growing sense of intellectual destiny, he comes to mistrust feelings in general and attachments in particular, and sees the prospect of progress only in the complete suppression of the emotional life. Accordingly, he seeks sexual outlet only, his imagination a ready vehicle for crude and 'monstrous reveries' – as we see on the trip to Cork. Discovering the word 'foetus' carved in a college bench, he is suddenly and dramatically forced to confront his suppressed sexuality:

It shocked him to find in the outer world a trace of what he had deemed till then a brutish and individual malady of his own mind.   (p. 93)

Ironically, when the subject of girls is raised by one of his cronies, Mr Dedalus confidently boasts to them that Stephen 'doesn't bother his head about that kind of nonsense'! Furthermore, as we discover in Chapter 3, he is busy at this time penning erotic letters which he plants here and there for innocent girls to discover (p. 119).

Back in Dublin after the sale of the last of the family property, we are with him as he collects his essay prize money from the Bank of Ireland and, as well as pointing up Stephen's intellectual achievement, it offers the possibility of a reconciliation with his family. But instead, in the same prodigal manner of his father and Uncle Charles before him, he fritters it away on an effort of self-indulgence and then slumps into despondency, an emotional as well as financial bankrupt.

No life or youth stirred in him as it had stirred in them. He had known neither the pleasure of companionship with others nor the vigour of rude male health nor filial piety.   (p. 98)[8]

It is interesting to note that, as he reaches such a depth, Stephen too becomes aware of the emotional void within him. But do we sympathize with Stephen, now that he is at his lowest point, lonely and without direction? In fact, we take the opposite view. This passage, like so many others, really makes us aware of the older narrator speaking at some distance from the events, older and wiser, and if anything Stephen's self-awareness makes him more culpable; the fact that he reflects on his failure to reach the lives of other people and yet does nothing (as he himself indicates during the sermon in Chapter 3) is what condemns him.

Eventually, he finds relief from the nagging ache of shame, not by facing it, but by taking cover in the nighttown passageways of Dublin's brothel district where, in the languorous embrace of his prostitute, he also finds release from overwhelming sexual yearnings. Alienated from his family, particularly his father, mistrusting his school fellows and the clergy, and after failing with Emma, he finds the prostitute's almost maternal embrace offers peace from the unbearable reality of sexual tensions and of tortured egoism.

As a result of this escape we see that the poverty of his humanity ceases to trouble him now. This is important, since it is chiefly by the quality of his humanity that we must measure him as an artist. Later, Stephen himself draws attention to this by suggesting that it is the curse of the artist to be isolated from ordinary people, for instance like the moon, in those snatches of Shelley's poem that echo through the novel, pale and weary of loneliness, reflecting light through art. Thus, it is through such a romanticized posture that he eventually transcends the issue, snobbishly accepting his cold isolation as proof of his destiny in art. At this point he actively seeks detachment while at the same time overlooking the void within himself (see p. 156).

For the time being, before the artistic annunciation in Chapter 4, isolation is a necessary condition for both his intellect and his self-esteem. A serious-minded scholar, Stephen is cast with heavy ironic comedy in the role of 'farcical pedagogue', hailing his distinction among the other Belvedereans, and he appears to revel in the elitism of his role, unaware of the satire. In addition to styling himself a sober, humourless youth, monklike Stephen is also outwardly an exemplum of moral probity to his peers, having been elected as gymnasium secretary as well as prefect of the sodality of the Blessed Virgin Mary (another sort of gang leader); he is 'the noble Dedalus' (p. 77) and:

... Dedalus is a model youth. He doesn't smoke and he doesn't go to bazaars and he doesn't flirt and he doesn't damn anything or damn all. (p. 78)

INTELLECT

Stephen's pride finds great distinction in his intellectual abilities, more than compensating for his bodily frailties. There are many examples, beginning with his simple curiosity about purple clouds and green roses, his rivalry with Jack Lawton to win at Maths for York, exceptional sensitivity with the poeticism of words and their realities (riddles, sounds, puns, contradictions, beautiful noises and sweet airs), his great urge towards abstraction, the poems after the Christmas and tram episodes. Many of these came from Joyce's own life, of course, and like Joyce, Stephen too finds interest even in the scrawlings of the toilet (pp. 44 and 83). By Chapter 2 he is beginning to receive public recognition in this field too, reinforcing his excitement (though without exaltation) – his weekly essay is an object of pride and he wins a prize for his efforts. Inevitably, his exploring rebellious spirit comes up against Church doctrine and Mr Tate pulls him up over heresy. This is the springboard for Heron to taunt Stephen with thinly veiled animosity about his choice of authors, again revealing Stephen's unwillingness to toe the line and to keep to the approved list. We have discussed elsewhere his choice of authors (embracing Byron and Newman) but the dispute itself illuminates Stephen's increasing autonomy in the intellectual domain, especially literature, and of the growing esteem which this draws for him from among the other boys. Like Mr Tate, Heron can find no fault in this man, other than in his free ideas and he is castigated for heresy, the classic response of the bigot (see also Dante's attack, p. 8). The clash ennobles Stephen here, his Christlike pose striking a moral blow for intellectual freedom and integrity. But Stephen's frailty at this stage is marked by the ease with which he succumbs to the lure of the flesh at the end of Chapter 2 and to the terror of Father Arnall's awesome vision which follows it.

But why is Stephen clever? Why does he enjoy the intellectual life above almost all others? One reason is his ability, which makes it easier for him to get involved in the intellect, having a disposition for abstraction as well as for speculation. Another is that it gives him kudos and therefore happiness – his family has encouraged him (see pp. 74 and 99, and p. 167 where he reflects on this) – and it is an outlet for frustrations. It also gives him a special place among the other boys, a distinction in the politics of the classroom: they look to him to win half-days off and to divert the master's attention on theological quibbles; excelling sets him above them anyway. At the same time, cleverness is a duty to him, almost a religious duty, because it is a gift bestowed upon him – shown by his obligation to win for the sake of York and his monklike devotion to reason and intellect in Chapter 5.

In the first part of the novel, however, intellect is not explicitly linked with artistic destiny – it is only one of a number of talents which may come together at the right time beyond the time of the novel. The emphasis in the opening chapters is on intellect rather than on art – Stephen wins a prize for an essay but he finds the poems difficult and has to force them 'by dint of brooding' (unlike the villanelle in Chapter 5 which is inspired from within); writing poems at this age is a corollary of the intellectual life though he does use it therapeutically to relieve frustration. Equally it is not until later that we feel that it becomes a challenge to him. For instance, when in Chapter 5 he arrogantly confides to Lynch 'Aristotle has not defined pity and terror. I have . . .' (p. 208), the prelude to the great aesthetic theory is the climax of Stephen's intellectual development in the novel.

His vulnerability to Father Arnall's harrowing sermons is due as much to Stephen's guiltiness about these vegetating talents as to the priest's skilful penetration of his sensitive imagination. Yet the sermon is the great melting pot for these three areas under our analysis, at a time when he is beginning to find his way, and the priest's words fix a ready focal point in Stephen's attentions, shocking him from sloth and voluptuousness. At the same time, Stephen's pride and egoism, previously the guardians of his freedom, play essential roles in coalescing the priest's words to such an extent that he becomes entirely convinced that every word was meant exclusively for him. We can see that it is his vanity, ironically, which is at work here, triggering off embarrassment and shame (as it did after the pandying in Chapter 1) and disrupting that unique perspective which Stephen has been cultivating through detachment and intellectual progress. Now under Father Arnall's inquisition, all this crumbles rapidly away in the intense claustrophobia of his conscience as he becomes further isolated, this time by undeniable feelings of guilt; it is even more ironic that, when Stephen swings back in Chapter 4 from fanatical penitence, it is vanity again which is the prime mover, after the director's shrewd appeal to Stephen's conceit.

Father Arnall's sermon, however, does eventually tap some deep root of humanity in Stephen (even if it is centred upon himself) as well as intellect, when feelings of guilt and shame begin to stir within. We see this shame dramatically projected in dumb show, represented as an assault on female chastity in the virginal–maternal figures of Emma and the Virgin Mary, Stephen's personal deity (p. 119). It is again a fantasy 'love', an ideal worship which closely resembles in mood that which Stephen had for Mercedes in Chapter 2, the manifest prototype of later erotic fantasizing; he is capable of love only at some distance removed (idealized and abstract, the courtly and protective love of Emma, Eileen, or the Virgin) or institutionalized with the prostitutes (exclusively carnal and lascivious). Even by the end of the novel he continues to be tormented by his inability to approach Emma except in wild gesturing or fantasy – in spite of Cranly's assurance that 'she's easy to find' (p. 249).

The terrifying effect of the sermons on Stephen testifies yet again to his dogmatic piety – his propensity for obsessive zeal, 'over-scrupulous' as we have called it – which is vividly articulated by Stephen's terror of imminent death at the close of the retreat and his subsequent violent sickness as his imagination conjures up grotesque and bestial nightmares (as it had previously conjured erotic reveries), and thus his sudden swing from one extreme of faith to another. Whereas before the retreat Stephen idly ridicules the niceties of Catholic doctrine, he now drives himself furiously into fits of intense devotion to them (he later becomes as passionately resolute in his total rejection of the Church).

It is with scepticism, then, that we watch Stephen devoutly in communion with his fellows at Mass. There is no spiritual communion with them – he is, in faith, as distant as he had been at the opening of Chapter 3; his alienation continues and increases further into the following chapter. Even when, alone again, he chastises himself there is no true contrition, no humility, only the ingenuity of the cash register; after he broods on the '. . . great mystery of love . . .' (p. 153), his religiosity is short-lived as he finds that the most difficult task is 'to merge his life in the common tide . . .' (p. 155). He briefly imagines himself as a priest, aloof and apart from his congregation, and his zeal subsides.

At first, though, there is a hint that Stephen may have come through with new humanity, that the catharsis of Chapter 4 may have reformed his stubborn spirit – he rejects the priesthood on account of its coldness and rigour, its unfeeling discipline, and out of an awareness of his own unworthiness. But, inevitably, pride reasserts itself – we had never really been convinced by any shows of humility. Even though he rejects the priesthood in terms of his unworthiness this, in effect, turns on his self-awareness and is another expression of the ego: a sort of double-bluff by Stephen's conscience to cope with his over-arching vanity by striking up the opposite position. In fact, he does nothing about his guilty feelings and celebrates his imminent fall amid chaos and decay as he walks home past rotting vegetation to the squalor of home.

When Stephen reaches the age of reason in Chapter 4, his arrival is marked by the coincidence of two distinct features – on the one hand he becomes aware of the importance of the activity of making decisions, and on the other he uses this awareness to articulate and bring about features of his character which he believes will further his career as an artist. In other words, he discovers that the need to make decisions is intrinsically a proof of his independence – as well as being the means to achieving his goals – and he realizes that his individuality as Dedalus must be asserted by insisting on those aspects of his nature which had previously been suppressed – for example, by the Church or his family or school life.

So, like a Nietzschean superman he reflects proudly on his commitment in rejecting the priesthood (he appears at times to have surprised even himself in this), and is convinced that he is right to reject it, though we feel that the rightness matters less than the deep sense of satisfaction he gets from having made the decision himself. However, Stephen's elation at his new-found independence is unmistakable and gives him the impetus to go further. He turns his back remorselessly on his mother's disapproval of the university and then leaves his father behind at Byron's pub to stride purposefully off towards the estuary – two significant departures which are both repeated in the opening to the final chapter.

At this time we are given brief but important glimpses of the squalor of Stephen's home life – in the first (Chapter 4) Stephen is briefly humbled and moved to join in the singing with his beleaguered siblings, but glad of the disorder (compare the order of the Jesuits), while in the second (at the start of Chapter 5) he is untouched by their plight, provoked by the voice upstairs, and irked by the sordid poverty which threatens to hold him back. He is now immune to their predicament, so absorbed is he in his own; he sets off smugly with relief to the university, firmly convinced that his own survival depends on cutting himself off from the 'net' which they pose against his soul, while bitterly loathing his background:

His father's whistle, his mother's mutterings, the screech of an unseen maniac were to him now so many voices offending and threatening to humble the pride of his youth. He drove their echoes even out of his heart with an execration . . . (p. 179)

We see also that this 'execration' is not reserved exclusively for his family. It reveals the ruthlessness with which he is ready to deal with such 'hollowsounding' voices. This is the second point – that he is no longer ashamed to follow such a line, seeing himself in a holy struggle of self-preservation against forces intent on destruction, from within himself as well as from outside. Whereas in Chapter 4 he penitently renounces pride as a vice, he now embraces it as a legitimate if desperate way of preserving his freedom, just as we may have to resort to vice to save virtue. Where we take exception, though, is in the matter of degree – that Stephen takes his strategies to insufferable lengths, abusing family, rejecting friendship, scorning love, dedicated to suppressing normal human response, for art's sake and the intellect. Whereas in Chapter 2 he had become isolated to some extent by his extra-sensitive nature, beginning to savour his solitude, we now see him a cold, loveless intellectual figure whose chief human characteristic lies, ironically, in the degree of his blindness to this.

If we sympathize with Stephen, as up to a point we are generally disposed to do, it is at least in part because of this blindness (like the blindness of a classic tragic hero such as Oedipus or Macbeth) and in part because of the dignity of his enterprise, the single-minded affirmation of his ultimate goal in spite of the negative methods he uses to try to reach it. He sets out to achieve in this what the characters of *Dubliners* only dream about, trapped as they are by their circumstances and their failure or disinclination to act on appropriate decisions.[9] But, more crucially (and this damns him in the eyes of the reader), he is blind also to the human comedy in which he is the chief actor and which this difference focuses on, even if within the limits of the novel he does not suffer – though we know that he will; the irony of Joyce's subtext directs us to this inevitable conclusion.

Exiled from the main bloodstream of life in order to experience 'life', he lives apart, detached and alienated from the life around him, perfectly captured by Joyce in the diaries at the end. He broods at a distance from the events which ought to touch him on deeper levels than the wretched villanelle would indicate; now condemned to live through fantasy, the legacy of his imagination, we see him as something of a dreamer living and partly living as an Elizabethan courtier, a form of coming to terms with his failure to reach Emma, unable to act, para-lysed, without love and impotent. Almost completely emotionless, his intellect now dominates – as the over-rational art theory attests – and he teeters on the brink of becoming an insufferable bore. In his lecture to Lynch he fulfils the role of the humourless 'farcical pedagogue' hinted at in Chapter 2. His rejection of all ties, and the love offered by his mother and Cranly, is symptomatic of a more general urge to reject, aspects of which also find their way into the art theory.

The stress here is again on the need to differentiate between things, as it was in the beginning and has continued throughout the novel – at first recognizing distinctions in the world and then later imposing his own distinctions. And Joyce makes it one of the conditions of the artist and his theory – seeing the differences and accepting them – as when Stephen tells MacCann, 'You are right to go your way. Leave me to go mine' (p. 203). But MacCann's reply, while less aphoristic, is more pene-trating:

—Dedalus, said MacCann crisply, I believe you're a good fellow but you have yet to learn the dignity of altruism and the responsibility of the human individual.   (p. 203)

MacCann's advice anticipates that of Stephen's mother on the final page and goes similarly unheeded in the uncompromising drive to express himself in art 'as freely as I can'. Like Macbeth, his future is foretold, but not the means of achieving it. Stephen becomes a prisoner of his own stultifying silence and exile; it is left to Cranly to plant the ultimate doubt in his mind: 'Cunning indeed! ... You poor poet, you!'(p. 251). And though Stephen parcels this up with all the other voices it hits at the very foundation of his ethos, the rationale of his whole life-view, making him dimly aware of the possibility of his own hollowness, as it ominously does in the first section of *Ulysses*: 'The void awaits surely all them that weave the wind: ...' *Ulysses*, p. 18). But here in Stephen's mind it is scarcely hinted at, though it yawns un-mistakably before his feet on the last page, and its uncertain threat resonates ineluctably beyond the prayer at the end.

Other characters

Having examined some features of Stephen's character we can turn now to consider the other characters of the novel, remembering that because of the novel's point of view they are seen very much through Stephen's eyes – not objective portraits, but Stephen's idea of them. Many of them are present for what they represent in terms of Stephen's development, pointing up key moments or as a foil to his ideas, rather than for their own sake.

HOME

One of the striking things about Stephen's home in the first chapter is the ironic contrast between Stephen's conception of it and the reality which we discover there. Expecting an abode of bliss, filled by accord and sympathy, the Christmas dinner episode reveals one of terror and discord, humiliation and bitterness. In spite of the material comforts still prevailing in the early part of the novel, it is a place in which Stephen spends little of his time and, from Chapter 2, a sordid contrast to the homes of the other boys, the order of college life and the comfort of his dreams.

Simon Dedalus is the first person we meet – the storyteller of the opening paragraph. In the first chapters he is altogether a warm, generous man in company at home, and on the trip to Cork he is without pretension. Nostalgic and sentimental about the past (both his own and his country's, pp. 98–9), he is intensely loyal to the memory of Parnell which contributes to the Christmas row with its clash of loyalties. As a result he is only partly to blame for it, though he is often insensitive about what he says (see also the visit to Cork) and this certainly helps to prolong the row.

In financial matters, however, Mr Dedalus is a non-starter. In Chapter 2, Stephen at first attributes the family's social decline to his father's 'enemies' and his 'financial problems', though these are never fully explained, and Stephen himself learns only gradually and dimly from hearing the servants whisper and seeing the family portraits collected before another removal (just as in Joyce's own household). Because of Stephen's minority position he, and consequently we, do not get to know the exact reasons for the spiralling decline. On the Cork trip where the last of the Dedalus property (what should have been Stephen's patrimony) is auctioned to repay Simon's debts, we see him a spendthrift and a fool for flattery; although he is genial and cordial towards his friends he is bitter to Stephen and resents his youth. He, too, comes to regard his family as a trap, yet at the same time he appears protective towards his son.[10]

His advice to Stephen as they part on the first day at Clongowes Wood, 'never to peach on a fellow', typifies the importance he places on a code of honour and on being accepted by others. We see too that Mr Dedalus is the source of his son's strong sense of pride – on the visit to Cork he struts before his cronies stuffed with pious self-assurance and bluster. Stephen is as much humiliated by his drunken bragging as by his father's account of the interview with Father Conmee and the priest's tactlessness.

Some of this can be explained by the tensions and insecurity arising from his decline, especially if we consider that he has already proved his loyalty to Stephen by fighting for a place at Belvedere and a Jesuit education. We do not hear of him again until the final chapter, but in Chapter 4 he has put up a similar fight to get Stephen into University College. He is not seen again in the novel, though at the beginning of Chapter 5 he shouts from upstairs, a man floundering, a tyrant dominating the shabby household intemperately, and at the end of the chapter Stephen squirms under the memory of seeing his father trying to beg a drink from Davin in the street, having lost virtually all self-respect.[11] His son no longer remembers him with pride, seeing him now languishing, a 'praiser of his own past' (p. 245) and an idle dreamer about the list of shifting, shiftless occupations and activities he has followed. By the end Stephen has become indifferent to him.

Although we see little of Stephen's father, we see even less of his mother, a shadowy but forceful presence felt more through Stephen's consciousness. At school he has affectionate, fond memories of her, such as the tears in her eyes as she left him on the first day at school, her kissing him at night and her warm maternal love. She is conciliatory too: at the Christmas dinner, Stephen is impressed by her vain attempts to pacify Dante and her warring husband, and Dante and the other characters respect her – for the brief period of the peace anyway.

But Mary Dedalus plays a complex role and, though she appears but little, her prominence in Stephen's consciousness (true also of *Ulysses*) testifies to her profound influence over him, revealed in the profusion of manifestations into which she is transmuted by him. At the same time as she is caring for him she also serves to question his own actions and course in the novel – disapproving of the university because of its conflict with her religious conviction. The moment provides a rare example of poignancy in the novel, brief-lived:

Yes, his mother was hostile to the idea, as he had read from her listless silence. Yet her mistrust pricked him more keenly than his father's pride . . . (p. 169)

Her disapprobation is unrelenting both in Stephen's life and in his mind yet, as Cranly says, whatever else is uncertain in this world a mother's love is constant. She is last seen packing his bags for him with the same devotion as when she washes and kisses him; her reward is his rejection of her love, yet she still wishes that Stephen may perhaps eventually discover in his own way the meaning of that word. In spite of her affection, slavish dedication and unquestioning loyalty, she is – from beginning to end, prosperity through to poverty – the archetypal victim of her own virtue, of her husband's facile vanity and her son's conceited dogmatism.

We see even less of Stephen's brothers and sisters (unlike in *Stephen Hero*), shadowy figures too of innocence and suffering who play no direct part in Stephen's development. Among rare references are those which tell us that, unlike Stephen, they are excluded from the table at Christmas, that Maurice is a 'thickheaded ruffian' (p. 74), and his sisters are enlisted as part of the domestic service (see p. 178). As elsewhere in the novel, Stephen's siblings appear to serve its demands only in terms of what they represent *vis-à-vis* Stephen himself, namely that as a group they represent a trap to him and their futures are to be sacrificed for his.

Stephen's early home life is filled with a variety of religious bigots, failures and jokers, lacking will or strength of character, both demanding and intimidating; so much so that it strikes us as curious that, until he reaches the age of reason, the one thing he desires is to return to it (and afterwards to leave it). Among these is Dante Riordan, one of the guardians of his boyhood and an important formative presence in his early consciousness. A brooding and irascible harridan, her strong influence on him is revealed when he idly rehearses her judgements on Protestants in general and the Vances in particular, with whom she forbids Stephen to have any dealings. Although she is a sort of nanny for him, he remembers her less vividly for any kindnesses (such as the cachou she gives him for fetching a piece of tissue paper) than for the terrifying vengeance and intimidation which she represents to him (see p. 8). Described as a 'spoiled nun' (p. 36), she is really a frightening religious bigot, typified not merely by her disdain of the Vances but also by her fanatical support for the Catholic clergy which makes her violently antagonistic towards the memory of Parnell. From the beginning (even before we hear about the revered 'Chief') we recognize her to be a callous and poisonous force of indoctrination, precisely the extreme sort of 'net' which Stephen has in mind at the end.

By contrast, the warmth and amiability of John Casey and Uncle Charles in Stephen's early recollections are unmistakable. In Stephen's thoughts these avuncular figures of mercurial wit are guaranteed good gas – promising the sort of banter and *bonhomie* which Mr Dedalus himself occasionally exudes in the early chapters. And so it seems, from the start of the Christmas section (p. 27). Mr Casey's deception over the silver purse and his hoax about Queen Victoria's birthday present amuse and perplex the young Stephen but, from our more objective viewpoint, we are wary until we know more, and our caution is proved right by his phlegmatic tale of the 'famous spit' (p. 35). He is a crafty old fox, deceptive, beyond the pale, a cynical old man; his evocation of past heroes only stresses the stubborn recalcitrance of history in popular memory. An antagonist at the dinner, his bitter story of revenge reveals how mistaken Stephen had been about him, and yet behind the resentment and ferocity we see in him the crisis of the Irish Parnellite, desperate to reconcile intense loyalty to Parnell's memory with the orthodoxy of the 'renegade' Church. Egged on by Mr Dedalus's emotive bantering and by Dante's taunts, he eventually loses control, railing against both Church and God in Ireland.

To Stephen it is a revelation of the snares of political fanaticism, however much we may admire his commitment. By comparison Uncle Charles is a figure of moderating virtue, pious, a quiet complaisant counsel for Stephen, fulfilling the paternalistic role which his true father abrogates.[12] Though well-meaning he represents, on the one hand, like Casey and Mike Flynn, a decaying generation (compare the early *Dubliners* stories too) which Stephen must soon shake off and, on the other, he is the incarnation of what his father will become, broken by failure and bankrupted by frustration, another sort of warning signal to Stephen.

CHURCH

Like the home, the Church is one of the central institutional influences of Stephen's youth. But where the home is a confusion of voices, all making clamorous demands on Stephen and threatening to humble his pride and integrity, the Church is unequivocal and monolithic in its many voices in the novel. Where the image of Stephen's family is neutral (that is, from Joyce's point of view), the picture of the Church is very much the embodiment of Joyce's mistrust of the Catholic influence on the individual and the national spirit, both in its principles and practice.

Though his hatred of it was never as acrimonious as his brother's, Joyce thought Catholic power was the root of Ireland's paralysis and inertia. In August 1904, at about the same time as he began *A Portrait*, Joyce wrote to Nora Barnacle:

Six years ago I left the Catholic Church, hating it most fervently. I found it impossible for me to remain in it on account of the impulses of my nature. I made secret war upon it when I was a student and declined to accept the positions it offered me. By doing this I made myself a beggar but I retained my pride.   (*Letters* II, 48)

However, although in Chapter 3 Stephen highlights several theological quandaries, Joyce does not attack the Church head-on but through its clergy. His presentation of Father Conmee is a case in point. At first we, like Stephen, see him perhaps as an archetype of paternal wisdom (yet another father model) and of prudent benevolence,[13] although we later discover this to be a misapprehension (as with Casey and Dante) when he betrays Stephen's trust, first as a big joke with the other staff and then with Stephen's father (p. 74).

Initially, however, he appears in Chapter 1 as a foil to the cruelty and sadistic humour of Father Dolan, another in the series of archetypal figures of intimidation and humiliation whom Stephen encounters during his youth. In his impatient, peremptory manner threatening eternal punishment ('Tomorrow and tomorrow and tomorrow . . .'), Father Dolan anticipates Arnall's portrait of the vindictive God of his sermon in Chapter 3. Equally, the image which Joyce gives us of the Jesuit school system at Clongowes is of terrifying hostility, peopled with cold disciplinarians in a regime of intolerance, and even when he seeks the reassuring ear of Father Conmee Stephen still expects retribution.

As it is represented in *A Portrait*, the Church has three arms: education, morality and theology. But of these Joyce merely hints at the theological aspects, implying that the Church does too.[14] And this is borne out with Father Arnall's return in Chapter 3. Even though his sermons have been conceived on a theological model, their primary thrust is by way of a staggering moral assault on the boys, with the prospect of a more enduring one in the long term. Shock tactics are the order with the stress on gruesome and horrendous suffering, Father Arnall's penchant for which is medieval and almost psychopathic.

However, because the narrator directs his sermons through Stephen's point of view, it is not so easy to get a full view of Father Arnall's personality; it can be argued anyway that he is not really in the novel as a rounded character so much as both a mouthpiece of the Church and a ghost of Stephen's lost innocence, returned to torment him. He is a cold impersonal figure, distant, and relying on fear for communication with his listeners, though it cannot be denied he is an articulate speaker with vivid and energetic imagination, who clearly understands the way into his audience's sensibilities. Yet, when looked at more soberly than Stephen can, his words are empty rhetoric, formulaic; by Chapter 3 he is become an old man, an old servant of the Church, a physical reminder of the past ever-living in the present and of Clongowes Wood College, paradigm of the historic context, one of the ever-present snares of the novel.

We know even less about the Director of Belvedere College. Along with Father Arnall and the other clergy, his role is partly to contribute to the composite character of the Church which Stephen rejects principally on account of its threat to his freedom, but also because its ethos cannot satisfy his search for truth. While its public face is human and ostensibly open, its absolute authority is undeniable and monolithic, and not exclusively within the spiritual domain; its influence permeates all aspects of Irish life, political, educational, cultural (p. 230). It works to perpetuate the opposite of that which Stephen seeks, intellectual emancipation, artistic as well as secular freedom and truth; its ideal adherent is typified by the tractable mindless peasant, Davin, whom Stephen describes as having '. . . towards the Roman Catholic religion, the attitude of a dullwitted loyal serf' (p. 184).

Although Dante describes the priests as 'the apple of God's eye', Stephen makes a distinction (just as his father had) between the ordinary Catholic priesthood, the 'Paddy Stink and Mickey Mud' of the Christian Brothers, and the more esteemed Jesuit order, the élite missionaries of the Society of Jesus. The humble Brothers, with their simple names and simple piety, make Stephen squirm as they pass him on the Dollymount bridge in Chapter 4, but it is as a Jesuit that he prides himself when, in the same chapter, he considers a vocation. For Stephen they represent an intellectual élite within Catholicism, the thinkers as the 'fishers of souls' and for Joyce himself they raised the religion above the depths of 'ritual and acquiescence', as he put it. As we can see from Stephen's reaction to the Director at Belvedere College and his reflections on the Dean at the university, the Jesuits are personified as chilly, single-minded zealots but above all as crafty and secretive, powerful, self-assured and worldly, totally devoted in worship and service. It is because of this that Stephen derives immense satisfaction from rejecting them, yet at the same time modelling his own secular life on their principles, by dedicating himself as 'priest of the eternal imagination' (see also 'Grace' in *Dubliners* for some different attitudes towards the Jesuits).

We have seen from the beginning of the novel that Stephen is embarked on a course of individuation and differentiation. But it is at school that this process is accelerated, where he meets all sorts of strange names and different ways, all of them challenging his home experience, making him feel strange and small: the way God spoke in French to French people, and Mr Barrett mysteriously calls his pandybat a turkey, Nasty Roche and Tusker Boyle, the Spaniard allowed to smoke cigars and every fellow had a different way of walking.

At first it is all a confusion of voices; gradually, though, some few identifiable characters emerge from it. Wells is a cowardly bully, who shoves Stephen into the ditch for his snuff box and then begs him not to peach. At the other extreme is Fleming, who is kind to Stephen when he is ill, colours his geography book with some originality, but is a duffer at Latin in which he provides some entertainment, a foil to the pandying. However, these characters are not further developed; the boys in general at Clongowes are, for the most part, present only as a body of obscure voices, considered by Stephen to be deceptive and unreliable: 'The fellows had told him to go but they would not go themselves' (p. 56). His school experience challenges that of home, and almost without exception the challenge is in the form of a rude aggressive shock, a sort of vulgarity to him. His experience in school is marked by bullying (from both boys and masters), by deception and intimidation in humourless claustration, but school is above all a place where Stephen comes into contact with and excels in the intellectual sphere, where he distinguishes himself.

At Belvedere the other boys are even more obscure, moving mainly in that darkness which is characteristic of Chapter 2. Only Heron, another bully, steps out from the shadows with his sycophantic cohort but, unlike Wells, he threatens Stephen out of motives of insecurity and envy towards a rival. His hostility to both Stephen and his free ideas is priestlike, reminiscent of Father Dolan and the other figures urging conformity in his schools. His voice, like the voices later of the boys on the estuary in Chapter 4, represents for Stephen what he would put behind him: coarseness and provincialism, chaos, and the unreliable, shifting world of forms and bankrupt rivalries – following instead the call of the artist.

But none of the boys at either school comes across as clearly defined, the narrator's reticence in drawing them out emphasizing Stephen's own reticence and isolation, and the contrast between the vividness of his character and the obscurity of theirs underlines Stephen's individuality as well as the gulf between them.

This changes, of course, in Chapter 5 during the university period, at a point where the narrator's 'neutrality' in favour of Stephen becomes conspicuously diminished. While we see Stephen in the process of shaking off the influence of Church and home, the narrator skilfully disposes the figures of MacCann, Davin and Cranly as foils to highlight the weaknesses of Stephen's life and its plans.

Davin, the first to appear in Stephen's memory, is uncomplicated, placid and direct. He is intimate with Dedalus, calls him 'Stevie' affectionately and comes closer to him as a confidant than anyone else previously in the novel. With an awe reminiscent of some of Synge's characters, he tells Stephen of his mysterious encounter one night with a seductive peasant woman, and its tameness clearly contrasts ironically with Stephen's visits to the prostitutes, highlighting Davin's simple, docile virtue. Moreover, he has the naïve but vigorous and idealistic nationalism which springs from a sympathy with the heroic peasant way of life. He despises anything suggestive of England and Empire. For Joyce as well as for Stephen, he represents the contemporary nationalist revival of traditional Irish sports, culture and language, whose figurehead at the time was Michael Cusack (see pp. 184 and 206; Joyce later used Cusack as the model for the fanatical and bigoted 'Citizen' in the Cyclops chapter of *Ulysses*).

In vain, Davin urges Stephen to join the national movement and to rejoin the Irish language classes, hoping to play on their friendship to coerce him, making him confront unpleasant facts about himself, calling him 'always alone', and a 'born sneerer' (p. 206) with 'pride too powerful' (p. 207). Stephen, however, while he enjoys Davin's company, cannot accord with his politics. His ideas represent a backward step for Stephen, however revolutionary, into the Irish past through hatred and betrayal rather than towards European futurism.

—Too deep for me, Stevie, he said. But a man's country comes first. Ireland first, Stevie. You can be a poet or mystic after.   (p. 208)

And Stephen also highlights the pervasive hypocrisy in the movement as well as it naïve optimism, by calling Davin a 'little tame goose' on account of his romanticized idealism (p.206). (Compare the 'wild Geese', exiled Irishmen who fought the English in various parts of the Empire in the eighteenth century.)

MacCann too is an idealist and, like Davin, his youthful idealism is translated into a sort of altruism, this time on an international scale, with his support for the Tsar's pacifism.[15] Ironically, though, he becomes hostile towards Stephen when he refuses to sign the petition. Stephen rejects it – chiefly because he sees this type of idealistic altruism as an inferior form of religious devotion; in any case he is also reluctant to endorse any one movement by committing his name to it, another extension of his alienation theme. Their sparring eventually concludes when MacCann, as Davin before him and Cranly after, warns Stephen that he is yet to learn fellow feeling and the need for humanity (p. 203).

As Stephen and MacCann cross swords they are interrupted by the heckling of other students. hopeful for a drama. Their quips and banter project a flattering image of energetic student wit and repartee, in marked contrast with Stephen's solemnity as the dissenting outsider (though in *Stephen Hero* he is depicted as a master of such wit). Because of the narrator's oblique approach, most of these other students remain undifferentiated, a flux of confused voices and forms which Stephen strips away before he faces Cranly alone.

Based on J. F. Byrne, Joyce's closest friend at university, Cranly is the last of Stephen's contacts in the novel before the diaries section. On the surface at least, he has a highly cavalier, worldly attitude to his student life, so that when he is missed from the physics lecture back comes the retort, 'Try Leopardstown!' (p. 195).[16] He has no academic aspirations or pretensions. (When later in life a friend asked Joyce if he was surprised to learn that Byrne had written a book, Joyce replied that he would have been surprised to learn that he had read one!) But his casual attitude to life makes him an ideal attendant, in contrast with Stephen's intensity. However, though he appears imperturbable at the start of the final interview, at other times his calm is quickly and inexplicably ruffled, for example by Temple's interjections – in fact, during his conversation with Stephen, he takes a particular, capricious exception to Temple's presence as a whole.

Joyce's friendship with Byrne was many-sided, and even in the short space of Chapter 5 we can see how Joyce tries to capture some of this complexity through the relationship between Stephen and Cranly. As Horatio, Cranly is Hamlet–Stephen's confessor and his closest friend in the novel; he provides for Stephen both a sympathetic ear and a worldliness which neither Davin's simple nationalism nor Lynch's dull insensitivity will admit. But, at the moment of Stephen's rejection, as Banquo he is sacrificed to his companion's ambition, and coming as this does immediately before Stephen's resolution to depart, it is ironic that this intimacy should become most clear exactly at the moment of its conclusion. Eventually Stephen denies both directions and, at some distance removed, conceives of Cranly in terms of John the Baptist, though the justification for this lies more in Cranly's loyalty and the advanced age of his parents than in any parallels between Stephen and Christ.

Cranly, unlike Davin and MacCann, is a realist and an apt foil to Stephen's own idealism. Among company he speaks with nonchalant ease and wit but with Stephen he is frank and direct. He confronts Stephen with the humanity which his friend himself has successfully denied, speaking with maturity and prudence, exposing to Stephen the full and potential implications of his decisions as well as his contradictions (p. 250). Accordingly, Cranly appears as an externalization of his friend's muted conscience, and his failure to bring about Stephen's comprehension of his responsibility within the novel – the expected but deferred anagnorisis of the book – condemns Stephen as implacably selfish and misguided. Their conversation is in the form of a catechism, Cranly's questions seeking to sustain what Stephen's laconic postures continually threaten to halt, the confrontation highlighting Stephen's (as well as his own) loneliness, until finally he forces Cranly into silence, and Stephen's ultimate question to Cranly heralds his own silence, turning his back on reason and fellowship. It is a significant contrast that Stephen in the novel rejects the sort of very deep friendship which in real life Joyce valued most highly.[17]

WOMAN

Throughout his life Joyce was occupied, often facetiously, on a scheme to define a generalized picture of woman – he collected what he took to be common traits of womanhood such as a dislike for soup and a tendency for replacing books on a shelf upside down. Commenting on his celebrated portrayal of Molly Bloom, the psychologist C. G. Jung exclaimed that Joyce's comprehension of the female psyche must have been inspired by the devil himself; however, untouched by this lofty commendation, Nora replied soberly of her husband: 'He knows nothing at all about women.'[18]

The subject of the presentation of women in the work of Joyce is a major and growing area; within the scope of this study we can do no more than introduce some aspects relevant to *A Portrait*. The world of this novel is predominantly masculine, chiefly because most of the novel covers Stephen's time at boys' colleges and at a university which was a male preserve; the general picture of women and girls reflects the time and place – women are seen on the one hand as chiefly serving the needs of men (for example, Stephen's sisters and his mother, especially in Chapter 5, or the prostitutes in Chapters 2 and 3), or on the other as idealizations of a variety of stereotyped aspects, usually as distant but vaguely importuning figures (though there are exceptions, such as Dante).

In Chapter 1, woman is presented most prominently as the mother, homely figure of emotional refuge and security which is promised by the approach of the school holidays. However, Stephen also remembers her as an ambiguous figure, both faintly threatening (p. 7) and peace-making. Female sexuality (or is it really Stephen's own sexuality?) is hinted at in his recollections of Eileen Vance's hands, though when Stephen idealizes these as ivory-like he ironically equates her more with the Virgin, the *Tower of Ivory* (p. 37).

The virgin image continues in Chapter 2 where the opening asexual, platonic image of a woman in the idea of Mercedes is gradually transformed by the action of Stephen's maturing, and increasingly frustrated, libidinous imagination into woman as an object of sexual gratification, the prostitute at the end. 'E.C.' (Emma Clery) appears here as a transitional point between the two, at least in Stephen's imagination, by assimilating the exalted virginal elements of the Virgin Mary with the sexual aspect realized later in the brothel episode (where, euphemistically, Stephen again records the girl's 'vanitities').

This confusion and yet polarization of the two aspects of woman, a legacy of the Church's medieval vision, is a feature of Joyce's own ambiguous attitude to woman; as he wrote to Nora:

I wonder is there some madness in me. Or is love madness? One moment I see you like a virgin or madonna the next moment I see you shameless, insolent, half-naked and obscene! (Letters II, 243)

Whatever Stephen does see, it is not the individual herself, and accordingly Stephen's response to this dual nature is itself dualistic, swinging between high sexual excitation and deep spirituality and shame.

Both of these extremes are prolonged and then eventually merged in Chapter 3. Speaking for the Church, Father Arnall recites its medieval image of woman, describing her as the 'weaker vessel' (p. 121), although by contrast we see Stephen's own mind ironically conjuring up the images of Emma and Mary (which represent for him archetypal figures of innocence) in order to intensify his own shame (p. 120). Then later in the same chapter, Joyce uses the old woman who directs Stephen to confession to represent the old Church in whose soothing voice he finds solace (p. 144); the figure of the Old Woman is archetypal in Celtic mythology and in *Ulysses* Joyce uses a similar old woman who delivers the milk to symbolize old Ireland, wrinkled and weary but still providing metaphorical sustenance (see *Ulysses*, p. 12).

Related to the notion of woman as sexual entity is the archetypal beckoning woman or the 'temptress' – in *A Portrait* she is linked inextricably with both the Call and the Fall syndromes in Stephen's situation: woman is both annunciation or inspiration as well as source of sin, guilt and decline, and there are many examples in the novel including the whores, the flower girl in Chapter 5, in addition to Emma herself (the 'temptress' of Stephen's villanelle), but the figure is given its most distinct treatment in the estuary epiphany of Chapter 4. Here the bathing girl draws together and brings to a climax all these other archetypal elements – she is a distant beckoning figure of unattainable sexuality, transmuted as a physical embodiment of artistic inspiration, but above all she is the annunciation of Stephen's destiny in art, in one of the most enduring of female images in the novel.

Woman is represented then in a wide range of figures and images and yet, partly because of his denial of the emotional faculty and partly because of the pre-eminence of the mother/virgin model, Stephen appears incapable of reaching her in all aspects simultaneously, as she is represented in Chapters 2 and 5 by Emma, and with the possibility of love. He is unable to conceive of her except in fixed, polarized terms and at best, as in many of Joyce's presentations of women, Stephen can only come to terms with 'her' symbolically as a strong maternal figure, ideally in the form of the Virgin Mary (even the prostitute mothers him). It is an extension of his conception of the victim but it is of course a less than satisfactory reconciliation for him, and his frustration is demonstrated graphically by his tormented readiness to suspect Cranly and Father Moran, by his sexual fantasizing, and also by his swinging to the other extreme and adopting a monklike withdrawal into the 'spiritual-heroic refrigerating apparatus', as he describes his clumsy response to Emma (p. 256).

It is sometimes argued that Joyce's women are most often portrayed as passive and complaisant, an observation frequently sparked off by focusing strongly on the figures of the recumbent Molly Bloom in *Ulysses* and the fluvine Anna Livia Plurabelle in *Finnegans Wake*, both of whom are almost exclusively restrained by their respective beds. But this is not borne out either by *A Portrait* or by *Dubliners*, where woman is typically seen trapped within the constraints of a strictly stereotyped cast, assigned by both a male-dominated society (characterized by extreme poverty and prolific child-bearing) and a Madonna–Virgin

Critical Studies: A Portrait of the Artist as a Young Man

orientated Church (whose symbolic deflowering becomes Stephen's avowed aim). Instead, women in general are represented as by far the more active and positive beings, holding the family together, realistic, and resourceful, inspiring, and yet ultimately and ironically reinforcing the very regime which suffocates them. With the possible exception of Molly Ivors in 'The Dead', Emma is the nearest to an intellectual woman in Joyce's work.

98

4. 'the spell of arms and voices': Joyce, Dedalus and the Idea of the Artist

> *... that odious and still today insufficiently malestimated notesnatcher (kak, pfooi, bosh and fiety, much earny, Gus, poteen? Sez you!) Shem the Penman.*
>
> *(Finnegans Wake* p. 125)

'John,' I said, seeking an ally, 'he's codding the pair of us.'

But John could not be enlisted to resent.

'A great artist!' he exclaimed, using 'artist' in the sense it has in Dublin of a quaint fellow or a great cod: a pleasant and unhypocritical poseur, one who sacrifices his own dignity for his friends' diversion.

'A great artist! He may be codding the two of us but he's codding himself!'   (Oliver St Gogarty, *As I was Going Down Sackville Street*)

What does Joyce mean by the word 'artist'? Does he intend it in this same comic, 'marketplace' meaning of the word, or in the broad Daedalian sense of a craftsman ('artificer'), or perhaps in a very narrow sense of an accomplished poet? Before we can judge Stephen, we must try to understand Joyce's use of the word and something of the general nature of the artist in his relationship to society.

Like Byrne, Gogarty was, at least in student days, a great friend of Joyce – in fact, their relationship resembled that between Stephen and Cranly – and like Cranly, Gogarty became the model for another of Joyce's characters: the ribald medical student Malachi 'Buck' Mulligan in *Ulysses*, Stephen's doubtful ally. His reminiscence above, concerning the real Dean of studies at University College, makes explicit one of the major difficulties in discussing the idea of the 'artist' in *A Portrait* – deciding in which sense or even senses Joyce is using the word. It is a difficulty which Cranly's own 'You poor poet' merely hints at.

The title of the novel is crucial in this respect, in setting up its chief challenge or expectation for the reader: simply, is Stephen an artist? (and the title is the sole direct authorial comment in the novel). But the effect of Gogarty's definition is of course to suddenly jerk the carpet away from under our feet as we wonder just what it is we are supposed to be judging. Moreover, it also gives a resounding smack to what we understood was the implied relationship between Stephen, Joyce and the reader since, if by the word 'artist' Joyce really means something like 'piss artist' in the modern idiom, then we also become immediately aware of the narrator's irony, and that after all Joyce has been codding us and deprecating himself through his novel.

We have already noted Stephen's capacity for cunning and deceit ('schemer') – his predisposition to make feints and to pretend (pp. 9 and 14), to adopt roles or to pose (pp. 64 and 180), and to dream (pp. 24 and 223) – and we will also see how the language seeks to do exactly the same, shimmying and evading. So, by combining the uncertainty of Stephen's genuineness and the treachery of Joyce's use of language, we are indeed in treacherous waters; to get an answer to the question of what sort of artist Stephen really is, we will need first to examine the novel in the context of Joyce's own ideas of the artist and of the clues which are dotted about *A Portrait* and *Stephen Hero*.

Romanticism and the Place of the Artist

The notion of the artist as a celebrity coincides with the rise of Romanticism in the early nineteenth century and especially in the concept of the poet-artist as hero figure. Its origins lie in the emergence of the professional writer (and the consequent decline in the function of the art patron, until then an indispensable *sine qua non* of the artist), the arrival of a class of writer who could make an independent living from his pen (such as the poet Robert Southey and the critic William Hazlitt). The old requirement of being born into a privileged class or having to court the continuous favour of an influential and beneficent patron dwindled rapidly at the end of the eighteenth century. This in turn loosened the artist's dependence on the power-base of aristocratic society and encouraged both an intellectual and geographical separation of the writer from the nobility. Wealth and status were still of course powerful obstacles to be considered but gradually this reorientation resulted in a new and increasingly close relationship between the artist and his public (and not least the financial one between the artist and his publisher).

The ensuing financial independence and professional aloofness gave rise in turn to the mystique of the artist and the establishment of a separate writer class with an emphasis on the detachment of the artist – an absence of cohesion was inherent in this stress on individuation, a source of its vigour and originality. At the same time there also developed an impulse to form loose groupings, such as circles or schools and cliques (for example, the Lakes school centred on Wordsworth and his associates; the medievalists on Scott, Southey and Keats; and the cosmopolitans on Byron and Shelley). The increasing detachment of the artist from his public naturally engendered a popular interest in the doings of artists, resulting in the literary biography and a general curiosity about the day-to-day private life of the writer, ranging from his views on Continental unrest to what he had for breakfast. Coinciding with a renewed interest in the natural landscape, the detachment of the artist-writer led to a flight from the city into a self-imposed exile of contemplation and inspiration surrounded by the revitalizing genius of Nature – in marked contrast to the metropolitan urban focus of the preceding Neo-classicists (and the succeeding Modernists).

The primacy given to the imagination during the Romantic period led to a pre-eminence of intuition, idealism and individuality, and ultimately to subjectivism, all of which worked to reinforce the focus on the concept of the artist as a sort of weather-vane, further heightening his role as guide or leader: the gifted writer became a mystical teacher figure, the poet guardian and moral conscience of society. In turn, this exalted status, together with a new-found independence, gradually encouraged an impulse towards non-conformity and bohemianism, with the idea eventually that the artist was actually in conflict with society and that it was his duty to be so, a rebel, a source of alternative visions and radical political values: hence Wordsworth's active involvement in the French revolution and Byron's fierce commitment to Greek independence from Turkey.

However, towards the middle of the century, with the violent deaths of some of the movement's leading lights and with no high priests to lead it into new directions, Romantic attitudes fell into abeyance, and in their place Realism began to take hold as the dominant approach; the Romantic emphasis on individual temperament and the subjective imagination as the sources of perception and poetic truth gave way to the doctrine of careful observation and photographic reproduction (in line with the general nineteenth-century spirit of progress through science). However, this idea that a novel can correspond closely with reality is at heart a futile pursuit, literature having its own unique reality and, as the Impressionists made clear, this quasi-photographic realism is in fact already the artist's own subjective version of reality.

With this new shift, poetry gave way to prose as the primary medium of expression, yet because the writer was accorded only the position of a recorder of events, scenes, people and so on, there soon developed an anxiety about his exact function in the transaction of fiction, especially regarding his moral position.

Theories about the artist's relationship to his material began to arise, especially concerning his detachment from the work – for example,

Gustave Flaubert, whose influential theories had a profound effect on the Naturalist school and succeeding generations of writers, considered the place of the writer in terms very similar to those expounded by Stephen Dedalus:

An artist must be in his work like God in creation, invisible and all-powerful: he should be everywhere felt, but nowhere seen.   (Letter to Louise Colet, 8 March 1857)

Not only did the idea of the artist as a God-like figure in his work persist but so also did the subjective principle: the coalescence of Realism with Romanticism is just as evident in Flaubert as it is in Wordsworth. Romanticism did not die out so much as become transmogrified and consequently the heroic figure of the artist also prevailed (though the prevailing realism of novelists such as Dickens and George Eliot worked to diminish the mystique and magic of the writer, compared with the days of Scott or the early Romantics).

So, towards the close of the nineteenth century, Romanticism re-emerged and in the wake of Tennyson and Browning 'flowered' in a variety of forms (sometimes grouped under the title of 'Neo-Romanticism') – including *Fin-de-siècle*, the Decadents, the Yellow Book, and the Symbolists – all exhibiting to different degrees the features of the early Romantic movement: its radical individualism, strident imaginativeness and its stress on the probing of the subconscious. Symbolism was one of the precursors of the Modernist movement with its insistence on organic internal structures rooted in recurrent image and motif, the exploration of myth and the fluid dynamics of place and time. On the other hand, there were the 1890s' poets of the Rhymers club, and the Aesthetic movement of the so-called Decadents such as Dowson, Swinburne, Wilde and the young Yeats, with Walter Pater as their pre-eminent inspiration. While looking back to the Romantics and Pre-Raphaelites they began to point in a new direction. They converted the anarchic individualism of the early Romantics into mere affectation and fey bohemianism while at the same time relegating the integrity of the art work to the ethos of 'art for art's sake'. Although Pater offered the movement its intellectual backbone his overtures to beauty and intense and expressive experience became translated into sensuality and superficial sensationalism, eroticism and linguistic posturing.

The Aesthetic movement, with its search for inner justification and internal integrity, favoured an attitude of withdrawal from the real world into a principle of art for art's sake in which the art object takes its reference not from the real world but from within itself. This was characterized ultimately by an obsessive preoccupation with style and form (compare Stephen's villanelle), with carefully rehearsed spontaneity and, since external reality was irrelevant, with excessive whimsicality. Melodiousness is replaced by monotony of repeated sounds and mannered tones, imagination by sentiment, sensation and gesture.

The figure of the artist at this time, however, owes much to that which the early high Romantics had evolved and established. But in place of the Romantics' close intimacy and special relationship with the reader, the Aestheticist poet, in line with his scorn for realism, is now not merely physically detached from his community but spiritually divorced from it too. He almost resents his readership and his special contempt is reserved for the bourgeoisie (on whom he nevertheless relies both for his readership and his image). In fact, the image of the artist as celebrity, the pose and the role, now dominates the creative aspects – the need to strike outrageous attitudes and to scandalize, to elicit shock and vilification is more important than the work: reputation almost completely precedes achievement. Through these gestures the artist manoeuvres himself so as to be able to peer scornfully down on a public which he now pompously regards as intolerant and philistine, the stock reply to a hostile society's charges of decadence and immorality. He insists on absolute freedom, on free choice of subject matter without extrinsic political or moral reference, on musicality, and on subjectivism.

Where traditionally a work had been judged in terms of its moral force, the 1890s' poets tried to reverse this by the principle that a work of art was morally good simply if it was good art:

... a work of art can be judged from only two standpoints: the standpoint from which its art is measured entirely by its morality, and the standpoint from which its morality is measured entirely by its art.   (Arthur Symons, *Silhouettes*, 1896)

A work became morally acceptable to them only on the grounds that it be a beautiful piece of work – whether it conformed to society's conventions of acceptable behaviour was irrelevant and even undesirable.

There are faint echoes of this in Stephen Dedalus's theory which judges works as 'improper' if they find their justification outside of themselves, thus arousing kinetic emotion (for example, pornographical or didactic ends) – a work is to be judged primarily on its internal qualities (harmony, radiance, etc.) not necessarily on its correspondence to the real world as previously in Naturalism (that is, imitation) – though at the same time Stephen also strives for an objective assessment of his criteria by placing the emphasis on the work of art being assessed rather than on the motives of the artist.

The demise of the 1890s' ethos eventually lay in its very inability to articulate – it even encouraged a diversion of attention away from art; even though many of its adherents were important innovators (such as Symons with regard to the French Symbolists) the search for new material and approaches led merely to novelty and frivolity. The artist, isolated from the demands and realities of the outside world, surrounded by art and artifice, is in almost full control of his existence. Art is pretentious, precious. Amorality eventually gives way to immorality. From a position at the opening of the century in which the artist is the initiator, custodian and arbiter of society's values (albeit by challenge and conflict), the artist has moved by the close of the century to one in which he is in constant conflict with society, courting its censure and inviting its disapprobation through the outrage of received values, not with any intention of revising them, merely for the sake of confrontation itself. Where the high Romantics were affirmative and positive, working ultimately within the community, the Aestheticists (Yeats's 'tragic generation'), precursors of Joyce's age and of the Modernists, were essentially anarchic, negative and insular.

The Artist as Hero

By the time that Joyce wrote his defiant essay 'The Day of the Rabblement' in October 1901, the Aesthetic movement was well in decline. It had become introverted, incestuous, irrelevant, the early sensationalism having lost its power to outrage, and what remained was already discredited as a sham of hollow gesturing.

Taken to its illogical conclusion, Aestheticism had lost its reference points and alienated its public. Yet Joyce himself is to a large extent a child of his own times and 'The Day of the Rabblement' reflects this. An important manifesto of his early ideas about the artist and his role, the essay had been initially written with the earnest intention of its being published in *St Stephen's*, a new literary magazine run by students of University College. But soon after submission, it was summarily rejected – not by the editor but by his 'adviser', Father Henry Browne, on the grounds that it made reference to a banned book, D'Annunzio's *Il Fuoca*. Incensed by this rejection, Joyce immediately set about publishing it privately, a fact which, together with the *risqué* books it referred to, worked to lionize Joyce's reputation, transforming him instantly into a minor Dublin celebrity and at the same time confirming his own role as *poète maudit* in the mould of a Parnell-like victim – a feature which the article itself sets out to demonstrate:

No man, said the Nolan, can be a lover of the true or the good unless he abhors the multitude; and the artist, though he may employ the crowd, is very careful to isolate himself. (*The Critical Writings of James Joyce*, p. 69)

Although ostensibly setting out to slate the Irish Literary Theatre for its provincialism and timidity in bowing to popular commercial taste, it effectively lays down Joyce's own impression of the artist and the necessary precondition for the aspiring poet: if the artist is to flourish he must first assert his individuality by ridding himself of all the diverting and distorting commitments to the collective world of society which threaten to compromise his honesty and freedom.

In an angry passage he reproaches W. B. Yeats for his equivocation in the face of the public outrage which followed his play *The Countess Cathleen*. The point is mirrored in *A Portrait* too, when Stephen Dedalus draws attention to this storm of protest as he recalls his recent visit to the theatre:

. . . The catcalls and hisses and mocking cries ran in rude gusts round the hall from his scattered fellow students.
　　—A libel on Ireland!
　　—Made in Germany!
　　—Blasphemy!
　　—We never sold our faith!
　　—No Irish woman ever did it!　(p. 230)

The moment leaps to Stephen's memory later as, watching the birds wheeling above the library, he agonizes over whether or not to imitate them by leaving the country, and he vividly remembers this hostility to the artist and the drama. The protests come from his fellow students but through them too Joyce also indicts the sterile culture of Dublin in general (which Joyce called 'hemiplegia of the will'):

A nation which never advanced so far as a miracle-play affords no literary model to the artist, and he must look abroad. (*Critical Writings*, p. 70)[1]

The students at the theatre echo the blustering hollow-sounding voices of the Church and of state politics, their shouts resembling those insults aimed at Stephen near the estuary in Chapter 4 (p. 172) and their jeering outside the lecture theatre in Chapter 5, urging him to support their cause and threatening to humiliate his ascendant pride.

105

'The Day of the Rabblement' refers specifically to the outcry at the first night of Yeats's play, a large proportion of whose audience was made up of Joyce's fellow-students, and he pinpoints their insidious threat: 'placid and intensely moral,' he calls them but the rabble regard the theatre and the arts in general as just another vehicle for their propaganda, through which to impose and consolidate their own political and religious prejudices, rather than promote innovation and progressive ideas.

Joyce finds their pervasive influence both insipid and insidious because it operates not through argument and truth but through bigotry and dogma. For Stephen its worst feature is that essentially it is non-rational (the world of the 'trolls', in Joyce's own words), uncivilized and therefore anathema to the true artist. But the rabblement is only half the story of Dublin's cultural malaise – the other is that breed of cowardly artist himself, a sort of simoniac who is ready to prostitute his talents for commercial success or popular acclaim.

If an artist courts the favour of the multitude he cannot escape the contagion of its fetishism and deliberate self-deception, and if he joins in a popular movement he does so at his own risk. (*Critical Writings*, p. 71)

Though we can see that on the one hand Joyce found it easy to dismiss such philistines, on the other we can wonder what sort of available models of the artist there were at that time for a young and aspiring Irish artist such as Joyce or Stephen; the Aesthetic movement discredited, the English impotent – what models were there in Ireland itself in the opening decade of the century? There was Yeats, of course, but his dabbling in the occult and other mystic arts (as many of the other Dublin literary lights did) made him unsuited by temperament to Aristotelian Joyce, and Joyce himself was out of sorts with the nationalist revival of vernacular poetry. The only Irishman of any repute was the exiled novelist George Moore, towering head and shoulders above any other. And yet, ironically (Moore too had quit Ireland's stifling atmosphere) Joyce reserves his especial contempt for this most esteemed Anglo-Irish novelist who, again like Joyce, spent much of his artistic life in Paris and consciously sought out and absorbed the influence of the European avant-garde. So why should Joyce have done this?

For one thing, in the eyes of Joyce, Moore's cardinal sins had been to bastardize his talents and demean his art in an ignoble pursuit of acclaim, in fact the precise objects of Stephen's contempt in *A Portrait*. But there was more – Joyce considered him a toady to popular taste, which had made him complacent as well as complaisant, and his landed, Anglo-Irish background identified him so firmly with a played-out bourgeois culture that, in Joyce's 'Gas from a Burner', a bitterly ironic verse satire on Irish letters, his work is derided as:

> Written by Moore, a genuine gent
> That lives on his property's ten per cent.

In 'The Day of the Rabblement' Joyce also considered that 'Mr Martyn and Mr Moore are not writers of much originality'.[2] On the other hand, Joyce's frustration became even more thwarted when Moore apparently informed the celebrated Dublin poet A. E. (George Russell) that he found Joyce's article 'preposterously clever' – adding also that he doubted if Joyce himself would make a successful writer. In the same vein, W. B. Yeats (another victim of Joyce's spleen) very much admired Joyce's 'Rabblement' article, to the extent that he later played a crucial part in securing publishers for Joyce's early work.

Unashamed, an ebullient Joyce dismissed Moore as a flashy chameleon who was ready to absorb or adapt himself to almost any influence however low for public acclaim and, in a broadside against one such influence, Joyce exposed the general thrust of his own artistic aspirations: 'his new impulse has no kind of relation to the future of arts'.[3]

Although this smacks strongly of Joyce flexing his youthful artistic muscles, Moore himself truly courted such vilification, not only by being a populist author but also because he consciously played out in full the role of the Great Author. (As a popular success Moore's career also marked a recognizable increase in the distinction and snobbery against the commercial artist with the rise of the avant-garde.) Consequently a cocky young Joyce could readily find in Moore a convenient old guard target, an icon of conventional taste and outmoded sensitivities – and through this Joyce also found a useful outlet to express his own embryonic ideas on art and the proper function of the artist.[4] In any case it was itself an implied fundamental condition of the Joycean artist-hero that the artist ruthlessly reject his forebears in order to stake his own claim to the muse. And as a con-man, 'Shem the Penman', Joyce the littérateur could be as sanctimonious as he could, in ordinary life, be Joyce the Jokey.

So, with no available living Irish model then, the obvious step for a young writer to take was to reject his home shores in favour of a foreign artist, and the more obscure or esoteric or outlawed the more likely he was to fit Joyce's ideal of the artist-hero. If Henrik Ibsen was obscure it was because of his homeland and native tongue, as well as the fact that his work was proscribed by the Church and the state. So it was that Joyce found his ideal of the artist, 'old father, old artificer', in the figure of the Norwegian playwright, giant of the Naturalist theatre, who was then in the final, great period of his career but whose work had almost single-handedly transformed the European stage, exercising an enormous influence on late nineteenth- and early twentieth-century theatrical attitudes. Moreover, through his influence, Joyce at once discovered a new type of heroic figure, the artist-hero, and then eventually through this new figure a method of uniting the themes of the Romantic hero, the biographical novel and the portrait of the artist.

An exile from his homeland since the age of thirty-six, Ibsen exercised a profound effect on Joyce both in his concept of the artist-as-hero, self-assured and uncompromising, and both directly in his naturalistic play, *Exiles*, as well as indirectly in the novels.

Specifically, Ibsen looked upon the creation of art as a means to the creation of life – he despised Aestheticism with its dogmatic *l'art pour l'art*, preferring instead to work in hard, material reality. Although Ibsen's works are more explicitly philosophical or sociological, Joyce absorbed many of his key themes, such as the conflict of the ideal and the everyday moral life, and the relationship of the individual with the forces of modern society. Joyce also assimilated Ibsen's craftsmanship, a rich, symbolic and ironic texture, meticulously crafted within a complex, prosaic naturalism.

A distinctly singular figure, Ibsen too believed that the way forward lay in shunning the 'rabblement' – as he wrote to Georg Brandes in 1882:[5]

Never in any circumstances shall I be able to belong to a party that has the majority on its side ... The minority is always right – that is to say the minority that is leading the way.

For him the writer is a questioner, a dissenter, a trouble-maker, challenging and provoking, at war with his age – an attitude that Ibsen translated most convincingly through *An Enemy of the People* (1882) in the character and predicament of Dr Tomas Stockmann, the medical officer in a small spa town who, discovering that the town's water supply is contaminated, stoically elects to suffer the violent contempt of the people rather than compromise his principles and conceal the danger.

DR STOCKMANN: Oh, my dear Mr Hovstad, don't talk to me about accepted truths! The truths that the masses and the majorities accept are the truths that the leaders of thought accepted in our grandfathers' day! We leaders of thought of the present day don't accept them any longer.

Ironically, Stockmann is found guilty of moral corruption by the town council who declare him a Public Enemy, and the mob stone his windows. After first considering exile he defiantly resolves instead to stay and educate the poor and oppressed of the town and to drive out the real villains even though by the end of the play he finds himself almost completely alone.

DR STOCKMANN: . . . You see, the fact is that the strongest man in the world is the man who stands most alone.

Joyce too found reassurance in this type of heroic situation, and there are parallels with Stockmann of Parnell's victimization too. In a letter to Ibsen, Joyce revealed those features of his plays that he found most useful, including the inspirational model of the heroic artist, resolute and uncompromising, absolutely convinced of his way in truth and art:

. . . your battles inspired me – not the obvious material battles but those that were fought and won behind your forehead – how your wilful resolution to wrest the secret from life gave me heart, and how in your absolute indifference to public canons of art, friends and shibboleths you walked in the light of your inward heroism.(*Letters* I, 52)

Joyce held fervently that, in order to find his voice, the artist had no choice but to cut loose from both the rabblement and from the paralysing moral influence of the old order – to set himself apart from sterile forces both physically and spiritually, fully aware of all the attendant peril that such an existential leap would entail.

So, although Joyce embraced Ibsen's inspirational ideas of the heroic artist, his translation of it into his own life was less extreme or intense than Stephen's is in the novel. For Joyce, the priority was not to break away from family nor even from friends but from the stifling ghosts of the past.[6] He had to cut himself free from outdated voices like those of Moore and his contemporaries in order to find his own, as Stephen says, to 'express his soul', to meet the problems and situations of a radically different world. In the novel this is the real motive for freedom. From the end of Chapter 4, once Stephen becomes positive of his way ahead as an artist, he also becomes aware through experience of the nets flung about him. After the liberating epiphany on the estuary, he is convinced of the need to escape and he translates this into absolute terms, abandoning almost everything, to leave family as well as Church, and the dispiriting squalor of home life (even though he had begun to find some redemption in its disorder). Subsequently he rejects too the possibility of love in Cranly, Emma, and his mother, abandoned along with the clamourings of MacCann and Temple, and not to have even 'one friend . . . who would be more than a friend'.

He tells Cranly, of course, that he is not afraid, that he is not frightened by the consequences of his decision – he is even quite offhand about it (see p. 251). But even if he says what he believes to be true, we can still ask if this makes Stephen a hero, that he faces up to this prospect of imminent oblivion with such stony composure? And are his values heroic?

Although Stephen pictures the artist as a heroic individual we are still not readily convinced of his own heroic values, even if we admire his readiness to commit himself to his ideas. His claim to heroism lies solely on the strength of his commitment, not on his solution to a moral dilemma (to which his only answer is flight).[7] But, instead of feeling that his commitment issues from some deep moral and humane engagement with life, we are left with the profound suspicion that his strength derives from exclusively negative urges (principally to deny rather than to create) and a strong impulse for the anti-life. In spite of his high-sounding words at the close, and even as anti-hero, the values he represents do not on the whole endear him to us.

His inner strength stems, of course, chiefly from the annunciation at the end of Chapter 4, filling him with a 'knowledge' of his way forward. As a result, Stephen interprets his duty now to be a sometimes painful campaign of cutting himself away, and pain and suffering are thus fused as inevitable corollaries of the heroic theme. Such is the strength of his conviction that we are now forced to reappraise the early part of the novel and see it, as Stephen does, as only a preparatory stage and to see his early ordeals as a form of necessary suffering – this element is one of the few real senses in which we can accept Stephen as artist-hero, in other words as 'victim': victim like Parnell of the prejudices and antagonism of other characters (from Dante and Wells to Temple), victim of his own struggle, of his own sensitivity and even victim of his own conviction . . . or illusion.

But at this point we become aware of two important paradoxes concerning Stephen's idea of freedom. The first is that although Stephen struggles to alienate himself from other people – rejecting their overtures and fellowship so as to avoid getting too close – in fact they also very much reject him too. They reject him as much as he rejects them – until, that is, we reach the final sections with Cranly and Stephen's mother, the only exception. He is often seen alone, simply because he is not popular. His company is not sought, he is cool, snobbish and is bullied by other boys, a solitary at parties in Chapter 2 and 5, with almost no contact at all even with his brothers or sisters, and he is apparently also rejected by Emma who (if Stephen's interpretation is any guide) sympathizes with him but keeps her distance. No wonder the director of Belvedere considers him a worthy candidate for the 'chill and order' of the priesthood!

Of course this is an aspect too of his heroic suffering as artist – he fulfils the role even before he shows signs of any convincing talent. This element of suffering, tempered in our eyes by a large measure of haughtiness as well as blindness, balances the novel, reverberating between potential tragedy and potential comedy – which is ultimately Stephen Dedalus's tragicomedy of exile and blindness. It is a paradox which is never fully resolved, at least not within this novel, nor do we seek its resolution, working as it does to generate and brilliantly focus the tensions of Stephen's equivocal destiny, his ambition and his struggle.

The second paradox concerning Stephen's freedom is that if he is destined to become an artist as he says he is, then surely he is not free to choose – he is born an artist – and if not, then why go to all the trouble of trying to free himself of all the nets which he supposes will hamper him? Moreover, if Stephen is not free but destined to become an artist (indeed he may already *be* an 'artist') then the decisions which he makes do not in fact set him free nor are they crucial to his becoming a writer: if he is predestined then his decisions, far from establishing his autonomy, merely *show* how the finished artist deals with such situations.

Consequently, although we admire Stephen's courage when he complains to the Rector at the end of Chapter 1, he is really forced there anyway by the voices of his conscience and his classmates who thrust upon him a decision which in any case he would rather not make – perhaps it would be better to forget it and just hide out of the way as usual '. . . when you were small and young you could often escape that way' (p. 56). And in the early part of the novel this is exactly what he tries to do – though his environment is continually intervening and imposing itself on him, forcing him into confrontation, even as he turns away. He is forced by the action of Father Dolan and his classmates in Chapter 1, by Father Arnall in Chapter 3 and in large part by the Director in Chapter 4; Stephen would really prefer to avoid decisions in the real world – he avoids rather than rejects and where he cannot avoid his responses are involuntary.

Instead of watching Stephen freely and fervently acting to initiate events in his life, what we do see is an individual either reacting to situations brought on him by others or simply remaining passive, with the result that it severely diminishes his status as artist-hero according to the terms which he sets up. We have already seen in Chapter 3 the importance that Stephen places on freedom as a pre-condition to the life of the artist, so the danger is that he is not free at all to become an artist but, as he himself points out, he is 'born to serve' this end (p. 173). It is only after the end of Chapter 4, after the annunciation and his arrival at the age of reason, that Stephen consciously makes informed decisions relating to a determined life in art.

However, a number of resolutions to this paradox of freedom also offer themselves. One is to separate the inherent aspect from the environment – Stephen may be a born artist but he still has to struggle in the world to assert his individuality in order to create worthwhile art; or that Stephen must make himself free in order to understand in full the meaning of his destiny, not committing himself too early to one exclusive course. Another possibility is voiced by those critics who see the novel as autobiographical, that Stephen does not need to make decisions – in other words, that Joyce had been this way before him. Yet this merely begs the question, since someone had to make the decisions in the first place, whether it is Stephen or Joyce – the paradox would not be resolved merely by saying someone else had the problem.

But we can reach a more satisfactory answer if we consider that at the heart of these two paradoxes there is a question of semantics, hinging on the keywords 'artist' and 'destiny' (and in Chapter 5 Stephen himself draws attention to their different uses).

We can say that Stephen used the word 'destiny' partly for effect – it has the right mythic sound to it and fits in with his Catholic notions of a vocation, an omnipotent idea which he can justly serve (he often sees himself as serving, and serving is yet another manifestation of the victim mode which he successfully exploits in the decisions he is forced to make). He sees his 'destiny' not strictly as something he is fated to become, but perhaps something for which he has been prepared by birth and early experiences – in other words, having the potential he would still need the freedom to express his voice truly and unreservedly, 'to express myself as I am'.

But then a problem arises because, in the literal sense of the keyword of the book's title, 'artist' (as opposed to Gogarty's con-man or poseur) is a goal-orientated word, implying some success in the activity – like the word 'teacher' or 'poet' – and Stephen has not yet achieved this. Where Joyce uses the word 'destiny' in the broad sense, he uses the word 'artist' in the narrow, except insofar as Stephen is an artist by temperament or inclination, and unless we see this in action we are unlikely to consent. So, because of the very nature of the word, there is a large element of competence implied in it, a challenge to the reader in the title of the novel. Yet, if this is so then we are thwarted because the novel closes before we are fully convinced – it all hinges on the villanelle which is poor matter and also unfinished – and Joyce himself is silent.

The final aspect of Joyce's concept of the artist-as-hero to consider appears only in the closing pages of the novel. We have seen already how Joyce presents Stephen as a dichotomy, as both a rejector and an embracer, placing most stress on Stephen the rejector – a feature of his own youth which Joyce sought to purge through this book. But, although there is little evidence of Stephen consciously affirming life to the full, there is one sense in which he goes forth to engage with reality at the end of the book, and that is of the artist as missionary. And, because it stems from Stephen's only deep-felt conviction about life and art, it is the principal sense in which he emerges as anything like heroic.

Undoubtedly this idea of the poet as missionary stems from Joyce's Jesuitical background,[8] but we can understand his two opposing aspects of rejector and embracer more clearly if we briefly examine Joyce's own longer verse where he bitterly articulated both aspects: in 'The Holy Office' (1904) he sets out his thesis of the poet-missionary, a crusader and rousing reformer, vigorous blaster of cant and smug hypocrisy, while in 'Gas from a Burner' (1912), as we have seen already, he gives us the poet as scourge of decadent values and moral paralysis, a portrait of the poet-missionary in action.

In 'The Holy Office', written in the same year as his initial essay 'A Portrait of the Artist', and three years after 'The Day of the Rabble-ment', Joyce unleashes his intense fury against the established writers and their circle in Dublin, lashing out at them for their meanness of vision ('timid arse') and provincialism:

> But I must not accounted be
> One of that mumming company . . .

However, scattered among the scurrilous and ironic wit of the poem there are conspicuous hints of Joyce's artist-missionary, the self-appointed crusader and defender of the faith:

> Myself unto myself will give
> This name, Katharsis-Purgative.
> I, who dishevelled ways forsook
> To hold the poets' grammar-book,

> Bringing to tavern and to brothel
> The mind of witty Aristotle . . .

Again we see him set apart from the others, the majority – the mystic poets of A.E.'s circle, nationalistic idealists, mercenaries, fellow-travellers, and hypocritical moralizers in particular. It is the Irish artist's solemn duty to expose these dissemblers for all their worthlessness and to purge Dublin of its moral meanness.

> But all these men of whom I speak
> Make me the sewer of their clique.
> That they may dream their dreamy dreams
> I carry off their filthy streams . . .

This is, in essence, the task of the poet-missionary lying behind Stephen's going forth at the end of the novel; though we meet hints of such fierceness only at rare moments in *A Portrait*, the tone is most familiar in *Ulysses*, in the 'Scylla and Charybdis' and 'Circe' sections. In *A Portrait*, the nearest that Stephen comes to such defiance is in the petition episode with the other students in Chapter 5, and then later with Cranly when he declares 'I will not serve' (p. 243):

> I stand, the self-doomed, unafraid,
> Unfellowed, friendless and alone,
> Indifferent as the herring-bone,
> Firm as the mountain-ridges where
> I flash my antlers in the air.[9]

Beneath the cocky, scathing irony (a foretaste of Joyce's mature stylizations) the 22-year-old Joyce's rancour is plain to see – and so is the youthful petulant ego.

On the other hand, in 'Gas from a Burner', though Joyce submerges his ego through the character of the Dublin publisher George Roberts, his effect is actually more direct, venting his anger now against the timidness of Irish publishers in general. And by adopting the ironic voice of Roberts himself, Joyce works a personal revenge on the man who had timidly prevaricated over, then tried to censor, and ultimately rejected *Dubliners*. The verse stresses the idea that through its squeamish morality Ireland has always betrayed her writers, forcing them, like Stephen Dedalus and Joyce, into exile:

> This lovely land that always sent
> Her writers and artists to banishment . . .

The only writers who have been acceptable to the publishers are syco-phants to public taste, simoniacs prepared to compromise their talents to produce work 'sad, silly and solemn' – work which is as daring as *Irish Names of Places* and the 'quite illegible railway guide'. The poem is a broadside against the stultifying philistinism of Irish morality, and Joyce's gaseous counter is a flatulent blast of frustration: 'Shite and onions!'

Joyce himself is also of course the 'Burner' of the poem's title, betrayed by mean-minded 'Dear Dirty Dumplin'; in a real sense too the poem represents Joyce's ideas in action, having been written on the train journey back to Trieste after his failure to get the stories published.

With echoes of Dedalus's final words Joyce too, stag-like, saw himself as setting out on a mission as a writer, and in writing his first substantial prose work, the *Dubliners'* short stories, he clearly regarded his task as a mission:

My intention was to write a chapter of the moral history of my country and I chose Dublin for the scene because that city seemed to me the centre of paralysis. (*Letters* II, 134)

And likewise, Stephen's endeavour is equally messianic: '. . . to forge in the smithy of my soul the uncreated conscience of my race' (p. 257), an ambitious resolution and one whose rhetoric seems to promise some noble purpose; yet it is not what it seems. The mission is not, as it may at first appear, a sort of self-effacing crusade to regenerate his fellow-countrymen's cultural status or even one through which to represent his people on the stage of European art; he is neither that selfless nor that patriotic. Instead, he turns his back on them, as he has threatened to do, seeing them as betrayers of their birthright and unworthy of his effort. Rather, his is a personal mission, ordained by the spirit of art: to appraise the consciousness of his own racial experience and to convert it through art into a permanent vital expression of his soul. And only in this sense of his stature can we consider Stephen to be heroic – not in terms of the values he portrays, but in terms of the conviction and sacrifice which he shows at the end.

The Artist as Priest

. . . a priest of eternal imagination, transmuting the daily bread of experience into the radiant body of everliving life. (p.225)

We should not be surprised that Stephen should conceive of the artist in these terms, as a priest – an extension of his concept of the artist as a hero (and also of the artist as a server)[10] – and in a novel in which the hero is early saturated with religious symbolism. We have been prepared for this, too, in the idea (though not the word) of the 'epiphany', a revelatory vision or manifestation by which the essential character of something is made known. Although Stephen never mentions the word in this novel, in *Stephen Hero* he explains that it is the duty of the 'man of letters' to record them, to intercede between the apparently incomprehensible world of artistic inspiration and the artist's audience. The closest that Stephen comes to naming it in *A Portrait* is in his definition of *claritas* in the aesthetic theory: 'the supreme quality of beauty being a light from some other world . . .' (p.217), though he immediately hastens to qualify this idealist interpretation. However, whereas in *Stephen Hero* the emphasis is placed on a passive artist whose job is merely to record these moments, in *A Portrait* Stephen's idea of the artist-priest is more active, more engaged, as inferred in his notion of 'transmuting'.

We have also been prepared by Stephen's unconscious (as well as conscious) adoption of priest- and monklike attitudes and postures; for example, directly (as in the quotation from p. 225) and the picture of the 'acolyte' (server again) in Chapter 4, but elsewhere indirectly in the priestly modesty at the end of Chapter 1, in the monklike scholasticism of the gymnasium secretary in Chapter 2, in the penitential and theological motifs in the opening of Chapters 3 and 4, as well as in the novel's general aura of sacerdotal reverence and Jesuitical cunning. Indeed, in Chapter 5, Stephen actually compares himself to a monk both explicitly, where he describes his mind as 'in the vesture of a doubting monk' (p. 180), and implicitly, 'steeled' in the school of old Aquinas and the heretical Bruno (p. 253); his dedication to 'silence, exile, and cunning' sounds unmistakably like holy vows:

How often had he seen himself as a priest wielding calmly and humbly the awful power of which angels and saints stood in reverence! (p. 161)

Furthermore, Stephen also closely identifies himself with Christ (pp. 246 and 253) and loosely in the form of martyr and messiah. Both of these are key elements too in his image of Parnell, and are also features which in *Ulysses* are mocked by Mulligan in calling him a 'fearful jesuit' and by Stephen himself reflecting on the wreck of his former ambitions: 'You were going to do wonders, what? Missionary to Europe after fiery Columbanus' (*Ulysses*, p. 135).

Yet, in *A Portrait*, even when he describes his vocation as a 'priest of

the eternal imagination' Stephen is self-consciously ironic: partly with
the intention as always of alienating himself from the words and the
concept, but chiefly with the aim of striking a moral blow against
Emma's (supposed) flirtation with Father Moran, a real priest, '...
coarse railing at her paramour' (p. 225). The irony is a consolatory
gesture for Stephen, an aside to himself, as well as an explicit part of
the novel's rub against the Catholic clergy in general.

So how does Joyce assimilate this essentially ironic conception of the
priest within the role of the artist? We can now examine in more detail
Stephen's vision of the 'priest' and so obtain more fully and clearly an
understanding of Joyce's wider concept of the artist.

Firstly, Stephen's artist-priest is again a being apart. He is essentially
separated from the rest of society, his readers and so on, by analogy
with the traditional image of the priest as exalted leader of his flock. It
is an hierarchical concept, with its origins in the strict idea of the order
(picked up early by Stephen, pp. 49 and 165) itself founded on prescrip-
tions of ritual, duty, obedience and seniority. As we can see though
from Stephen's picture of the priest in Chapter 4, the chief instrument
which sets the priest apart is his ordained power: 'No king or emperor
on this earth has the power of the priest of God' (p. 161), the power to
grant absolution for sin and, most importantly, the power to invoke
God into the bread and wine. But in art the artist-priest has an even
more divine power, as a being set apart by his gifts: he has both the gift
of inspiration and the gift of communication, being able to speak to his
fellow men through his creations. For Joyce the paradigm of the artist-
priest is William Blake as both visionary/seer and communicator.

Rejecting the received idea of Blake as a mystic or madman, Joyce
described him instead as a 'visionary' – a man of deeply penetrating
intellect, animated and directed by a powerful imaginative sensitivity
for humanity. Nor did Joyce interpret Blake's visionary faculty simply
as the means for escape into a fantasy world outside real human life –
he regards it as the capacity to see into the very heart of human life itself. In
his Italian lecture on William Blake (1912) Joyce explained that:

It seems to me that Blake is not a great mystic ... In him, the visionary
faculty is directly connected with the artistic faculty. One must be, in
the first place, well disposed to mysticism ... [but] Blake naturally
belongs to another category, that of the artists, and in this category he
occupies, in my opinion, a unique position, because he unites keenness
of intellect with mystical feeling. (*Critical Writings*, pp. 220–21)

By the nature of the writer and the nature of his work, the artist-priest lives in both spheres, the world of the muse and the world of the commonplace; he sees into the transcendent essence of beauty and fashions it through his own creation as an image accessible to his fellow men. He is both Daedalian craftsman and magus.

We can see, though, that for Stephen the balance is not quite exact – the dual nature of the artist-priest is both blessing and curse, and he lives more easily in the sphere of art. He has not yet learned to cope with its duality and, as the villanelle and the art theory reveal and confirm, the inspirational side of the formula is more convincing than the performance, at least as far as the aesthetic theory and his villanelle go, and he is limited to the 'visionary' aspects. He is isolated too through the inability to communicate his extremely powerful sensitivities and is tricked into inexpert rhetoric and clumsy gesturing, as when he tries to explain his plans to Emma and manages only inept flourish (p. 256) – the art theory too reads better on the page than it would sound aloud.

As well as Blake there are other precedents for the idea of the artist-priest, especially among the early English Romantics – for instance, Shelley:

Poets, according to the circumstances of the age and nation in which they appeared, were called, in the early epochs of the world, legislators or prophets: a poet essentially comprises and unites both these characters. For he not only beholds intensely the present as it is . . . he beholds the future in the present, and his thoughts are the germs of the flower and the fruit of the latest time. (*A Defence of Poetry*)[11]

Stephen's conception of the artist-priest also encapsulates both: a seer into truth because of his special sensitivity and a translator of that truth into beauty through his imagination and special gifts of craftsmanship. But, for the same reason, we can see that Stephen's emphasis does not exactly coincide with Shelley's view: that artistic inspiration is heavily idealistic, seeing and dipping into a Platonic world of perfect forms to copy through art, whereas Stephen's is a more Aristotelian approach starting out in the everyday, with the 'daily bread of experience' and imbuing it with his own special vision.

If the artist is a sort of priest then is this analogy worked out consistently in other aspects of art – the art object, the artistic process and the audience or reader, too? In spite of his deprecation of sculpture as an 'inferior' art form, for Stephen the art object or 'image' as he calls it can be anything which has been worked on. But what about the artist's intention behind the object – is that essential? When Stephen asks the question:

—If a man hacking in fury at a block of wood . . . make there an image of a cow, is that image a work of art? (p. 218)

he raises the old 'intention' issue, but he forgets to give the answer. On the other hand, the reply is really implicit in the general preamble to his own theory when he argues that 'art' is objective, depending neither on the artist nor on the reader but on the three criteria of 'wholeness, harmony and radiance'.

Within his aesthetic theory in Chapter 5, Stephen Dedalus has little else to say about the image itself but his attitude is made clear elsewhere, most notably in the section which follows it, where he composes the villanelle. It is clear here that it is the esoteric ideas, the words themselves and their 'rhythmic movement' rather than the concrete form recorded on a humble cigarette packet which constitute the important object of our interest. Nothing new here, but it does contrast strongly with an example in Chapter 2 when the ritual of the performance of writing receives more attention than the inspiration or the creative impulse: 'Before him lay a new pen, a new bottle of ink and a new emerald exercise' (p. 72). By dint of brooding in monklike solitude he mechanically forces out a series of unsatisfactory verses, framed within ritual Catholic mottoes, which he then hides as the mood passes.

Even here, though, something of the artist's self passes into his work, something of his own vulnerable soul, and he must hide the verses. To the mature Stephen of Chapter 5, the art image – his verses – is still an object of reverence, eucharistic and sacramental, handled as the priest handles the delicate fragile host. The dedicated artist resembles closely the devoted priest, instrumental but also protective, and the executor of the verses fulfils the same function as the ordinary of the Mass fulfils with all its elaborate ceremony. By *Ulysses*, however, a grounded Stephen looks back on these youthful efforts with a colder eye as, sceptically, he scribbles some new verses, once more on the back of a cigarette packet;[12] in *Finnegans Wake*, Joyce acknowledges the full implications of the consubstantial artist-priest-god, of the poet writing on and with his own body, the word having truly been made flesh:

. . . this Esuan Menschavik and the first till last alshemist wrote over every square inch of the only foolscap available, his own body, till by its corrosive sublimation one continuous present tense integument slowly unfolded . . . (*Finnegans Wake*, pp. 185–6)

Just as the priest intercedes between the divine and the secular, so the artist and his image intercede between artistic inspiration and everyday

119

experience, forging significant meaning out of the chaos and commonplace of ordinary life. This is most clearly seen in the writer's use of symbolism, in which everyday objects such as the rose powerfully and mysteriously irradiate meanings beyond their immediate reality – the everyday transmuted into everliving life.

Joyce himself does this to greatest effect in *Ulysses* where, through the character of Leopold Bloom, he draws attention to the minutiae of ordinary events, showing how even apparently trivial events and the details of life have sublime significance in themselves as well as enriching and magnifying the web of life's experience. This process has its fullest effect in *Ulysses* through Joyce's use of Homeric and other mythological parallels, with the result that the Everyman, Bloom, is transfigured into a man of heroic stature as we come to realize through new perspective the eminence of his reactions. But even in *A Portrait* we can see the possibility of this – the example which comes first to mind is the importance which Stephen attaches to his own surname (and others attach to his first name) thereby setting up expectations for himself and the reader, acting as a form of comment on the action and Stephen's ambitions; but there are other examples: the red and green roses with their political symbolism, and the importance of the 'moment', the coincidence, the element of chance, the chance remark, the filth and drudge of Dublin, all become the stuff of personal legend.[13]

The key to all this is the artistic process and the key to the process is the faculty of the artist-priest's imagination, described by Stephen in the moment of inspiration in Chapter 5:

In the virgin womb of the imagination the word was made flesh. Gabriel the seraph had come to the virgin's chamber.   (p. 221)

Joyce also told his wife that he too had been pregnant with the word when he was writing *Dubliners*:

I went then into the backroom of the office and sitting at the table, thinking of the book I have written, that child which I have carried for years and years in the womb of the imagination as you carried in your womb the children you love . . . (*Letters* II, 308)

Of course the artist as represented here is womanly but Joyce also has the religious process of annunciation clear in his mind; the artist is again, like the priest, an exalted vessel of the mystery of artistic inspiration and creation, whose moment reminds us of Stephen's breathless feelings about the college chapel in Chapter 1, a 'strange and holy place', awesome and sacramental (p. 42).

This supreme quality is felt by the artist when the aesthetic image is first conceived in his imagination. The mind in that mysterious instant Shelley likened beautifully to a fading coal. (p. 217)

Clearly the moment is adventitious, contingent upon a necessary Wordsworthian tranquillity – at least at first – in which experience as well as emotion can be recollected, a painless transformation process carried out in elemental, etherized silence. The process contrasts however with Joyce's own creative experiences in which perspiration outweighed inspiration (he himself claimed that he had no imagination), and also with Stephen's own previous, failed efforts in earlier chapters where his mood is anything but tranquil (p. 72).[14]

When Stephen comes to write the villanelle, however, Joyce invokes a beautiful image to capture the mystery of the moment, in a 'rose and ardent light' born of a white flame through which amorphous forms gradually materialize within the imagination of the artist – and after Stephen has recorded the words there is a 'hymn of thanskgiving'. The whole labour is steeped in religious symbolism, transliterated into the lofty periods of ecclesiastical rhetoric. Yet, because the novel records only this moment of inspiration (artistic conception, as opposed to gestation and birth) and whatever we think of the formulated verses, this stage of the process appears exclusively passive on the part of the artist-priest whose involvement is as a fortuitous medium, emerging from sleep into an enchanted fertile medium of warmth, music and light and is passed over by the spirit of the angel Gabriel. We are not shown the inevitable working over of these lines, the effort and decisions which might wrench such raw stuff into art (though even here Joyce has compressed the process, omitting the sweat which Stephen must have exuded to find such taut rhymings in such a short period).

And what of the reader in this? What is the reader's correlative to the artist-priest? Although Stephen Dedalus in *A Portrait* makes little reference to the reader or to the reader's relationship with the written word or with the artist, he does occasionally refer to or imply the role of the reader – after all, Stephen himself is emphasized as both reader and writer at different periods in the novel (for example, when Heron quizzes him in Chapter 2); and the art theory is based on his experiences as a reader.

Just as the Church stresses the primacy of the leader as the active element, so too does Stephen. The reader is conceived as a passive celebrant, mere observer of the holy office; the vital office is that of the priest-artist (after all, no one strives to become the reader, even though

121

as readers we strive for meaning). The reader is the silent 'other' towards whom the artist works to place his image since it is the distance between these three components which determines the mode – lyrical or epical or dramatic (p. 218). But the reader in himself is irrelevant to the art, just as the Mass would take place without the congregation. The reader is only assumed.

The act of artistic creation, then, is centred exclusively on the artist who remains objective about his work and about the world into which it is released, 'beyond or above his handiwork' (p. 219). In fact, he cannot heed it since his voice would not then be free, not 'expressing myself as I am'. And the villanelle bears this out – its creation is enough. For Stephen, there is no reader and the work comes into its own life partly by a form of catharsis for the author – just as we shall see that *A Portrait* partly serves a similar function for Joyce. The central concern is the creation of art and the artist himself is only marginally more important than his reader. The reader is irrelevant both to the artist and to the work of art. Whether he understands the work or even enjoys it, he leaves it untouched – it has a life of its own, without collaboration with the reader, its life breathed into it by the artist alone.

But this fact, that the reader is irrelevant, also makes it all the more difficult to assess Stephen as an artist on his own terms: both the aesthetic value of the object and the skill of the creator are independent of the reader as they are independent of everything else. The word 'artist' is not then prescriptive or evaluative (based on achievement) but descriptive – it is the reader who must adjust to the contours of its dictates:

When you have apprehended that basket . . . *you make the only synthesis which is logically and aesthetically permissible.*   (p. 217)

As he expounds his art theory, Stephen talks of the reader, the recipient, exclusively and continually as the 'other' and we can detect in this something again of both the Church's own élitism and Stephen's, in the notion of the 'rabblement'.[15] The reason for this lies, unexpectedly, in Joyce's own attitude to printers and publishers because through bitter experience, he had developed a mistrust of both, especially in their role as self-appointed custodians of redundant bourgeois morality. He saw them as a constant danger, threatening to alter his work, however slightly, and so destroy the fabric of his meaning (Joyce's protracted negotiations over the publication of *Dubliners* had been a harrowing and salutary catalogue of squabbles, in which a host of stop-go publishers timidly prevaricated and printers refused to set up, then, after doing so, destroyed the page proofs of the book).[16] In a different way, the reader, like the publisher, the politician and the Church, is a constant threat to his autonomy, his artistic freedom, ever-threatening to trespass on his art work, and Joyce's weaving of games and traps into his text to manipulate the reader is an effort to limit this.

Stephen's ideas, though, cannot risk this. It is all very well saying that art should not move its reader – but once the work enters the melting pot the reader's response is uncertain. Heron, Mr Tate and the director of Belvedere all put forward their own private prejudices as informed, disinterested, readerly evaluations. For Stephen the laity is represented as a 'dullwitted loyal serf', peasants and children, simple and ingenuous. For the artist-priest, the reader is the 'indispensable informer' of this triangular relationship, always ready to betray and subvert the text; once the image is released, it has to make its own way and begins to slip and slide, partly at the mercy of interpretation and partly also at the mercy of the instability of the language – a point which Stephen reveals to the Dean of Studies at university:

—One difficulty, said Stephen, in esthetic discussion is to know whether words are being used according to the literary tradition or according to the tradition of the marketplace. I remember a sentence of Newman's in which he says of the Blessed Virgin that she was detained in the full company of the saints. The use of the word in the marketplace is quite different. *I hope I am not detaining you.*
—Not in the least, said the dean politely.
—No, no, said Stephen, smiling, I mean . . .
—Yes, yes: I see, said the dean quickly, I quite catch the point: *detain.* (p. 192)

As we will discuss later (Chapter 8), the crisis of language is one which characterizes Modernist writing and which Joyce confronts most fully. We have seen Stephen's anticipation of it in his early experiments, exploring absurdities in the language, detaching the words from the reality to which they refer – the green rose impossible in the real world but existing in art and the imagination as vividly as Fleming's maroon clouds (p. 15). For him, as for Joyce, words and reality are to exist at their most vivid only in their oppositions – the conflicts of Stephen's life are mirrored in the tensions in the world of words as a constant state of confrontation (hot and cold, wet and dry, green and red, pandybats, turkeys and tundish, straps, belts and thighs, smugging, foetus and fetid). The mystery of the world is the mystery of its words:

123

'What did it mean?'
'Why did Mr Barrett call his pandybat a turkey?'
'What was the name . . .?'
'How beautiful the words were . . .'

He detects early what cunning instruments words are and rather than be deflated by it he rises and resolves to exploit their multifariousness, translating elusive experience into evasive language, the 'spell of arms and voices', making the word flesh and fresh, again and again.

5. The Method in His Madness: the Narrator

The teatimestained terminal (say not the tag, mummer, or our show's a failure!) is a cosy little brown study all to oneself and, whether it be thumbprint, mademark or just a poor trait of the artless, its importance in establishing the identities in the writer complexus ... will be best appreciated by never forgetting that both before and after the battle of the Boyne it was a habit not to sign letters always. Tip.
(*Finnegans Wake*, pp. 114–15)

Before evaluating Joyce's unique narrative technique, it is first essential to evaluate some of the other chief narrative techniques which were available to him and whose strengths he sought to assimilate within his own.

When Stephen declares that the author of a work ought to be:

... within or behind or beyond or above his handiwork, invisible, refined out of existence, indifferent, paring his fingernails.   (p. 219)

he is putting forward a view similar to that of the French realist Gustave Flaubert (1821–80) who, in energetic pursuit of realism, advocated a scientific approach to writing. Flaubert expressed his aim as 'treating the human soul with the impartiality which physical scientists show in studying matter ...' This scientific approach necessitated the narrator's exclusion of all his own direct moral comments from his material, limiting himself instead to the presentation of facts in the form of descriptions and explanations, so that he should be 'everywhere felt but nowhere seen'.

In this naturalistic approach, the narrator neither explicitly approves nor disapproves of his characters' actions or personalities but they are treated as facts. Flaubert himself attempted the method in *Madame Bovary* (1857) and as a result it became the centre of a fierce controversy, its critics accusing him of being too candid in presenting a study of Emma Bovary's adultery: because the narrator was not explicit in censuring the heroine, Flaubert was roundly denounced as celebrating adultery.

The chief problem involved in pursuing impartiality, however, is that it is impossible to achieve in any absolute sense: the narrator's views will always come through, in his choice of words, the selection of material and his arrangement of it – on its simplest level the narrator sets the menu. Another important problem is that, without a commentary, the narrator's attitude to his material can easily be misinterpreted by the reader since there would be no opportunity to step in and make his attitude clear.

There are thus two conflicting demands at work here – one for realism and the other for some sort of commentary – and to reconcile these two demands authors have resorted to a variety of strategies or narrative modes. One of these, the first-person narrator, in which events are related by someone with personal experience of them ('I' stories), was used by Dickens in his biographical novels:

> But the agony of mind, the remorse, and shame I felt when I became conscious the next day! My horror of having committed a thousand offences I had forgotten, and which nothing could ever expiate – my recollection of that indelible look which Agnes had given me – the torturing impossibility of communicating with her, not knowing, Beast that I was, how she came to be in London, or where she stayed – my disgust of the very sight of the room where the revel had been held – my racking head – the smell of smoke, the sight of glasses, the impossibility of going out, or even getting up! Oh, what a day it was! (*David Copperfield*, 1849–50, Ch. XXIV)

Overwrought with shame at the previous evening's drinking bout, Copperfield's self-reproach is clearly manifest in the moral tone of the diction: 'remorse', 'shame', 'offences', 'beast that I was', and at the same time the realistic presentation makes us intimate with the feelings of the narrator too.

But there are also disadvantages to this. The narrator's self-reproach too often sounds self-pitying, or at least self-conscious and oversensitive. Moreover, the narrator must be present at all the important events of the novel, though only on the outside. Since he cannot dip into the feelings or thoughts of the other characters, being limited to drawing conclusions solely from their outward appearances, he is therefore less than perfectly reliable, and his version of events is coloured by his own character and his point of view. A good example of this in *A Portrait* is the diaries sequence of Chapter 5, in first-person narrative:

> Read what I wrote last night. Vague words for a vague emotion. Would she like it? I think so. (p. 255)

Comparing Stephen's version of his conversation with Cranly (p. 252: 20 March) against the narrator's version (pp. 242–52), we can see how Stephen's is undoubtedly distorted, partly by his nature, but also by his strong feeling against Cranly created by the conversation itself. Stephen records: 'He had his grand manner on. I supple and suave', which is clearly not true since Cranly is explicitly supplicating (according to the narrator anyway).

But even if the first-person narrator actually tells the 'truth', and there is no guarantee that he will, then his views on moral points still need not be those of the author: David Copperfield is not Charles Dickens, Stephen Dedalus is not Joyce.

Alternatively, to overcome this latter obstacle and to make his views clear, an author may adopt the other major approach, the 'third-person' narrator, an implied narrator (rather than a named character) used to present the stuff of the novel as if he knows everything and is able to dip into the minds and motives of everyone else in it ('omniscient narrator'). D. H. Lawrence's *Sons and Lovers*, written about the same time as *A Portrait* and also dealing with the development of the artist, is typical of this mode. In Chapter VI, the narrator describes Mr Morel:

As he grew older Morel fell into a slow ruin. His body, which had been beautiful in movement and being, shrank, did not seem to ripen with the years, but to get mean and rather despicable. There came over him a look of meanness and paltriness. And when the mean-looking elderly man bullied or ordered the boy about, Arthur was furious. Moreover, Morel's manners got worse and worse, his habits somewhat disgusting. When the children were growing up and in the crucial stage of adolescence, the father was like some ugly irritant to their souls.   (*Sons and Lovers*, 1913, Ch. VI)

Although in this type of approach there is a loss of intimacy with the subject, Lawrence's disapproval of Morel is unmistakable.

This is basically the type of narrator that Joyce uses in *A Portrait* – but with modification. To retain some of the intimacy as well as the flexibility of the first-person mode, the narrator tells the story using Stephen's point of view – Stephen is present at everything which happens in the novel which is told with all the events filtered through his consciousness, using his perspective as the window on them. They are accordingly far more interesting, not only for their moral commitment, but also for what they reveal about Stephen himself: his inner, intellectual and moral development revealed through his response to externals.

Hence, the second section of Chapter 1 is presented from the point of view of a very young Stephen – mystified, intimidated, not understanding the motives of Wells – picking out the points which are important to a child rather than to an adult narrator, such as the mysterious temperatures of the body, the size of people, going home. For the same reason the narrator does not give the reader information which is not available to Stephen – the meaning of 'smugging', the reason Mr Barrett

127

calls his pandybat a 'turkey', and why Dante is described as a 'spoiled nun' remain enigmatic since to do otherwise would undermine the consistency of the narrator's point of view and, in any case, this approach perfectly captures the awe of childhood itself. In Chapter 2 the point of view of the tram episode, the scene in general and of Emma in particular, is narrowed down exclusively to that of Stephen (p. 71) and, further, when the older Stephen recalls that moment in Chapter 5 the narrator uses almost exactly the same words to indicate the vividness of Stephen's recall (p. 226). Meanwhile, in Chapter 4 a slight variation on the approach is used, again to reinforce Stephen's point of view. There the thoroughness of Stephen's penitence is implied in the scientific description of his atonement, breaking down his penitences into sections and groups in the way that Stephen's own excessive zeal does. Working through this type of expressionism the narrator attempts to recapture some intimacy with the character; to express shades of the mood and feeling of the subject, the narrator occasionally imitates some of the subjects's characteristics, namely Stephen's points of view at different levels of development (by contrast, in Lawrence's *Sons and Lovers* the narrator's point of view is consistently mature and stable throughout). We shall also see in the next chapter how Joyce reinforces this by modulating linguistic styles to parallel these levels.

In fact, *A Portrait* uses at least a dual consciousness[1] – one, from Stephen's point of view, enables Joyce to capture the intimacy of a first-person narrator (recording and observing, experiencing at different levels, ages and sensitivities) while the other, from the point of view of the mature narrator, allows Joyce to retain legitimate control of the form and to comment indirectly on the subject matter, through a surrogate, the principal advantage of the third-person narrator.

A simple instance of the narrator's presence is in the selection and arrangement of the episodes to generate a form of 'comment', as in Chapter 2, where we see first Mr Dedalus investing the money from the sale of his property in a pub crawl, and then Stephen squandering the essay prize money in a similar riot of spending. Another example which bears closer analysis is the conjunction of the close of Chapter 4 with the opening of Chapter 5. As we saw earlier, the former closes with Stephen's spirit soaring in ecstasy at the discovery of his destiny and the narrator reflects this in the language:

A wild angel had appeared to him, the angel of mortal youth and beauty, an envoy from the fair courts of life, to throw open before him in an instant of ecstasy the gates of all the ways of error and glory. On and on and on and on!   (p. 176)

The scene reaches its rapturous climax, and then ecstasy subsides into the tranquillity of evening, as Stephen reflects on his achievement, the language again reflecting his mood in its soft sibilants and looser sentence structure:

... and the tide was flowing in fast to the land with a low whisper of her waves, islanding a few last figures in distant pools.   (p. 177)

Then Chapter 5 opens with the sudden shock of anticlimax in the picture of Stephen's squalid home life:

He drained his third cup of watery tea to the dregs and set to chewing the crusts of fried bread that were scattered near him, staring into the dark pool of the jar. The yellow dripping had been scooped out like a boghole and the pool under it brought back to his memory the dark turfcoloured water of the bath in Clongowes.   (p. 177)

Because of the great difference in time (perhaps two or three years) between the two moments, the contrast in the two moods undoubtedly originates in the narrator's arrangement and is clearly aimed at the reader as an ironic comment on Stephen and his home: Stephen apprehending the vision of artist in an exalted, idealistic condition, but before he can achieve his aim he must come to terms with a home life which continually threatens to drag down and destroy his spirit. At the same time it also expresses the contrasting directions of Stephen's and his father's fortunes, especially as Chapter 5 continues by listing the items which his father has recently pawned. On the other hand, some critics have responded to this sort of ironic juxtaposition more sharply, finding in it proof positive that Stephen is misguided in seeing himself as potential artist, citing this dramatic cadence between the chapters as Joyce's ironic pointer of an inevitable rude fall in the months after his departure at the end: in other words, that the irony is a comment on Stephen himself rather than his home.

This mature consciousness, which runs parallel with Stephen's point of view, works to qualify Stephen's chiefly through irony and the humour which issues from it. In the above example the irony arises out of the narrator's arrangement of the material, and sometimes through his exaggeration of it. In Chapter 1, after Stephen is unjustly pandied, his outrage is shared by his classmates but one of the older boys puts it more deprecatingly: 'The senate and the Roman people declared that Dedalus had been wrongly punished' (p. 54).

Critical Studies: A Portrait of the Artist as a Young Man

This immediately sets off a train of thought for Stephen who, by a process of association, drifts away from the original context into a reverie about Peter Parley's Tales, Stephen's illustrated history book, until he eventually visualizes the first page of the book:

... Peter Parley had a broad hat like a protestant minister and a big stick and he was walking fast along the road to Greece and Rome. (p. 55)

With some exaggerated childishness and the contrast between its homeliness and Stephen's harsh punishment, the reverie works by opening up a gap between the mind of Stephen and that of the mature reader, who holds back from the sentiment of the moment, allowing him to judge Stephen and understand his situation (while also underlining Stephen's delicate youth). The narrator thus cunningly avoids any intrusion into the character's consciousness but also manages a situation in which to manipulate the reader's own consciousness.

The same process occurs in Chapter 2 with Stephen's exaggerated fantasy about the Count of Monte Cristo, and in Chapter 3 with his intense mental and physical response to the sermons (in fact, Father Arnall's sermons themselves exacerbate this atmosphere by their own excesses, see p. 127). Stephen's reaction to these sermons reaches a climax at the start of Chapter 4 in the form of his histrionic and ingenious self-mortification, especially in his rigorous control over the senses:

But it was to the mortification of touch that he brought the most assiduous ingenuity of inventiveness. (p. 154)

This is the unmistakable voice of the narrator foregrounded to make Stephen the butt of his irony; the two complementary perspectives eventually converge in joint climax at the moment when Stephen's piety expires: Stephen's in fanatical pursuit of absolute penance, the narrator's in highlighting and mocking his fanaticism. After this climax (p. 154), Stephen becomes suddenly and fatally attracted to the idea of surrender. This is mirrored in a falling-off in the mood which follows, and a new realistic narration (again hinted at in the irony) begins to emerge.

In all these examples, even in this last one, the narrator's ironic tone is still sympathetic towards Stephen, and its effect is in no way intended to denounce Stephen but instead treats his errors merely as the follies of youth. However, in the final chapter, the narrator's relationship to Stephen alters subtly yet radically as the latter arrives at the age of reason, as if to emphasize the point that Stephen now takes more complete responsibility for what he is and what he does – experiences being seen either through Stephen's eyes or in a fully dramatized form. An example of the first is the journey from Stephen's home to the university, during which he remembers Davin's story and his confession to Cranly:

... Stephen, remembering swiftly how he had told Cranly of all the tumults and unrest and longings in his soul, day after day and night by night, only to be answered by his friend's listening silence, would have told himself that it was the face of a guilty priest who heard confessions of those whom he had not power to absolve but that he felt again in memory the gaze of its dark womanish eyes. (p. 182)

Here the narrator sits close to Stephen's intimate thoughts about Cranly so that we can see him not through the narrator's eyes, but dramatized through Stephen's, and the 'dark womanish eyes' is Stephen's, rather than the narrator's, description. Other clear examples can be found (pp. 179–87) before Stephen reaches the university, and in the villanelle section (pp. 221–8). Whereas in previous passages involving Stephen's imaginative flights the narrator's voice has been conspicuous, qualifying them, its absence in the villanelle section is equally obvious. Nor is it followed, as we have come to expect, by the juxtaposition of the familiar reminders of sordid reality.

However, most of the chapter is presented in dramatic form – typically through discussions and conflict, such as Stephen's conversations with MacCann, Lynch and Cranly. In these situations, the narrator's 'commentary' is itself dramatized through other characters, to make Stephen and us aware of the criticisms of him: his pride, his loneliness and aloofness, and his lack of human feeling. And the concluding section of the novel, with Stephen alone and preparing for flight, is fully dramatized since the diaries consist only of Stephen's exclusive voice and his selection of material.

But if the last chapter exists by and large without the presence of the narrator's voice to 'comment' on Stephen, is there not the same problem which we found with a first-person narrator? How can we be sure that the conclusions which we draw are those which Joyce intends? And is authorial intention what we are necessarily seeking in the novel?

One critic, Wayne C. Booth, in his general study *The Rhetoric of Fiction*, highlights what he takes to be an ambivalence in Joyce's presentation of Stephen:

Well, which *Portrait* do we choose, that of the artistic soul battling through successfully to his necessary freedom, or that of the child of God, choosing, like Lucifer, his own damnation?   (*The Rhetoric of Fiction*, pp. 327–8)

He concludes that the ambiguity can be resolved only by going outside the novel and examining *Stephen Hero* and *Ulysses*, and biographies about Joyce himself, and that because of this *A Portrait* is a flawed masterpiece.

The natural reply to this would be to ask: why should Joyce make the decision for the reader anyway – that there is no obligation on the author to come down on one side or another in this type of moral situation, and that such ambiguities reflect those in life iteself with no recourse to any authoritative narrator: the Great Narrator? It is Stephen's dilemma too. At the same time, the author is not necessarily shirking any responsibility if he posits a number of plausible interpretations and leaves it open to the reader to make the decisions. And this apparent silence, one of the great discoveries of the Modernists, reflects not only the silence of life but also the Modernist preoccupation with the profound anxieties implied in the anticipated break-up of civilization at the end of the last century.

But it is not the case that Joyce is ambiguous in his attitude towards Stephen. Until Chapter 5, the narrator clearly endorses Stephen's position with regard to home, religion and nation chiefly through his ironic treatment of these topics; we only need to consider the devastating effect of the political fight at Christmas, the narrator's presentation of Fathers Dolan, Conmee and Arnall, and the effect on the family of Mr Dedalus's decline, to see his point of view. However, the narrator stops short of endorsing Stephen's character once it becomes clear in which direction he is moving and the price he is willing to pay in his single-minded drive towards his 'destiny', following Chapter 4. Beyond this point, Stephen's pride, his arrogant posture and his radical approach to what he justifiably perceives as nets (involving the rejection of love and fellowship) become clear and the narrator's gently mocking but sympathetic irony ceases, leaving Stephen isolated. The last chapter makes it clear: from Stephen's point of view he *is* breaking free, but from the reader's and the narrator's points of view he is cultivating his own damnation. While Joyce may be silent about the decision we might eventually reach, he is not silent about the clues which direct us towards a decision – the better part of silence here is only discretion.

Of course, this narrative approach of Joyce's is unsettling and places a greater responsibility on the reader, compared to one in which the narrator defines his position and holds the reader's hand. There is a greater onus on the reader not only to make decisions but also, in the first place, to recognize issues and pick out the information available. One of the consequences of Joyce's redrafting of *Stephen Hero* into *A*

Portrait was a marked economy of words; the surviving manuscript of *Stephen Hero* (which deals only with Stephen's time at University College) covers just under two hundred pages whereas the whole of *A Portrait*'s Chapter 5 is only about a third of this. One effect of such economy, in addition to producing a tighter, more succinct text, is that the reader is expected to interpret the subject and to make the necessary connections. Some of these are relatively simple – for example, the reason why Stephen changes the number in his desk (p. 10) and the meaning of the word 'smugging' (p. 43); but other connections are less distinct, such as the description of the director's skull-like head at Belvedere (p. 157) which should make us recall the skull on Father Conmee's desk at Clongowes Wood and so imply a comparison and assessment of Stephen's development between the two interviews. The imagery also directs the reader towards such comparisons and thus serves to outline Stephen's development – for example, the recurring ivory imagery (pp. 37, 44 and 182) and the red/green motifs running throughout.

These connected fragments naturally enrich the poetic as well as the thematic fabric of the novel, but they also represent a fundamental part of one of Joyce's most important narrative techniques both here and in other works: what has come to be called his 'free indirect style' or the 'stream-of-consciousness'. This technique attempts to present Stephen's inner mental life by imitating the working of the mind as it recalls ideas, etc., by a process of association, and is shown most clearly in Chapters 1 and 5. For example, Stephen's stream-of-consciousness (pp. 47–8) begins with the external description of Mr Harford and his being just a master; this leads on to the injustice of being pandied for the sins of the older boys who had stolen the altar wine; the awesome sin behind this makes Stephen recall the ritual of the Mass and then, through the smell of the wine, to his first communion, and a vision of grapes and ancient Greece, returning to the smell of wine and first communion, and finally to be reminded of Napoleon's first communion.

There is an abundance of such examples in Chapter 1, partly because Stephen spends a lot of his time in idle thought either because of illness or because he has been excused from lessons and sits through them, daydreaming. Another possible reason is that this stream-of-consciousness, with its random, apparently unstructured character, is a more rarefied form of realism since it more closely captures the subjectivity of life, the thought processes of a mind not directed towards any particular end, like that of the speculative mind of a young child.

It characteristically suggests the vivid imaginative awe of a child. But because the stream-of-consciousness reveals not only *what* is being contemplated but also *how* it is, then it perfectly communicates the states of mind of the character as well as the experiences that he recalls. Thus the consciousness of Stephen has a unique unifying function in the structure, since the development of Stephen's mind is both the subject matter of the novel and the structure which gives shape to that subject matter.

The technique is intended to represent the stream of life – ostensibly random moments but connected at some deep level. In *Ulysses*, Leopold Bloom unconsciously draws attention to the essence of the technique, by drawing attention to the way in which the consciousness flickers across the fleeting moments of experience in recollection: 'Always passing, the stream of life, which in the stream of life we trace . . .' (*Ulysses*, p. 71). Clearly the notion of a 'stream' refers not only to the fluid aspect of life moving on but also to the evanescence of its moments – and the transience of the moment is an idea which Joyce develops in his concept of the 'epiphany' (see Chapter 7 below).

In *Ulysses*, however, Joyce takes the technique of stream-of-consciousness to a more complex and studied level. In *A Portrait*, the stream-of-consciousness is principally used as a device of the narrator to organize his narrative, but in *Ulysses* it is also used to present the characters' thoughts more immediately (the term 'interior monologue' is usually used for the detailed content of the thoughts). In *A Portrait*, Stephen's stream-of-consciousness is expressed in complete words and regular syntax whereas in the later novel Joyce brings the technique to maturity, imitating the fragmentary nature of interior speech by breaking down the sentences and even the individual words. The following extract from *Ulysses* deals with Bloom's thoughts as he takes leave of another character:

Well, I must be. Are you off? Yrfmstbyes. Blmstup. O'er ryehigh blue. Ow. Bloom stood up. Soap feeling rather sticky behind. Must have sweated: music. That lotion, remember. Well, so long. High grade. Card inside. Yes.   (*Ulysses*, p. 235)

As Bloom begins to leave he remembers some soap in his pocket and an identification card in the band of his 'High Grade' hat, as well as his earlier promise to pick up some lotion at the chemist. The thought is more compressed than in *A Portrait* ('Yrfmstbyes' seems to be a condensed form of 'You're off – must be – yes', while 'Blmstup' is explained in the following line as 'Bloom stood up'; he thinks about his action before doing it). The stream-of-consciousness technique, given its first major treatment by Joyce in *A Portrait*, became a crucial cornerstone of his mature work; it was also later to be adopted by contemporary writers and to become one of the central distinguishing features of Modernist literature. In *Ulysses*, the subject alternates between the 'external' experiences of the novel and the character's internal responses to them. Yet while in *Ulysses* the difference between what characters do and what they think is still readily distinguishable, by *Finnegans Wake* the stream-of-consciousness takes over completely and itself becomes the central experience of the novel.

Although Joyce became the most renowned exponent of the stream-of-consciousness technique, he was not its inventor. The novelist, Dorothy Richardson, had already begun to experiment in its use, and its source can be traced back at least to Arthur Symon's *The Symbolist Movement in Literature* (1899), which Joyce read in 1901 and which was a seminal influence on Modernist writers. But Joyce never claimed that it was his device and fully acknowledged his debt; in a conversation about *Ulysses* with his close friend Frank Budgen he explained:

I try to give the unspoken, unacted thoughts of people in the way that they occur. But I'm not the first one to do it. I took it from Dujardin. You don't know Dujardin? You should.[2]

Joyce can take the credit though for refining the technique, taking it beyond the realms which Dujardin later modestly claimed for it:

In poetry, the internal monologue is the unspoken and unheard speech by which a character expresses his most intimate thoughts, those nearest to his subconscious before imposing on them any logical order, that is to say at their moment of creation through direct, plain sentences so as to give an impression of 'free flow'.[3]

Whereas in *A Portrait* the stream-of-consciousness traces the way in which Stephen's thoughts arise, in *Ulysses* and *Finnegans Wake* the interior monologue attempts to find a direct verbal equivalent for the units of thought themselves. But in *A Portrait* the stream-of-consciousness is used as the principle by which the narrator, using Stephen's consciousness, lays down the moments or 'epiphanies' which make up the novel. The chief manifestation of this is in the selection and ordering of the epiphanies – not necessarily chronological but, like individual sentences and paragraphs, arranged by association. Again, Chapter 1 shows the clearest evidence of this method of arrangement. The section begins with a football match, back through 'belt' to the day of his parents' departure, to the football match, thoughts of being indoors, and so on. We receive a dynamic picture of a fluid succession of presents, of images or epiphanies united by their continually returning to the present moment of the match and united also by their associations through the mind of Stephen. The rapidity of these flashbacks here also underlines Stephen's irritation at Wells's 'mean trick' and at having to play at outdoor sports.

A similar process occurs in Chapter 4 while Stephen is being addressed by the director of his college (pp. 157–64). Stephen's attention slips back to the moment he received the invitation from the director and then his subsequent reluctance to meet him. Then, once the director begins his introduction, Stephen's thoughts begin to slip back into the past, frequently recalling his earlier school, women's clothing, the Jesuits and the beating at school, the lawns there, its corridors and the baths. Unlike the previous example this one contains two focal points, the present at Belvedere and the past at Clongowes Wood; they are set up in Stephen's thoughts alternately, with the clear purpose of making the contrast between the two periods – between his obedient, respectful attitude in the past and that of the present which looks on the Jesuits in the light of his recent stirrings of freedom:

Lately some of their judgments had sounded a little childish in his ears and had made him feel a regret and pity as though he were slowly passing out of an accustomed world and were hearing its language for the last time.   (p. 159)

Again the contrast is used to measure Stephen's development without the need for explicit intrusion by the narrator. More important, though, from the point of view of the framework is that the structure of the novel appears to stem organically from within the novel itself, rather than to be imposed from outside, to stem from within the consciousness of Stephen, so that the structure obeys the subject matter rather than vice versa (compare this with Stephen's diaries at the end of the novel, a formal, externally imposed structure, with the opening section of Chapter 1). Therefore, although at first sight the structure appears to be random (even chaotic), there is method in his madness.

While the foregoing discussion has concentrated on the stream-of-consciousness and its influence on the structure of the novel, we must also take into full account its fundamental drive and rhythm. The course of Stephen's growth itself imbues the novel with forward impetus and rhythm, but Joyce intensifies these by making deliberate use of conflict to set up tensions and further rhythms. For this technique,

Joyce openly acknowledged the influence of the Italian philosopher Giordano Bruno, burned at the stake as a heretic in 1600 (see p. 253).[4] In a letter of 27 January 1925 to his benefactress, Harriet Shaw Weaver, Joyce explained something of this:

His philosophy is a kind of dualism – every power in nature must evolve an opposite in order to realise itself and opposition brings reunion etc etc. *(Letters* I, 226)

In *A Portrait* Joyce employs the conflict of oppositions from the beginning: in the first section, Stephen notes that his mother has a nicer smell than his father; the bed is first warm then cold; his father's nice and cosy story contrasts with Dante's threatening eagles. These images anticipate the world of conflict that characterizes Stephen's life and the novel as a whole. The schoolboy world at Clongowes and then Belvedere is characterized by it – Stephen's rivalry with Jack Lawton, with Wells over his snuff box, and the question of kissing one's mother, disputes and polemics with Heron and Mr Tate and eventually with Temple and parents. Joyce represents this through the imagery and the diction: red and white roses, red versus green, hot and cold, 'nice' versus 'mean'. Stephen himself unconsciously highlights the fluctuation of extremes: he reflects on the manner in which noises alternate as the refectory doors open and close, like a train in and out of tunnels, p. 13; then the progress of college as term follows vacation follows term. Similar alternations occur in other chapters: the noise of the audience, p. 76; the peacock's tail, p. 106; the coiling formula, p. 195. His perception of the world in these ways is especially characterized by Stephen's continual use of the word 'but', particularly in Chapter 1:

But you could not have a green rose. But perhaps somewhere in the world you could.   (p. 12)

But was there anything round the universe to show where it stopped before the nothing place began? It could not be a wall but there could be a thin thin line . . .   (p. 16)

How pale the light was at the window! But that was nice.   (p. 27)

The contrast helps to clarify, in Stephen's mind at least, the realities of his world and their relationships with each other and with himself. The narrator uses the conflict to convey the state of tension which is ever-present throughout the novel, its particles held in uneasy balance,

137

especially later when he interprets such polarities in terms of the claims upon him of religion and politics.

Moreover, a rhythm is also set up by Joyce's alternation of settings, which also helps to shunt the action forward as well as emphasize the surface tensions; for example, in Chapter 1 the attention of the narrator and the reader switches alternately between the outdoor football scene and the indoor scenes, open and closed settings, pleasant and unpleasant, home and school, past and present, real and imagined.

The various rhythms set up by these alternations in Chapter 1 eventually reach their climax and resolution first, partially, at the Christmas dinner and then more fully in the pandying episode, in which the conflicts are personalized and made explicit; but they are not resolved either satisfactorily or finally in this chapter (nor even in the novel as a whole). At the Christmas dinner, Stephen is only a spectator of the conflict and, after he complains to Father Conmee about the pandying, what appears to be a resolution with authority is undermined in Chapter 2 when Mr Dedalus reveals the Rector's betrayal and mockery of him. Instead of resolving these tensions the two confrontations become translated as archetypes and rumble on, occasionally surfacing in new forms (the confrontations with Heron, Mr Tate, his own conscience, his family and the students), and Stephen comes to terms with them with varying levels of competence and maturity. Thematically they too become articulated as a dialectic of oppositions: the Call and the Fall, flight and paralysis, imagination and reality. Indeed, the conflict can also be traced as the two opposing movements in the viewpoints of the novel: Stephen continually attempts to avoid personal confrontations, while the narrator continually makes them the subject and the technique of the novel. For example, the narrator uses starkly realistic and austere scenes and language to force the focus of the narrative on to areas which Stephen finds uncomfortable (pp. 115 and 177). In the first, congealed food makes Stephen face up to the condition of sin which he has evaded, and in the second a gross food image collides with the flight of the imagination, a reminder of the squalor of home. Overall, the dualism of this dialectic together with the use of twin consciousnesses, Stephen's and the narrator's, and the changing distances between them has a cumulative effect, gathering creative momentum through the reverberation of perspectives, tensions and surfaces by which the whole experience of the novel is communicated.

Though we have seen how the distinctive narrator works in the novel, does the narrator have a separate, distinct personality? Who is the narrator of *A Portrait* – Stephen Dedalus himself? Joyce is silent and does not draw attention even to his imaginary, implied narrator, nor does he attempt to justify him within the world of his novel as some authors have done (such as Marlow in Conrad's *The Heart of Darkness*). However, it is tempting to regard the anonymous narrator as Stephen Dedalus himself. Because the novel aims at realism in other aspects and because it adopts the same intimate point of view as a first-person narrative it is inviting to link the two points of view, one of the bewildered child, and later ebullient youth, and the other a mature, detached and perhaps penitent Stephen Dedalus.

In support of this the narrator and Stephen also have facets in common – both have a tendency towards abstraction (compare the villanelle with Stephen's original attempt to write verses, and with the original tram episode, pp. 71–2), neither explains the initials 'E.C.' and, if we have the diaries as evidence in addition to Stephen's character, it is clear that both he and the narrator have a tendency for silence and cunning – in fact, Stephen is actually more reticent than the narrator, advocating an author who is invisible and beyond his work. Furthermore, they appear to have identical approaches to the theme of time; in his diary for 6 April Stephen records:

The past is consumed in the present and the present is living only because it brings forth the future.   (p. 255)

And, as we shall see below in Chapter 7, this is identical with the narrator's conception of 'epiphany': a timeless moment in which times past and future are embodied in time present, and that life is a fluid series of presents (compare with the stream of consciousness). Stephen's potential for cunning has its equivalent in the narrator's shifting stylistic agility, in his fluctuating relationship with the reader as well as his tendency for evasion.

While Joyce does not anywhere acknowledge any connection explicitly, it is not unreasonable to regard the novel, on the one hand, as the achievement of an older and a wiser Stephen Dedalus and, on the other, as an older Joyce's ironic expiation of the sins and folly of his youth as portrayed in the enlarged defects of Stephen. If so, then there is after all some of that irony and much hope in Mrs Dedalus's wish at the end:

... that I may learn in my own life and away from home and friends what the heart is and what it feels.   (p. 257)

6. Language and Style in *A Portrait*

> *Let manner and matter of this for these our sporting times be cloaked up in the language of blushfed porporates that an Anglican ordinal, not reading his own rude dunsky tunga, may ever behold the brand of scarlet on the brow of her of Babylon and feel not the pink one in his own damned cheek.*
>
> (*Finnegans Wake*, p. 185)

Again and again we can see in *A Portrait* that Joyce's subject and the manner in which he writes are fused. In a real sense the novel's subject *is* its manner or style, and it is crucial to avoid regarding them as separate. In a real sense too Stephen Dedalus himself is the language of the novel. This comes about because another of Joyce's major innovations in *A Portrait* is the modulation of styles throughout, using a different style in each section to underline each stage of the main character's development. Each style is intended to represent a different stage in Stephen's progress towards full maturity and accordingly each of the styles themselves is lacking in maturity in order to parallel that of Stephen. Joyce makes this clear by deliberately foregrounding the novel's styles in the reader's attention.

This use of parallels (including the stream-of-consciousness technique) is a direct manifestation of Joyce's general disposition towards imitation, onomatopoeia and parody; for example, in *Ulysses* Mr Bloom contemplates the noise made by a guillotine and tries to imitate it:

... Doing its level best to speak. That door too sllt creaking, asking to be shut. Everything speaks in its own way. Sllt.   (*Ulysses*, p. 100)

In *A Portrait*, Mr Dedalus draws attention to the same idea and as a natural storyteller (see p. 245) he too feels the need to tell a story in a style appropriate to it. There is the moocow story on the opening page, of course, told in a style which adults think is appropriate to children, but then at the Christmas dinner when he talks of the Wicklow Hotel keeper he takes some trouble to imitate his voice:

Stephen, seeing and hearing the hotelkeeper through his father's face and voice, laughed.   (p. 30),

and in Chapter 2, as he repeats what Father Conmee had told him of the interview with Stephen, he '... imitated the mincing nasal tone of the provincial' (p. 74) – Stephen too is encouraged to do the same by Heron when he plays the part of 'a farcical pedagogue' (see p. 75).

This is precisely what Joyce himself attempts to do: to make the reader see and hear Stephen Dedalus through the narrator's face and voice. He had experimented with a similar technique in some of the stories of *Dubliners*, occasionally adapting language to reflect a character's viewpoint, but in *A Portrait* the technique is given full-scale treatment for the first time and it reveals in full the great range of Joyce's stylistic virtuosity.

This is clear from the stream-of-consciousness approach in the opening chapter, beginning in baby-talk, monosyllabic in the main, with short direct sentences. The simple vocabulary with the repetition of the conjunction *and* helps to create the simplicity of childhood, showing how childhood apprehension of the world is limited by position in the family and to sense-impressions, at the same time setting up Joyce's theme of the role of the senses. Stephen's growth is implicit in the change of style between the first and second sections but we can also see here a characteristic of the later sections in Stephen's interest in words themselves – their meanings and sounds, and the relationships between the two. In the second section he notes the double meaning of the word 'belt', the relationship between sound and meaning in the two onomatopoeic words 'suck' and 'kiss', and the relationship between the words 'hot' and 'cold' on the water taps in the lavatory. The latter is part of a more general preoccupation with the temperature of things and its relativity as he becomes feverish. His still naïve point of view is clear in the use of direct sentences and simple vocabulary but also in the elementary moral judgements he makes – people are invariably either 'nice' or 'decent', or 'mean'. The limitations of his vision are underlined by the way in which Stephen adheres to the standards and advice of his parents, while home is very much a point of reference. The continual use of 'but', as well as implying the conflict mentioned earlier, also emphasizes the qualification imposed on his vision at this age. However, we see the influence of school widening Stephen's outlook, as shown in the subjects of his formal education and the schoolboy slang which he meets in the chapter: rump, dog-in-the-basket, stink, scut, feck, smugging, pandied, wax, twice nine. It richly animates Joyce's rendering of the school life, and Stephen's awe at these expressions underlines both his youthful naïvety and his isolation from the groups who use them.

This awe is evident too in the Christmas dinner section for which

Joyce adopts a dramatic, impersonal mode – to add weight to the intimidation of the experience and also to parallel the fact that this is Stephen's first Christmas at the grown-ups' table. There is a shift away from the previously sympathetic discourse towards impersonal language, and the reader too experiences something of the strained atmosphere through the shift. The occasion is presented dramatically, through dialogue chiefly, the objectiveness of the narrator and the savage frankness of the dialogue contrasting with the subjective prose of the previous section now that the world of adults takes over. However, there are occasional deferences to childhood as Mrs Dedalus reminds everyone of Stephen's presence at the table and it is ironically in terms of the language they use that they are the most sensitive about their influence on Stephen:

—O, he'll remember all this when he grows up, said Dante hotly – the language he heard against God and religion and priests in his own home. (p. 35)

The contrast between the outside world of harsh reality and the inner one of imagination is to be one of Stephen's enduring preoccupations; it is here anticipated in the Christmas dinner section in the contrast of styles as well as in the explicit argument at the table.

In the final section of the chapter, the style returns to that of Stephen's subjective viewpoint when, once more, outside reality encroaches at the moment of the pandying, although in this section the subsequent conflict is very much internalized. Before the prefect enters the room, the narrator's prose imitates the idleness of Stephen's meandering thoughts, which take a loose conversational form, beginning usually with a fact, proceeding to a vague speculation about the fact, which is then arrested by a qualification ('but') as Stephen realizes an objection, and finishing off with a conclusion or a consolation. For example, Stephen notes how Father Arnall is in a 'wax' (p. 49), then speculates 'was that a sin . . .' – but as he is a priest where would he confess it? – and Stephen concludes that it would be up the line of the 'order' to the minister . . . The drifting nature of these speculations is emphasized by the loose syntax – direct sentences strung lazily together by a succession of conjunctions. However on the arrival of the prefect, the style sits up straight, brisk and abrupt, and the narrator again adopts the dramatic mode, to indicate urgency and fear. To describe the details of the pandying the narrator's objective approach concentrates on the swift encroachment of external reality, cataloguing the progressive stages of the event. Only after does the style resume Stephen's subjective point of view. As it does so it is characterized by continual repetition of key phrases:

It was *cruel and unfair* to make him kneel in the middle of the class then: and Father Arnall had told them both that they might return to their places without making any difference between them. He listened to Father Arnall's low and gentle voice as he corrected the themes. Perhaps he was sorry now and wanted to be decent. But it was *unfair and cruel*. The prefect of studies was a priest but that was *cruel and unfair*. (p. 53)

As well as sticking on these highlighted phrases, Stephen's attention also focuses on eyes and hands, especially as he thought that the prefect was going to shake hands with him. The repetition conveys clearly Stephen's outrage, and his continually returning to the same images and phrases expresses his frustration at his own weakness. The prose after the pandying is a good illustration of the narrator's stream-of-consciousness method too, with Stephen's thought patterns and associationism feverishly accelerated by anger. It repeatedly gives the impression of someone talking with himself – through self-questioning (How could the prefect know? What would happen?, pp. 53 and 55) and his statements of reassurance (Yes, he would do what the fellows had told him, p. 54). We can see too the strength of Stephen's internal monologue clearly sustaining the high level of tension, defused only after the interview with the rector when the mood changes to dramatic form.

The second chapter, tracing Stephen's adolescence from the first awakening of sexuality and his growing isolation from his family, has a greater fragmentariness of styles than the first and the styles themselves rub and collide as Stephen's inner and outer realities come into contact with each other. Yet there is little suggestion of this in the opening section with its relaxed though forthright style. On the one hand, Joyce makes the theme of time more evident in the heavy adverbial openings to the sentences of this first section: 'Every morning', 'On week days', 'When ...', 'While ...', 'On Sundays', 'His evenings', 'At night ...' especially in the context of Stephen's accompanying Uncle Charles. Then, on the other, after the third page of the chapter, the narration switches to finite verbs of activity as Stephen is released to his own leisure: 'the gang made forays ...', 'the boys would take turns in riding ...', and 'Stephen sometimes went round with the car ...' p. 66). Stephen eventually recognizes this play for what it is and as he becomes disillusioned, he returns to reading romantic literature. Whereas in Chapter 1 Stephen came into contact with words through the reality of life in school and at home, in Chapter 2 the reverse happens and he begins to apprehend reality imaginatively through words and reading, underlining his sensitivity for language:

Words which he did not understand he said over and over to himself till he had learnt them by heart: and through them he had glimpses of the real world about him.   (p. 64)

But against this escape into the labyrinth of language the narrator contrasts vivid descriptions of cheerless reality; for example, 'stale odours of the foreshore . . .' and 'foul green puddles and clots of liquid dung . . .' (p. 65), with echoes of the square ditch images in Chapter 1 and throughout the novel. The first section of Chapter 2 ends with a typical example of Joyce's stylistic adroitness as Stephen, nauseated with both the reality of his life and the available avenues of escape, looks outwardly towards a meeting with an idealized woman, presented in a parody of sentimental romantic fiction, the consciously esoteric style exactly matching that of Stephen's romantic reading and his own studied posturing:

They would meet quietly as if they had known each other and had made their tryst, perhaps at one of the gates or in some more secret place. They would be alone, surrounded by darkness and silence: and in that moment of supreme tenderness he would be transfigured. He would fade into something impalpable under her eyes and then in a moment, he would be transfigured. Weakness and timidity and inexperience would fall from him in that magic moment.   (p. 67)

Repetition of the word 'would' together with other terms of uncertainty ('as if', 'something impalpable', etc.) work to create a melodramatic image in which gestured movements, separated rather than fused by the word 'and', prolong his ecstasy. The fantasy quality of the language and of the experience anticipates that at the end of Chapter 4 (where he does eventually meet this figure).

As we have seen happen often, Stephen's flight of spirit in language collides violently with a subsequent image of external realism – and in section two it is in the form of the two yellow removal vans. In *A Portrait*, but to an even greater extent in *Dubliners*, yellow and brown are colours which Joyce associates with paralysis and decay (see also pp. 19, 103 and 158). So the diction in the paragraphs which follow carries presages of despondency, 'lumbering heavily', 'weak light', 'muddied', 'gloomy', 'bare', 'cheerless', 'made his heart heavy' (p. 67). Now Stephen's escape to the labyrinthine streets of Dublin is followed in an objective, explicit style, in contrast with the earlier romantic posturing and with the concealing prose of the three epiphanies which follow, each beginning with the words 'he was sitting . . .' (p. 69–70). In each the language is intended not so much to reveal as to conceal what is happening and although in all three the peripheral details are clear, the focus is either blurred (as in the first two) or eccentric (as in the third) and each takes place in a gloomy, obscure setting leaving the reader grasping after the details. In the third of these epiphanies, dealing with the tram episode, Stephen himself attempts an evocation in verse – he selects out all the 'common' elements, there is no trace of the tram, 'nor did he and she appear vividly', only some 'undefined sorrow' (p. 72). If the subject of both Joyce's scene and Stephen's recasting of it is 'sorrow' then it is also absent from both, and the language prevents us from seeing it by continually veering away from the essential point. Even Stephen's poem, unlike that in Chapter 5, is hidden from sight. The scenes are represented through Stephen's subjective point of view and it is one which is beginning to evade and deceive.

Two years pass between the second and third sections and in the latter the Belvedere College play takes place (for the most part) in the darkness backstage. The theatre is likened to an 'ark', an image which merges the novel's imagery of water with its themes of messiah and flight. Flight is often hinted at elsewhere in this section, especially in the bird imagery behind the names Heron and Tallon, and the latter also takes up references to claws and fingernails (see pp. 8, 44, 46 and 219). The style of the section is restrained, punctuated by the dialogue of the conflict between Stephen and Heron. Although we have noted above how Stephen found words such as 'suck' and 'kiss' to correspond with their reality, he now remarks on the ironic coincidence that Heron should have 'a bird's face as well as bird's name' (p. 78); in Chapter 4 he also notes that the simple names of the Christian Brothers reflect their simple piety (p. 170). Yet, strangely, he never finds it as ironic that he himself should bear the name of the archetypal artist.

By contrast, the restraint of the narrator's prose here points up the emotional energy of the first confrontation between the rivals, but, in addition, it mirrors Stephen's growing distaste for such rivalries and his growing aloofness towards others: 'The question of honour here raised was, like all such questions, trivial to him' (p. 86). But his poise is eventually ruffled by the prospect of meeting Emma, and then is thrown into chaos by her absence. The prose matches each in its furious agitation which returns to rest only as Stephen encounters the familiar strains of crude reality, the rank odour of 'horse piss and rotted straw' (p. 89).

There follows a miserable trip to Cork (for Stephen anyway), done in a prose style peppered with adult slang: 'come-all-yours', 'drisheens', 'kick out for yourself', 'Maneens', 'the governor', 'Peter Pickackafax', 'Dublin jackeen', 'fireeater', 'Draw it mild'. Although Stephen regards this common talk as clinching evidence of his father's decline, the vigour and colour of their patois has the effect of intensifying and enlivening the encounter for us. And then Stephen's own prodigality with money is brilliantly evoked, with more than a whiff of smug detachment in the narrator's image when 'the pot of pink enamel paint gave out' (p. 101).

The chapter ends with memories, both in Stephen's mind and in the prose style, of the fantasizing wit with which it began. No longer is it the static heroic posture of the Count of Monte Cristo style, though the prose implicitly invites the reader to make comparisons between the romantic style at the opening to the chapter with that at the close, when 'the image of Mercedes traversed the background of his memory' (p. 102). The glossy seductive prose style in the brothel eventually parodies that of the earlier romantic-erotic literature as Stephen swoons helplessly in the arms of the prostitute, whose yielding embrace ironically fulfils Stephen's long-suffering romantic ideal.

As he searches the backstreets of Dublin's brothel district the prose finally articulates the brutal lust which lurks behind his yearning:

He burned to appease the fierce longings of his heart before which everything else was idle and alien ... A figure that had seemed to him by day demure and innocent came towards him by night through the winding darkness of sleep, her face transfigured by a lecherous cunning, her eyes bright with brutish joy ... (p. 101)

The assonance of this second sentence (night, winding, eyes, bright) beautifully evokes the seething allure of expectation, while its alliteration (by day, demure, face transfigured, bright with brutish joy) induces an almost tangible sensuality. The narrator's use here of suspended sentences, snaking through embedded and mazelike subordinate clauses, seeks to hold off the reader and thus create in miniature the frustration which Stephen himself undergoes – each sentence swelling the momentum in increasingly pulsating vocabulary towards his final embrace. But then, with the relief of that first embrace the prose, like the momentum, suddenly subsides and Stephen, having reached his goal, surrenders himself to the girl's arms.

But the prose does not continue its imitation by attempting to emulate Stephen's arousal, and instead it is addressed towards the reader and attempts to stir him through its subtle cadences and seductive poetry. Although the prose is momentarily of that porno-kinetic type scorned by Stephen in his art theory it is insidiously effective, striking the balance between Joyce's stylistic decorum and Stephen's almost uncontrolled lust, yet at the same time sacrificing neither meaning nor mood. We can also see here how Joyce's technique sets up a rhythm of converging and releasing movements over previous sections; these are now reconciled, briefly and sublimely, in a subtle sexual metaphor, together with the subjective and objective realities of the prose – the vague speculative probing of Stephen's inner world together with the coarse insistent external reality.

In Chapter 3, the latter of these two – the imminent external reality – eventually takes over. An indication of it comes in the first paragraph of the chapter with the focus of the language on the appetite, in those same gross terms which we meet again and again in *A Portrait*:

... he felt his belly crave for its food. He hoped there would be stew for dinner, turnips and carrots ... Stuff it into you, his belly counselled him.   (p. 104)

Back at school the arithmetic equation of Stephen's scribbler is another thread of the maths and number imagery which runs throughout the novel (pp. 12 and 106) but it also anticipates the mathematical preoccupations of Father Arnall's sermons.

These are presented dramatically in direct speech but, as we discussed above (in Chapter 3), they appear eventually to filter through Stephen's own inner consciousness having completely overwhelmed it. Although manifestly dealing with theological themes, they do not discuss theology at all but ram home its morality through fear. They are instead masterpieces of technique rather than doctrine, aimed with meticulous skill at the precise level for their audience.

Amongst the devices of the sermons one of the most manifest is Father Arnall's repetition of certain key ideas throughout – 'separation' and 'selfishness' are two which stand out, and also have special significance for Stephen. Not only this but the ideas themselves are also treated in hyperbole. As Mr Tate remarks during one of the intervals: 'That's what you fellows want: and plenty of it to make you work' (p. 128). Of course the sermons use the diction and imagery characteristic of the Church, biblical and often archaic – asunder (p. 131), illgotten (p. 132), wherein (p. 133), admixtures (p. 134), vouchsafed (p. 136) – as well as the rhythms and tone associated with church rhetoric, thus displaying Joyce's anti-clericalism:

—I pray to God that my poor words may have availed today to confirm in holiness those who are in a state of grace, to strengthen the wavering, to lead back to the state of grace the poor soul that has strayed if any such be among you. (p. 138)

They are indeed masterpieces of rhetoric, relying on sound as much as on semantics for their effect. We hear the preacher's voice flexing artfully between the various modes, at times supplicating 'help me, my dear little brothers in Christ' (p. 114), at other times interrogative 'Why did you sin?' (p. 127), or imperative 'Depart from me ...' (p. 128) but insistently intimidating 'tender eyes flaming like molten balls' (p. 125). Sentence structures reveal a similar use of rhetorical devices: repetition of key words – 'That time is gone: gone for ever' (p. 133);[1] parallelism in sentence construction:

—Time was to sin and to enjoy, time was to scoff at God and at the warnings of His holy church, time was to defy His majesty ... (p. 116)

and the use of inversions, 'Be not afraid' (p. 138). The pace is carefully varied by fluctuating the length and structure of sentences, occasionally inserting short monosyllabic phrases to drive home the climax of a progress; for example, 'But that time had gone' (p. 116) and 'Yes, a just God' (p. 137). In addition to these there is Father Arnall's conspicuously heavy use of alliteration and assonance, such as in: 'The blood seethes and boils in the veins, the brains are boiling in the skull ...' (p. 125), and the use of grotesque and ingenious metaphor.

It is a terrifying vision relying for its effect on the sheer overwhelming nature of the suffering as well as on the size of the punishment and its intensity and inevitability, an inevitability which is implied by the intricate logic of the structure of the whole piece, each of the separate sermons reaching its daunting climax to leave Stephen increasingly more horrified. Such is their force that, ironically, Stephen's own inner prose eventually comes to imitate Father Arnall's as he becomes overwhelmed by guilt, his feverish imagination concocting images almost as grotesque.[2]

And yet, although the sermons are, of their type, accomplished and highly effective, they remain only a partially mature prose style. We can see that at each stage of Stephen's growth the prose becomes increasingly more mature, though it never becomes completely so. Where the prose used for the brothels can be described as 'kinetic', for sexual ends, the sermons are kinetic for didactic ends (and therefore fail to meet even Stephen's own criteria for judging prose, pp. 209–10) – which is one reason why we cannot consider them as a fully mature style, only as a step towards it. Moreover, apart from the fact that they are geared to suit a young audience, they rely heavily on a crude rhetoric which, to the objective ear, eventually sounds hackneyed and weary, at times clumsy, making their application too limited.

Where Father Arnall's sermons are based on medieval and seventeenth-century models, the three sections of Chapter 4 are done in a spirit and in styles adapted from nineteenth-century writers. That of the first section approximates the style of the comic novelist, chiefly evoking Dickens in its ironic tone and detachment (with hints of Meredith and Thackeray) though at the same time also taking up and parodying the solemnity and earnestness of the recent sermons. The vocabulary has an exactitude and bearing associated with more moment-ous import but when applied to Stephen's zeal it highlights his mis-guidedness:

A brief anger had often invested him but he had never been able to make it an abiding passion and had always felt himself passing out of it as if his very body were being divested with ease of some outer skin or peel. (p. 152)

In fact, the language's exactitude and discipline attempt to contain Stephen's zeal by defining rather than explaining it. Defining the experi-ence makes it formulated and objective, whereas expressing the experi-ence helps to share it with the reader – as in the opening page of the novel where the prose attempts an exact parallel of the subject, explain-ing the child's point of view (and thus drawing our sympathy). Accord-ingly we find a conflict between the language and its subject. The style and irony of the first section eventually sound clichéd and stale (and again is only a partially mature style), drawing downwards as the language tries to contain the subject, Stephen's exaggerated penitence, which instead aspires upwards, Icarus-like. At length, both subside and merge when Stephen reconciles himself to failure, at which point the prose becomes once again sympathetic, approaching what we may expect to be Stephen's own mode of reflection: 'Perhaps that first hasty confession wrung from him by the fear of hell had not been good?' (p. 156).

In the second section Joyce takes the style of his beloved Cardinal Newman as his model. When Heron challenged him in Chapter 2, Stephen himself nominated Newman as the best writer of prose (p. 82) and Joyce, in a letter to Harriet Shaw Weaver asserted that '. . . nobody has ever written English prose that can be compared with that of [Newman]'.[3] It is a typically Joycean conceit that discussion of a vocation in the Jesuits should be presented in the exquisite style of Newman, himself a Jesuit. Joyce's own mature style has the same dignity and poise, without ornament or ostentation (even as Stephen momentarily envisages himself in the priesthood he shuns the pomp of the celebrant in favour of the austerity of the acolyte). It is efficient, prosaic, succinct, yet has a charm of words. Its vocabulary also reflects Stephen's increased maturity and discernment: for example, embrasure, deft, tremulous, diffident. However, the style is also apt, in another way, for reflecting the cool rational temperament of the Jesuit priesthood and, in the letter quoted above, Joyce himself rejected this temperament in favour of the artist, as Stephen finally does: 'The chill and order of the life repelled him' (p. 164).

In the final section of Chapter 4 (from p. 168), after a quotation from Newman himself, the style now swings freely and exuberantly to the other extreme, exultant and emancipated. The model parodied now by Joyce is the prose of the Victorian art critic Walter Pater, with echoes here too of the swooning sensual cadences of Swinburne. If in Chapter 3 Stephen was overwhelmed by the external reality of Father Arnall's sermons, here the rapturous prose of the final episode of Chapter 4 marks the triumph of the voice of inner reality. That the prose and Stephen's state of mind should coalesce is a point hinted at by Stephen himself as he approaches the river estuary, and he searches for the words to describe his buoyant mood. As he does so he reflects on his chosen phrase and on his love of the sounds in the words:

—A day of dappled seaborne clouds.

The phrase and the day and the scene harmonized in a chord. Words. Was it their colours? He allowed them to glow and fade ... (pp. 170–71)

In contrast to the elegant self-restraint of Newman's prose, that of the concluding section is subjective, even wild, the words themselves an intense personal experience of the particular moment rather than a definition of it, and the words are its fundamental reality for the reader.

The diction now reveals the narrator's renewed concern with emotional states (last seen at the end of Chapter 3): weary, ecstasy, aflame, lust, desire. Vividly emblazoned images abound, and the heart is the predominant inspiration of both the imagery and the highly charged metaphors of the section: 'his heart trembled', 'the flame in his blood', 'his heart seemed to cry'. Where Newman's antiseptic prose contained and restrained the emotion, the language now, after a hesitant start, begins to run riot, struggling to express direct verbal equivalents of Stephen's ecstasy as Joyce presses it to its limits, straining to capture and prolong non-rational inner states – the style is conceived in terms of sensation, wildness and emotion soaring almost beyond control. Individual words, however, matter less now than the cumulative rhetorical effect of their resonances. The focus of the narrator fluctuates rapidly between the outer scene and Stephen's inner state of pulsating joy, setting up a rhythm which gradually fuses the two in a rhapsodic climax. An unmistakable energy drives throughout, impelling the reader's attention forward in parallel with Stephen's own spirit.

This hurtling effect is created chiefly by two methods: firstly, Joyce's concentration on the present participles of verbs of activity (calling, throbbing, running, dangling, gazing, with much 'soaring') and, secondly, by the loose extended structure of the sentences in which phrase and clause are merely tacked breathlessly on in series, again prolonging initial states, as in:

He was alone and young and wilful and wild-hearted, alone amid a waste of wild air and brackish waters and the seaharvest of shells and tangle ... and ...   (p. 175)

The effect of the repeated constructions and the spate of conjunctions is unmistakable, building up and reinforcing the air of excitement and wildness, especially straining the limits of the normal syntax while the repetition of the key words evokes breathless rapture 'Yes! Yes! Yes!' (p. 174) and 'On and on and on and on!' (p. 176).

Yet, punctuating the rapid crescendo of inner sound and climax, Stephen swoons ecstatic but exhausted. To arrest the momentum now and to foreground this silence, the sentences on the final page of the chapter at first revert to a tighter, more regular construction, until at last in the final paragraph the grip is once more slackened, to finish in a quieter tone. The two key images of the section (soaring flight and the bird girl) unite the motifs of freedom, flight and escape which have rolled along through all the previous chapters, now becoming objectified for the reader as well as for Stephen. It is a triumph of style for Joyce, drawing together all the rumbling conflicts and unrest of the novel thus far into an impassioned climax of stylistic dexterity.

But, immediately following it, the outset to Chapter 5 is a total anticlimax, not simply in the heavy monosyllabic prose which opens it but also in the styles of the chapter as a whole, and the two anti-climaxes are related. After tracing Stephen's development, paralleled in maturing prose styles, our expectations are raised, as Stephen's spirit soars, to anticipate in the final chapter a mature style to represent Stephen's own maturity. However, there is none, not even a distillation of these other styles. There is only a sort of stylistic silence, since the absence of Stephen's own authentic style is really the equivalent of silence.

We have seen how Joyce's continual modulation of styles in *A Portrait* is a form of linguistic odyssey, a journey paralleling the progress of Stephen's development, especially so because in a real sense Stephen *is* the language of the novel, as we said at the outset.[4] But it is an unfinished journey since, at least within this novel, there is no destination, no final mature linguistic style. Instead, what we find in Chapter 5 is not the artist but a series of images of Stephen struggling to shake off the nets that threaten to stifle his aspirations. And we also find examples of the various styles we have previously encountered now held in a state of uneasy tension; so the art theory discussion exemplifies the chill impersonal style of rational discourse:

—Rhythm, said Stephen, is the first formal aesthetic relation of part to part in any aesthetic whole or of an aesthetic whole to its part or parts or of any part to the aesthetic whole of which it is a part.   (p. 210)

while that style in which Joyce describes Stephen's moment of creation closely approximates the subjective language of the estuary epiphany (although the villanelle itself appears to have had any true spontaneous feeling refined out of it).

The instant flashed forth like a point of light and now from cloud on cloud of vague circumstance confused form was veiling softly its afterglow.   (p. 221)

For Stephen's fantasies of Emma there are also echoes of that romantic-erotic style parodied in the closing section of Chapter 2:

Her nakedness yielded to him, radiant, warm, odorous and lavish-limbed, enfolded him like a shining cloud . . .   (p. 227)

while the moments of confrontation and dialogue between Stephen and his university colleagues are in almost pure dramatic form.

The linguistic styles of Chapter 5 are both fragmented and diverse, held together by the centripetal force of the two combined consciousnesses of Stephen and the narrator. So what we see is not the finished artist but one still coming to terms with the 'nets' around him and also with the voices both of the nets and of literature itself. While on the one hand his struggle is to free himself of these nets, on the other it is to transcend these voices or styles, no longer appropriate or adequate to his ambition. He must do so in order to find an independent, authentic and personal voice or style of his own with which to express his individual conscience – and since the conscience is uncreated so also is the mature linguistic style in which to 'forge' it. This is what Stephen means by the net or labyrinth of language, another symbolic correlative of the Daedalian labyrinth designed to contain and restrain the minotaur.

... You talk to me of nationality, language, religion. I shall try to fly by those nets.   (p. 207)

The final chapter is linguistically characterized chiefly by precision; for example, in his conversation with the dean, Stephen distinguishes between the marketplace and the literary uses of language. This precision is also reflected in an advance in the vocabulary of both Stephen and the narrator: technical (kinetic, gestation), classical (*claritas*, *integritas* etc.) and poetic (lambent, transmuting, querulous). There is a corresponding increase too in the complexity of sentence structures, now conveying more complex feelings and concepts. The bog Latin of the student banter as well as mocking erudition also shows a broadening of the perspective – but significantly (consistent with Stephen's European and Modernist perspectives) nowhere are there any Irish words used by Stephen or by other students (even those who urge him to rejoin the Irish class). His continual self-questioning still portrays Stephen as the speculative individual of Chapter 1, though his speculations are now less idle or fanciful, relating more closely to their immediate stimulus and to his artistic ambition. He is more rational as well as precise, and his concern with the immediate is imparted by the conspicuous increase in realistic detail and the use of proper nouns in his discourse, reinforcing the idea of the encroachment of reality following the estuary epiphany in Chapter 4; for example, the wealth of Dublin place names (see pp. 179 and 242), a catalogue of authors and influences corresponding with the expanding limits of his intellectual encounters (Bruno, Dante, Swedenborg, Marx, Collins, Galvani, Shelley, Cusack, Aristotle, among others), as well as a preoccupation with times and dates (even if he is always forgetting them they are still part of his reality – for example, the dates on the diaries impose a specifically formal framework of time).

This type of precision also portrays Stephen as coming increasingly to grips with language as an instrument over which he has some potential control, and he must overcome its net if he is to manipulate it for his own end. His response to the environment is increasingly more precise, even more scientific, though he is seen less to engage with that environment than merely to describe it at a distance. His mastery is ultimately symbolized by the scene with the dean of studies, an Englishman, when he instructs him in the meaning of the English word 'tundish' (p. 193).

Yet, though there is no fully mature voice in the concluding section of the novel there is, however, a hint of its development; if it is not yet a mature style then it is a maturing one – that is, in the diaries. On the threshold of exile, Stephen withdraws into the diaries, which are presented significantly without the intervening voice of the narrator. As such, these represent the most extensive example of Stephen's own writing in the novel and in their technique they are close to the mature stream-of-consciousness approach, the free indirect style, which Joyce will develop later in *Ulysses*. Their fragments are not, however, those subjective speculations characteristic of the immature stream-of-consciousness which the *narrator* arranged in Chapter 1 but rather a raw attempt by the mature Stephen himself to translate accumulated subjective impressions into the formal objective experience that is art.[5] They are the gropings towards a style, with all that is to be found in such gropings – fears, hesitations, experiments, mistakes and regret. The style once more parallels the content of the novel, not just in the sense that Stephen's maturity as an artist is not complete but also that, as often in Joyce's works, the final passage looks beyond the present work forward to some other time. In 'The Dead', Gabriel Conroy looks outward and towards the end of his life; in *Exiles*, Richard Rowan and Bertha look out to a new future together; at the end of *Ulysses*, Leopold and Molly Bloom, each in different ways, contemplate the prospect of the following day. In *A Portrait*, the prospect is outward and towards the future and the style, too, looks out, as important in what it promises on the final page as in what has already been achieved.

7. Content and Significant Form: Joyce's Concept of 'Epiphany'

> —*I bet you are. Well, he was wandering, you bet, whatever was his matter, in his mind too, give him his due, for I am sorry to have to tell you, hullo and evoe, they were coming down from off him.*
> —*How culious an epiphany!*
> —Hodie casus esobhrakonton?
> —*It looked very like it.*
>
> (*Finnegans Wake*, p. 508)

Fundamental to an appreciation of Joyce's approach in *A Portrait* is an understanding of his concept of the 'epiphany' and its use. As defined by Stephen and used by Joyce, it is crucially important not only to this novel but to all of Joyce's work, since in its implications it widely embraces the themes of time, truth, morality and art. However, *A Portrait* marks a step forward for Joyce's development as a writer in that, while all his previous work – *Chamber Music*, *Dubliners*, and *Stephen Hero* – also employs essentially isolated epiphanies held together in varying degrees of unity, *A Portrait* incorporates a sequence of related epiphanies in the form of a coherent narrative.

We have already met the idea of epiphany several times in above discussions, but what exactly does Joyce mean by the word? For a formal definition of 'epiphany' we must go outside *A Portrait* and to its earlier version, *Stephen Hero*, where Stephen, idly composing his 'Villanelle of the Temptress' in Chapter XXV, overhears fragments of a conversation between two people:

This triviality made him think of collecting many such moments together in a book of epiphanies. By an epiphany he meant a sudden spiritual manifestation, whether in the vulgarity of speech or of gesture or in a memorable phase of the mind itself. He believed that it was for the man of letters to record these epiphanies with extreme care, seeing that they themselves are the most delicate and evanescent of moments. He told Cranly that the clock of the Ballast Office was capable of an epiphany. Cranly questioned the inscrutable dial of the Ballast Office with his no less inscrutable countenance.

—Yes, said Stephen. I will pass it time after time, allude to it, refer to

it, catch a glimpse of it. It is only an item in the catalogue of Dublin's street furniture. Then all at once I see it and I know at once what it is: epiphany.
—What?
—Imagine my glimpses at that clock as the gropings of a spiritual eye which seeks to adjust its vision to an exact focus. The moment the focus is reached the object is epiphanized.   (*Stephen Hero*, pp. 188–9)

Joyce, of course, borrows the term from the religious context – the feast day celebrating the revelation of the infant Christ to ordinary mortal mankind represented in the three Magi. Clearly, Joyce's concept takes up this idea of a manifestation – a showing forth of the reality of an object, a person, an event, etc. to the observer, with the suggestion also of privileged spiritual insight. Joyce discovered the phenomenon early in his teens, and Stanislaus in his biography records his brother's practice of collecting such moments:

... manifestations or revelations ... little errors and gestures – mere straws in the wind – by which people betrayed the very things they were most careful to conceal. 'Epiphanies' were always brief sketches ... (*My Brother's Keeper*, p. 134)

In *Chamber Music*, almost every poem is centred on a single precise epiphany, presented with youthful reverence, while in *Dubliners*, each story consists of one or a number of epiphanies by which a character (and/or the reader) comes to realize the truth of his circumstances and the paralysing limitations of them. On the other hand, in *Ulysses*, an older, self-mocking Stephen scorns his own youthful reverence for epiphanies and his eager collecting of them, as he contemplates his languishing artistic ambitions:

Remember your epiphanies written on green oval leaves, deeply deep, copies to be sent if you died to all the great libraries of the world, including Alexandria? Someone was to read them there after a few thousand years, ... (*Ulysses*, p. 34)

In *A Portrait*, Joyce advances the use of epiphanies not only as a fundamentally significant literary technique but also as an important philosophical concept which was to become the cornerstone of his own mature works – and a cornerstone of Modernism in general (see below, Chapter 8).

In Stephen's definition and in Joyce's practice the term has two meanings: one is that an epiphany reveals the truth, the intrinsic essence of a person or of something which is observed, revealed perhaps through a 'vulgarity of speech or of gesture'; and the second meaning is a state of mind, a heightened spiritual elation of the observer's mind, what Joyce calls the 'memorable phase of the mind itself'. The first puts emphasis on the object and the fact that its reality can be revealed by an epiphany, while the second puts emphasis on the observer, for whom an epiphany can be a state of spiritual ecstasy. Consequently, although we would normally think of the acquisition of knowledge in terms of a rational process, both of these meanings involve non-rational states, and insofar as they involve knowledge (either about an object or about oneself), the process implies a subjective source of truth, knowledge as a sort of intuition. In fact, as Stanislaus records, epiphanies can even include dreams – especially so since Joyce considered dreams to be a subconscious re-shaping or sharpening of everyday reality.[1]

Taking the first meaning of 'epiphany', the example which Stephen gives to Cranly in *Stephen Hero* places the emphasis on the object rather than the observer: 'the clock of the Ballast Office was capable of an epiphany' – not that the clock has the ability, but that it is a potential source of epiphany for the person looking at it. A good example of this comes in Chapter 2 of *A Portrait* when Stephen's romantic idea of farm life is given a violent shock by the reality when he visits Stradbrook, and the vivid details of the cowyard bring home to him the distinction between the beauty of his idea and the foulness of the reality:

. . . the first sight of the filthy cowyard at Stradbrook with its foul green puddles and clots of liquid dung and steaming bran-troughs sickened Stephen's heart. (p. 65)

Similarly, in Chapter 4, Stephen recalls the rough feel of a woman's stocking as a shock to his preconception of the yielding softness of women (p. 158). And, as we have seen in *A Portrait* as a whole, Joyce likes to parallel the shock of reality for Stephen with a similar shock for the reader through a change of style, both to reinforce the impact of the sudden enlightenment and to rouse Stephen into an awareness of the sordid reality of Dublin.

But epiphanies have to be reliably interpreted – and this Stephen does not always do: to illustrate the subjective and therefore unreliable nature of epiphany as a source of truth, Joyce in Chapter 3 reveals how Stephen becomes convinced that his only correct course is to repent and to return to the Church and, in the ecstasy after the confession when he kneels in communion with the other boys, he considers:

Another life! A life of grace and virtue and happiness! It was true. It was not a dream from which he would wake! (p. 150)

Yet, as Chapter 4 reveals, although it had not been a dream, his former repentance is rejected by Stephen himself as misguided folly.

While Stephen nowhere refers to 'epiphany' by name in *A Portrait*, he does define a very similar phenomenon in his aesthetic theory, when he discusses the various stages of apprehending the beauty of a work of art. After identifying a work as first a single integrity (*integritas*) and then perceiving the harmonious rhythm of its parts (*consonantia*), there is a final stage or criterion for a work of art: *claritas*. Although the notion of 'epiphany' does not necessarily imply any moral or aesthetic content or comment – epiphany reveals only truth – its process has much in common with that of *claritas*, a phenomenon which Stephen has great difficulty in elucidating. He identifies it first as the relationship between, on the one hand, the observer's intellect and imagination, and on the other, the external physical stimuli. While he convincingly explains *integritas* and *consonantia* as relatively mechanical steps in the process, he gets stuck at *claritas* largely because its closeness to unintelligible religious experience makes it awkward to rationalize. After substituting the words 'radiance' and 'whatness' he eventually resorts to Shelley's analogy of a 'fading coal' before slipping into more esoteric territory with 'luminous silent stasis' and 'enchantment of the heart'. However, at this point, because of its elusive nature *claritas* ultimately defies this type of formulaic approach; in fact, the phenomenon is really much closer to the *Stephen Hero* definition of epiphany as a form of highly rarefied, spiritual manifestation.

The second meaning of epiphany concentrates on its effect on the individual and its ability to inspire him, rather than on the acquisition of knowledge. Again Stephen draws attention to this in his aesthetics theory when he talks of an 'enchantment of the heart' in the moment of epiphany – such moments as those at the end of Chapters 1 (after the interview) and 3 (after confession), rapturous moments for Stephen in which his whole being is exultant and exalted, even though neither moment involves knowledge or truth:

The cheers died away in the soft grey air. He was alone. He was happy and free ... (p. 60)

As we have seen, such moments are an integral feature of the special rhythm which Joyce sets up throughout the novel, a rhythm created in the systematic contrast of the meanness of Stephen's home life against

158

the airy flights of his spirit with which it is in conflict, imbuing the novel with its vital pulse and a source of indirect commentary for the narrator.

Of course the two meanings often coincide in a single moment and the most substantial example of this is the estuary epiphany. Here we see how, on the one hand, Stephen in a flash of insight recognizes the call of the artistic vocation, transfigured into the form of the wading girl, become for him the embodiment of beauty and art while, on the other, the second aspect of epiphany (an 'enchantment of the heart') is portrayed clearly in the wild transport of delight experienced by Stephen at this sight of the girl, and to some extent shared by the reader through the ecstatic language. The two aspects resonate and eventually coalesce to bring Chapter 4 to its rapturous wild climax.

However, because of its concern with time, this second meaning of epiphany also has a deeper, philosophical implication. Stephen himself draws attention to this implication in his diary and by doing so also draws attention to the important fundamental relationship between epiphany and Joyce's ideas on time:

The past is consumed in the present and the present is living only because it brings forth the future.   (p. 255)

Clearly, Stephen's view is that each moment partakes of times past and present, each moment being created or determined by the cumulative effect of past decisions and actions, etc. and itself bringing about future times by the same process. A prime example of this is that epiphany relating to the tram scene in which Stephen and Emma part after the children's party (p. 71). The moment not only embodies the past because as he stands with her, he recalls a previous occasion, 'the day when he and Eileen had stood looking in the hotel grounds', but it also consumes the past in the sense that all of Stephen's formative influences have led up to this moment – in the way he responds to Emma, the signs ('vanities') which he reads in her body, and especially in his failure to bring the moment to a satisfactory end by kissing her. Moreover, the moment also brings forth the future, partly in that he will recall this occasion in later moments (pp. 72 and 226), but chiefly in that it will also have a subconscious influence in his future life, Emma becoming for him an archetype: first of female virtue, then of unattainable sexuality (p. 119).

The epiphany thus encapsulates all time itself – past, present and future (racial as well as personal). This is the key to the epiphany's deeper, more fundamental significance in the form of Joyce's writings and Modernism in general, for no longer is the novel tied to the plod of strict chronological sequence. The psychological insights of the epiphany all at once open up a completely new, wholly natural method of organizing the subject matter – through the consciousness of the central character, around the ever-present and eternal moment, flashing back and forth spontaneously between the 'was' and 'shall' of now.

For Joyce, time is a dynamic sequence of fluid consecutive present moments, forever cross-referencing through memory and fate to the past and the future, represented in Stephen's stream-of-consciousness, and fluctuating between different times in the forms of memory and ambition. This idea, that in the evanescent moment all eternity can be glimpsed, is further developed by Joyce in *Ulysses* and in *Finnegans Wake* where it finds its ultimate expression. In both works Joyce takes full advantage of the epiphany technique by his additional exploitation of myth and fable, vastly expanding the connotations of the immediate material to embrace cosmic potentialities.

However, we can see the approach already at work in *A Portrait* both in the role played by the epiphany or 'timeless moment in time' (as T. S. Eliot called it) and also in his more limited use of archetype, myth and symbol: Daedalus, Icarus, Christ, St Stephen, Lucifer, Parnell.

But Joyce is not the only author to have held this view of time or to have used the technique of the epiphany, although the vision and the adaptation of it are uniquely his. For example, Wordsworth in his autobiographical poem *The Prelude, or the Growth of the Poet's Mind* describes a similar idea in what he calls 'spots of time':

> There are in our existence spots of time,
> That with distinct pre-eminence retain
> A renovating virtue, whence, depressed
> By false opinion and contentious thought,
> Or aught of heavier or more deadly weight,
> In trivial occupations, and the round
> Of ordinary intercourse, our minds
> Are nourished and invisibly repaired . . .
>
> (*The Prelude (1850) Book XII, ll 208–15*)[2]

Describing such moments as sources of 'profoundest knowledge' he differs from Joyce in that he emphasizes their moral function, moments of experience by which children are taught – though this of course is not excluded from Joyce's concept: one could still learn through Joyce's epiphany (as Stephen learns mistrust by way of his realization of Father Conmee's betrayal). The poet Gerard Manley Hopkins also comes close to Joyce's emphasis on the moment as the revelation of knowledge, in his own conception of 'inscape', a word which he coined to describe both the distinct essence of a thing and the process of experiencing that essence, its 'thisness' or intrinsic 'self'.[3] As a Jesuit, Hopkins considered that the inscape of a thing was what revealed the presence of God in it and he dedicated his poetry to achieving the same end. Yet, while Joyce's viewpoint too would not rule out the presence of God (and Stephen's sometimes intense epiphanies do approximate to a religious experience), Hopkins's idea is narrower in scope both in terms of the objects in which inscape is discovered (mostly objects in nature, as opposed to Joyce's mostly human and urban world) as well as in terms of the universe which inscape can embrace (this may seem ironic having said that Hopkins finds God in inscapes, but his view of God is a figure narrow and paternalistic). At the same time, Hopkins also places less importance on excitement and on the exaltation of the observer's ego:

> I kiss my hand
> To the stars, lovely-asunder
> Starlight, wafting him out of it; and
> Glow, glory in thunder;
> Kiss my hand to the dappled-with-damson west;
> Since, tho' he is under the world's splendour and wonder,
> His mystery must be instressed, stressed;
> For I greet him the days I meet him, and bless when I understand.
>
> ('The Wreck of the Deutchsland')

> Self flashes off frame and face.
> What do then? how meet beauty? Merely meet it; own,
> Home at heart, heaven's sweet gift; then leave, let that alone.
>
> ('To what serves Mortal Beauty?')

However, the writer who approaches most closely to Joyce in his view of the epiphany is his almost exact contemporary Virginia Woolf, whose work also shows other general similarities with Joyce's, especially in the relationship between the individual and his apparently bewildering and beleaguering urban environment. Each writer too sees literature as attempting to capture and penetrate truths about human life rather than, as previous authors tended to do, concentrate on aspects such as strong story-line, materialistic settings or the teaching of morality. At root, both Woolf and Joyce are profoundly concerned with life's essential evanescence:

The mind receives a myriad impressions – trivial, fantastic, evanescent, or engraved with the sharpness of steel. From all sides they come, an incessant shower of innumerable atoms ... Life is not a series of gig-lamps symmetrically arranged; life is a luminous halo, a semi-transparent envelope surrounding us from the beginning of consciousness to the end. Is it not the task of the novelist to convey this varying, this unknown and uncircumscribed spirit, whatever aberration or complexity it may display, with as little mixture of the alien and external as possible?[4]

Although this evanescence necessarily eludes definition or capture, the experience of it can be paralleled for the reader through what Virginia Woolf called 'moments of being' and which she also used for the structure of some of her greatest novels:

But somehow into that picture must be brought, too, the sense of movement and change. Nothing remained stable long ... That is what is indescribable, that is what makes all images too static, for no sooner has one said this was true, than it was past and altered.   ('A Sketch of the Past')[5]

This confirms me in my instinctive notion: (it will not bear arguing about; it is irrational) the sensation that we are all sealed vessels afloat on what it is convenient to call reality; and at some moments, the sealing matter cracks; in floods reality ...   ('A Sketch of the Past')[6]

The concepts of 'moments of being' and epiphany are thus strikingly similar in their action and function. However the essential difference is one of scale. While Virgina Woolf's moments are personal and domestic, exposing truths about a character's relationships with other people in his circle in addition to truths about himself, Joyce's epiphanies can ultimately be truly cosmic in their revelation since as well as intimating to Stephen (and to the reader) truths about himself and his relationships, they also enable him to see his situation in wider racial, historical, cultural and religious contexts encompassing a vast human universe. So at the end of Chapter 4, Stephen's epiphany with his artistic vocation as its central subject reaches out to embrace countless other contexts – the decline of his family and his own estrangement from it, the sterility of Catholic Dublin, 'ancient kingdom of the Danes' (with echoes of the nationalist issue), the call of European culture, and archetypal flight in the myth of Daedalus, the 'hawklike man', (pp. 173–4; see also pp. 15, 101 and 229 for other examples).

Having hit upon such a brilliant concept, to what uses did Joyce then apply the idea of epiphany in *A Portrait*? There are chiefly two: to communicate information to character and reader, and to impart a structure to the novel. Since epiphany reveals new information, this is naturally an effective implicit method of allowing the story to unfold itself, again reducing the need of the narrator to intrude on the story, and of indicating what is significant in the story (and also alleviating the difficulties of selection and significance discussed above in Chapter 6).

Sometimes the epiphany is for the reader alone, such as at the start of Chapter 4 where we can see how the intensity of Stephen's exaggerated zeal is clearly unsustainable; also the 'smugging' episode (p. 43) in which Joyce reveals the gap between Stephen's limited understanding of what is happening, and the reader's mature point of view, here to bring out graphically Stephen's lack of maturity – but elsewhere in the novel Joyce uses such gaps to bring about an indirect comment on Stephen through humour or distance (for example, Cranly's criticism of Dedalus in Chapter 5).

At other times, in tune with the ever-fluctuating relationship between the reader and the novel's subject matter, the epiphany appears to be exclusively for the benefit of Stephen or the narrator and the reader is kept in the dark. Examples of this occur in Chapter 2 when Stephen is visiting his relatives, in enigmatic circumstances and amid a general atmosphere of doubt and uncertainty in which the point of view is kept rigorously limited to that of Stephen's. The two moments concern the 'beautiful Mabel Hunter' (p. 69) and then Stephen's being mistaken for a girl called Josephine (p. 70); while we can see that these enigmatic glimpses touch obliquely on the theme of sexuality, the reader can only approach without fully reaching their precise meaning. However, in general terms, they do sharply communicate that same obscurity of life's meaning as that which Stephen undergoes at this moment in the novel, the angst which Stephen faces in taking decisive steps being paralleled in the alienation of the reader.

The majority of epiphanies, however, are shared by reader and character, especially where Stephen acts as the intermediary between the experience and the reader, and so both appear to receive the information together simultaneously, making the reader more sympathetic to Stephen's situation; for example, in Chapter 2 when Mr Dedalus reveals Father Conmee's betrayal, it is as much a revelation to the reader as to Stephen (p. 74). On the other hand, although the epiphany may be simultaneous for reader and character the interpretation may not be the same. For example, when Stephen, searching for his father's initials in the university benches at Cork discovers the word 'foetus', although the word itself is neutral, even harmless, if bizarre for the reader, for Stephen it induces a paroxysm of anguish since it reveals how commonplace his recent crudities really are:

It shocked him to find in the outer world a trace of what he had deemed till then a brutish and individual malady of his own mind. (p. 93)

However, this example is also interesting because it illustrates the true power of words to trigger off epiphany for Stephen; as throughout the novel, the outer world of the senses opens up access to the inner world of sensitivity and imagination: words are Stephen's gateway to reality.

The other important use which Joyce makes of epiphany is a structural one. One of the most striking features of *A Portrait* is its use of parataxis – the unusual sequence of apparently unconnected events, its structure based on the stream-of-consciousness. On a first reading this may seem less a structure than the absence of one – a random hotchpotch of isolated items thrown loosely together, which it is but, as we have seen above, unlike the more conventional chronologically ordered approach in, say, *David Copperfield* or *Sons and Lovers*. Joyce uses the consciousness of the central character as the principle through which the structure of the novel grows organically and this is founded exclusively on the sequence of epiphanies (as the first page of the novel displays). By this method, the structure appears less to be imposed and regulated externally (on the basis of the order in which events originally happened) than to be generated instead from within the consciousness of Stephen Dedalus (in the order in which they are remembered). The structure thus appears to be justified within the world of the novel, to issue more naturally, based on the principle of what things Stephen considers most important even subconsciously. Stephen himself selects and imbues significance.

Further, this affords yet another advantage in that the structure both reflects and embodies the personality and moods of Stephen, at the same time reinforcing or challenging other perspectives on him. Consequently the chronological time sequence must of necessity be disrupted, especially so because one occasion can look back on another previous occasion, resulting sometimes in an epiphany within an epiphany, as happens in Chapter 4 during the epiphany which involves Stephen's interview with the director (p. 158). This occurs when the reference to 'les jupes', describing a friar's garment, suddenly diverts Stephen's thoughts first back to the time of his 'fall' with the prostitutes (pp. 102 and 104) and then even further back to his innocent days on the farm at Stradbrook (p. 65); the seemingly random and isolated moments are intricately connected through Stephen's mind but also, at a deeper level, through the senses (the touch of a woman's clothes and the

164

harness) and also through theme (the juxtaposition of innocence and sin implying Stephen's more mature outlook now). Thus, although the time sequence is momentarily disrupted, we can see that the diversion actually reveals through association the significance and interpretation which Stephen himself makes. Through Joyce's use of this structure, based as it is on significant form, the 'daily bread' of Stephen's ordinary experiences is transmuted into the 'radiant body of everliving life' (p. 225), giving permanence through art to the evanescent moment.

So significance is revealed or imparted not just by a single individual epiphany but also by the total arrangement of a series of them. While we have indicated above that this places more onus on the reader to interpret (since the arrangement is silent, without narrator's comment), the isolation and arrangement of such epiphanies can in fact deepen the reader's involvement in the novel. However, there are also potential difficulties with this approach. In order to intensify their impact, the epiphanies generally have an abrupt, occasionally even melodramatic ending. Joyce manipulates these into sequences which have a cumulative effect, working by progressive individual crescendos into a major climax at the conclusion of each of the five chapters. However, without the usual bridging material from the narrator these epiphanies can sometimes appear isolated, with the result that the novel frequently comes over as episodic, the reader being presented with bald, unprefaced moments. While it can be argued with some truth that this equates with the way that the mind works in recalling events (fetching up important occasions rather than proceeding smoothly from one item to the next) the experience of reading is not, after all, identical with the process of living. Also, by stressing the moment rather than the flow of narrative it could be claimed that, while Joyce's general thrust is dynamic, progress is actually being continually halted by short episodes and abrupt closes, and the reader's attention is continually being shunted back and forth.

Against these charges, however, we can say that to a great extent they are cancelled by the advantages, chiefly that the unifying consciousness and presence of Stephen helps to bridge the moments, especially as they all originate in him; that the archetypal nature of the epiphanies unites them, even if often at some deep subconscious level (in the same way that themes, images, motifs and symbols for which the epiphanies are a vehicle also serve to hold the novel together). The charge that Joyce's use of epiphany occasionally leads to a halting, fitful effect has more weight though it cannot be held up as a drawback of the whole; for example, in Chapters 1 and 2 the staccato effect created by the series of short, fragmentary and unresolved epiphanies effectively operates to underline Stephen's own feelings of frustration with his environment, especially in Chapter 2. Overall, the epiphanies project a generally fluid succession of presents generating their own intrinsic dynamism, their thrust being provided by Stephen's insistent internal maturation (represented in a variety of directions – intellectual, emotional, sexual and artistic), driving the novel forward through its climaxes.

8 the word made fresh:
Modernism and the Revolution of the Word

There lies her word, you reder! The height herup exalts it and the
lowness her down abaseth it. It vibroverberates upon the tegmen and
prosplodes from pomoeria. A widow, a hedge, a prong, a hand, an
eye, a sign, a head and keep your other augur on her paypaypay.

(*Finnegans Wake*, p. 249)

In Chapter 4 of *A Portrait* Stephen, disaffected, gazes out across the Irish Sea and prophetically contemplates the distant prospect of Europe, unseen and only dimly felt. He stands between two opposing revolutionary impulses.

Behind him lie the forceful, importuning voices of the Celtic revival, rooted in revolutionary nationalism and vocalized, on the one hand, through a Romantic culture which had already long ago had its day in Europe and, on the other, through a language long suppressed and almost extinct. In terms of European mainstream letters Ireland is for Stephen a backwater – as it had been for Joyce too.

Instead, both look to the distant preluding of a different revolutionary phenomenon in European civilization and culture, beyond the sea and beyond Britain, to the continent: to Paris, Berlin, Vienna and other centres where, amid widespread feelings of discontent and scepticism, a new movement was beginning to find shape and momentum: Modernism.

It is to the uncertain stirrings of Modernism that Stephen, like Joyce, flies at the end; though *A Portrait* is not a fully Modernist text (in the sense that *Ulysses* is), the novel appeared as a significant influence in the early days of the embryonic movement. Its subject and techniques anticipate many of the features of the later, more mature achievements of both Modernism and of Joyce himself, who became its prime mover. To fully appreciate these features in *A Portrait* it is vital to see it in the wider context of European artistic currents, and especially in the light of the crisis of values and uncertainties which took place during the period from 1890 to 1920, a crisis which occurred in the face of a widespread collapse of confidence in science, philosophy, religion and art.

To try to pinpoint the start of any movement with a specific date or work of art is inevitably a ticklish endeavour – Modernism more so since it was never a school, just a more or less simultaneous stirring among intellectuals and artists as a common but independent reaction to the failure of science and religion to offer a convincing definition of the changing world. There was never any consensus or manifesto among the artists and writers who have since been grouped together under its umbrella by succeeding critics. Thus Modernism has no easily identifiable starting date and indeed no *real* starting date – it grew instead as a late nineteenth-century reaction to Romanticism and a response to the world's social and intellectual changes. And while its achievements reveal its radically distinct approaches based on new perspectives, its initial rise was quite gradual.

While the break itself is difficult to pinpoint in time there is no question about the great divide in the terms on which art, literature, philosophical attitudes, social values, politics and science separated the Modernists from the age of Jane Austen, Wordsworth, George Eliot and Dickens.

But what differentiates the approach and style of Modernism from what went before? How can we identify the style of Modernism – its soul?

First of all, Modernism is not one style but many. Unlike Romanticism which was effectively a change of emphasis growing out of the unconscious reaction to Neo-classicism, Modernism is a concerted attempt to create a new artistic attitude through a new way of looking at the world and at the art which expresses it. This is typified for instance in the new styles of painting, such as Picasso's Cubism, with its rejection of representationalism in favour of significant form and expressive style based on experience – a sort of introversion turning on scepticism and mannerism, in which technique and form are unmistakably foregrounded. But unlike representational art, which finds its pretext in a close physical correspondence between the image and the real world, Modernist art finds its justification within itself; it is ultimately self-sufficient.

For Modernist art, there is not merely a crisis in reality but also a crisis in perception. On a wider scale, Modernism springs from and closely corresponds with the crises and anxieties of the age as a whole – industrialization and urbanization on a vast scale, rapid and uncontrollable change and chaos, together with the inevitable alienation of the individual. And all this is mirrored in the splintering of art into diverse schisms and '-isms'.

But if Modernism is characterized by a preoccupation with style, what is the character of that style?[1] As we have hinted, this is no simple task since paradoxically the movement is united by its own impulse for fragmentation, partly aimed at thwarting generalizations about itself. We can say, however, that it is typified on the one hand by flagrant artifice – it flaunts its technical underwear – yet also by a high level of abstraction, with a lack of piety for the conventions of language and form. It is characterized also by shock, crisis and discontinuity, obscurity and anxiety – all seeking to break down old comfortable reader relationships and to substitute instead new ones, to place the reader in a position of continual flux with his artist-author. At the same time there is a strong drive towards art which finds its form and being within itself through significant form, the ultimate end, according to Nietzsche:

a book about nothing, a book without external attachments, which would hold itself together through the internal force of its style.

This is an idea which is echoed in part by Stephen Dedalus in *A Portrait* when he talks about the artist being above and beyond his creation; Joyce's novel itself, though biographical in origin, finds its strength through internal referents as much as through correspondence with reality.

And yet, as we have seen in the previous chapter on epiphany, Modernism is also much concerned with time, especially with the transience of the moment, in particular the paradox that, while on the one hand the experience of a moment is evanescent, on the other its effects are permanent. Many writers struggled to capture the spontaneity and impact of the moment – in Virginia Woolf's phrase, to catch 'the atoms as they fall upon the mind',[2] to unfold its significance, and not only as the subject matter of their work. By exploiting it as the organizing function of the art form, they could also exploit its internal life. The inimitability of the moment is paralleled by the uniqueness of the form of the work in which it is reflected: the idea that for every work of art there is a uniquely individual form appropriate to its subject matter.

Fundamentally, the crisis in Modernism is underpinned by a profound intellectual readjustment, whose consequences strike at the formal conventions in art and literature, at the methods of characterization and the use of language and, as we have seen, at the very idea of the artist himself. Above almost all else it is associated with the idea of an avant-garde – in spite of the spirit of alienation, denial and scepticism.[3]

There is thus an inbuilt élitist tendency among artists implied by such avant-gardeism, and this is naturally reflected among readers too since Modernism evolved as an arcane and private art addressing an audience with a shared, educated culture. The result is an overall readership divided into those who regard Modernism as the ideal form of expression of the age, embracing even its hostilities, and those who find it marginal, temporary and above all incomprehensible.

It was in the beginnings of these stirrings that *A Portrait* first appeared in book form, almost unnoticed, and it was also during the horrifying abyss of the First World War and shortly after the Irish Easter uprising, two of the most critical and violent assaults upon British imperialism. It emerged into a world immersed in profound and far-reaching turmoil, through which many of the cosy assumptions and principles which had gone before would be swept away. In one of the most remarkable periods of dynamic growth and turbulent change, the thirty years before the war witnessed decline and transformation in a wide range of the most profound areas of the social fabric – in science, technology, economics, social philosophy, and psychology, as well as the arts.

At the turn of the century London, Paris and Berlin were the triple hubs of the capitalist, industrialized world, together dominating almost the whole globe through a web of industrial, commercial and imperialist forces, controlling between the three of them over 60 per cent of the world markets for manufactured goods. Yet the period between 1890 and 1914 also saw a rapid boom in heavy industrial output in the three countries with, at the same time, a momentous technological revolution which resulted in a great number of key technical innovations: the emergence of electricity and petrol as the new major power sources; the internal combustion and diesel engines, with the appearance of the motor car and trams and buses on the city street scene; the first powered flight; increased mechanization of industry and agriculture; the introduction of new synthetic fibres and plastic with a rise in the importance of the chemical industry; and in communications with the invention of the telephone, the typewriter and wireless telegraphy.

During this time the three major European capitals also underwent a massive surge in urbanization (in 1910 the population of London was almost 4.5 million, of Paris over 2.5 million, while by contrast that of Dublin was only 304,802) continuing the flight from the land begun in the industrial revolution. And in the cities themselves the routines of urban life were becoming increasingly dominated by the rigid routines of the office and factory.[4] The day of mass production had dawned, with industry gearing up to generate and sustain vast mass-markets through economies of scale and advertising: thus, with the beginnings of cinema and mass-circulation newspapers, the modern mass media had been born.

It is a picture of the individual overwhelmed and subjugated to colossal dehumanizing forces of industry, commerce and production. Yet, while the ancient aristocratic regimes of the imperial powers – Britain, France, Russia – still remained intact, the new emergence of wealth as a key force was beginning to dislodge the hereditary monopolies on status, materialism, education and leisure with the rise of a *nouveau riche* – parvenus who derived their new-found wealth from profit and trade; some, like T. S. Eliot, in *The Waste Land*, equated this new class with moral and social decline:

> One of the low on whom assurance sits
> As a silk hat on a Bradford millionaire.

Polarization of the prosperous leisured class from the slum-dwelling poor increased as the latter came to be regarded merely as a pool of cheap surplus labour and degraded humanity. Gradually, however, although the rich had by and large isolated themselves from the lower classes, the voice of mass protest was already beginning to make itself heard – the workers had already begun to organize themselves and membership of socialist parties across Europe was rapidly increasing, while at the same time the women's suffragette movement was gathering strength and momentum.

But, over this latent if awakening conflict, there still sat a high degree of smugness about the middle and upper classes. In spite of the spectre of organized labour, there was, before the war, no real threat yet to the established order of society. For the leisured classes of the three major colonial powers, *la belle époque* was characterized by freedom and security, grace, ease and privilege served by cheap and plentiful labour and material benefits, at the centres of empires equally untroubled by (and largely ignorant of) their deep social, racial and sexual inequalities.

But what of the intellectual life of the period? In 1895 Wilhelm Röntgen's discovery of X-rays and the Curies' discovery of the properties of radium heralded the onset of a profound revolution in physics. They were closely followed by the nuclear research of Thompson, Rutherford and Soddy whose immediate spin-off was the most profound reformulation of attitudes to physical matter since classical theories, the foremost concepts being Max Planck's Quantum Theory of Energy (1900) and Einstein's Special Theory of Relativity (1905). In twenty years the whole image of the physical universe, previously regarded as the most complete and secure foundation of scientific thought, was shot through with doubt and attempts were made to replace it with a new model.

Although we have an image of the individual beleaguered by the dehumanizing forces of industry on a huge scale, as a result of this we can see the social sciences beginning to make a closer, more scientific examination of him. Most renowned in this field is, of course, Sigmund Freud, founder of psychoanalysis. One of the most pervasive influences on twentieth-century thought in general and literary theory in particular, he has been an immensely seminal force in the widest range of social contexts as well as in his own specialist fields. His involvement in psychology itself dates only from the 1890s when, with Josef Breuer, he published *Studies in Hysteria* (1895) a landmark in psychoanalysis. However, his ideas, which created a revolution in psychology by focusing controversially on early influences and childhood sexuality, also contain many contradictions, a feature which identifies his work as a herald of Modernism while at the same time containing the seeds of its demise. Although aware of his impact, Joyce never acknowledged any influence of Freud on his own early works which, nevertheless, show a remarkable parallel development with Freud's concerns and reach similar discoveries by separate courses; for instance, Joyce's emphasis on the crucial role and influence of Stephen's mother and other early influences in *A Portrait*, and his exploration of father–son relationships in *Ulysses*.

By middle age though, Joyce had certainly studied some of Freud's ideas in depth and *Finnegans Wake* displays the undoubted influence – and inevitable parodies – of Freud's dream and symbol theories (Joyce described psychoanalysis sardonically as '... we grisly old Sykos who have done our unsmiling bit on 'alices, when they were yung and easily freudened ...' (*Finnegans Wake*, p. 115).[5]

A side effect of Freud's early work, the role and importance of mythology, itself later became very much a central concern of psychoanalysis through the exploration of cultural archetypes; the most notable theorist in this area is Carl Gustav Jung, an early pupil of Freud, who later wrote an appreciative account of *Ulysses*[6] and also became one of the many psychiatrists to treat Joyce's daughter, Lucia, during her illness.

As traditional concepts of 'fictional reality' were overturned and new attitudes to time – personal as well as cultural – started to appear, artists too began to turn to myth to fill the gap which had been left, seeing in it also a means of bringing order to the contemporary world and discipline to feeling and experience. For Joyce, myth became one of the fundamental features of his mature work, exploited for both theme and form, though he used it extensively throughout all his writing: from

172

his earliest published work ('Et tu, Healy'), through Daedalian and Odyssean fable in *A Portrait* and *Ulysses*, to the Celto-Christian myths (among many others) of *Finnegans Wake*.

But psychology very rapidly cast its attention across a host of human activities. In addition to mythology, Jung also worked on word association, an interest paralleled by the research of William James whose book, *The Principles of Psychology* (1890), not only anticipated many of Freud's concepts but in addition, and most significantly, outlined the phenomenon of the 'stream-of-consciousness', one of the most characteristic narrative devices of Modernism as a whole and of Joyce's mature work in particular.[7]

At about the same time as these advances in psychology, the foundations of modern sociology too were being laid from the theories of Emile Durkheim and Max Weber both of whose most original work appeared between the years 1895 and 1914. Both sought to find solutions to the crises in social living by confronting what they considered to be the heart of the individual's dilemma: 'a state of confusion in a rootless, incoherent world from which traditional values and rules had been dislodged'. And both proposed, among other things, a return to myths as a regenerative source of cultural values and coherence.

At the heart of many of these crises, however, is a deep philosophical scepticism – a profound sense of uncertainty. Hand in hand with new social realities, the early part of this century witnessed a revolution in philosophical perspectives and moral vision to cope with the widespread collapse of faith in monolithic systems of truth. Freudian theory, based though it was on a framework of nineteenth-century assumptions of determinism, rationalism and positivism, suddenly switched the emphasis on to the unconscious and causal factors which appeared outside the previously held views of personal responsibility. And the notion of absolutes in normal and abnormal behaviour was given a severe blast, with the concept that all individuals display neurotic symptoms in varying degrees.

It is difficult to comprehend now the hostility with which his theories were greeted, yet Freud's sturdy framework maintained similarly deterministic evolutionary assumptions as those which lay behind Darwinism, Marxism, and the philosophical ideas of Wittgenstein, Kierkegaard, Moore, Bergson, Russell and Nietzsche.

Against the view of the hapless citizen beset by oppressive megalithic forces in which he came to be regarded as the product of natural causal features and largely passive, philosophical outlooks began to react by redefining the nature of existence and the essence of the human personality. Friedrich Nietzsche's ideas in the 1880s of 'aristocratic radicalism' and the myth of eternal regeneration were momentous landmarks in the swing towards the reassertion of the individual. Though he had been published before, Nietzsche's views sprang to prominence in the last decade of the century through the popularization of his ideas by the Danish critic Georg Brandes, through whom they worked a powerful influence on the playwrights Strindberg and Ibsen and thus, indirectly, on Joyce. By believing firmly that mankind had reached a moment of destiny in which human ideas and values must become subject to radical reappraisal, Nietzsche prophesied and helped bring about the revolution in thought which would ultimately bring about Modernism itself.

Although many of his ideas have become discredited by a stress on his 'moral nihilism' and by their later annexation by the Nazis, Nietzsche's perspectives herald a significant change of emphasis, a challenge to the nineteenth-century idea that true values were located in the society rather than in the individual. Taking this up, Ibsen gave full expression to the new thinking by insisting through *An Enemy of the People* (1883) that the 'majority is never right', an idea which Joyce embraced to the full (see Chapter 4). But Ibsen was not alone; for instance, Hardy's naturalistic *Jude the Obscure* and *Tess of the D'Urbervilles* both present stark portraits of the alienated individual, outcast by society's intolerance, and G. B. Shaw was beginning to grapple with the theme of social tyranny, while Joseph Conrad's impressionistic world exposed the nihilism and moral bankruptcy of deeply accepted values.

The new thinkers and artists were turning their attention to the new arena in which flux, fragmentation and pluralism were key notions, in contrast to the fixed and stable positivist world of nineteenth-century thought. Reality was no longer limited by ideas of a fixed, palpable and solid world of phenomena; it could be evasive, evanescent, protean, like the fleeting, elusive images, mysterious associations and perceptions of the conscious and subconscious mind.

And just as late nineteenth-century aesthetics had come to explore confidently beneath the surface of reality, challenging traditional surface materialism, science blasted this view of reality and its materialism; to the dots, dashes and strokes of the impressionists were now added concepts of invisible particles and waves.

A concern for the abstract, a recognition of a special kind of subjective logic antithetical to the commonsense rationality of Naturalism and Utilitarianism, also emerged through the inspirational thinking of the psychologist William James and the philosopher Henri Bergson.

Bergson, an important influence on the young T. S. Eliot who attended his lectures in Paris, placed supreme emphasis on the intuition as the chief means of grasping reality, through 'intellectual sympathy' as he called it.

At once, ambivalence and imaginative philosophical speculation became respectable avenues of exploration and, consistent with Freud's theories, the dream and man's unconscious became germane areas of serious research. It was also soon recognized that the workings of deep structures of the mind offered radical new formulas for accumulating and shaping material into a distinctly special coherence which writers readily exploited to the full – opening the way for works such as August Strindberg's *A Dream Play* (1902) through expressionism, surrealism, and a range of experiments leading to Joyce's *Finnegans Wake* in 1939, its ultimate expression. In his preface to *A Dream Play*, Strindberg reveals his full cognizance of the new possibilities:

In this dream play, as in his previous dream play *To Damascus*, the author has tried to reproduce the disconnected but apparently logical form of a dream. Anything may happen; all things are possible and probable. Time and space do not exist; against an unimportant background of reality, the imagination spins and weaves new patterns; a blend of memories, experiences, free ideas, absurdities, improvisations. The characters split, double, multiply; they evaporate, crystallise, scatter and converge. But a single consciousness holds dominion over them all: that of the dreamer.

By the beginning of this century the old values and certainties had been severely challenged; the stable predictable world of the nineteenth century was in increasing crisis as the forces which would ultimately wrench it apart gathered strength, forces which would eventually culminate in the stark cataclysm of the world war. It is against such a scenario that Strindberg's statement needs to be set but, as his statement also implies, the vision of disintegration and uncertainty was too a powerful and exciting inspiration to the artist, a provocation to come to terms with it in a new order and a new sort of artistic order: Modernism.

When Joyce moved to Paris in December 1902, it was already the capital of progressive vitality and innovation in the arts, and Paris was to remain indissolubly linked with the Modernist movement throughout the rest of Joyce's lifetime. Among artists already working there at the time of his arrival were Braque, Utrillo, Derain, Matisse, Duchamp, Vlaminck, as well as Picasso and Cézanne. Like Joyce, many others too were drawn to the city about this time – Brancusi, Modigliani, Marc,

Klee, Chagall, Mondrian. In painting, the new vision is characterized by Matisse's fauvist interiors, Seurat's optical experiments in divisionism (for instance, in *A Sunday Afternoon on the Island of La Grande Jatte*, 1884), and in the colour–sculpture experiments of Cézanne, Picasso and others who sought to model subtle surface effects through a rigorous discipline of form and space (e.g. Cézanne's *Mont Sainte-Victoire*, 1885–7, and Picasso's *Les Demoiselles d'Avignon*, 1907).

In Paris and elsewhere the early 1900s saw an exceptional flowering of artistic talent – for example, in Dresden *Die Brücke* group (early expressionists), and in Munich the *Der Blaue Reiter* group whose influential talents, Kandinsky and Klee, laid the foundations of the later Bauhaus group and profoundly influenced post-war Abstract art. Elsewhere, other related talents were beginning to blossom: Edvard Munch, Norwegian expressionist; Oskar Kokoschka, Austrian expressionist; James Ensor, Belgian painter and etcher; and the artists of Italian futurism who strove to assimilate into their art the images and forms of the world of mechanization.

And then in music there is Stravinsky, the most prominent, strident figure among the new wave of composers, in the wake of Mahler and Richard Strauss, and his best work dates from the period before the war. Drawing inspiration from the Romantic twilight, Stravinsky's work heralds a neo-classicism in music, his ballet suite, *The Rite of Spring*, signalling the climax of his bold pre-war experiments in complex rhythms, fragmentary and repetitive melodies and polyphonal harmonies – its performance in Paris in 1913 provoked a riot in the audience. For twentieth-century music this is the most exciting period with Debussy, Ravel and Satie in France, Berg and Schoenberg in Vienna and Bartók in Hungary.

But it is in literature that there is the most prolific blossoming of Modernist talent – Gide and Proust, Paul Valéry and Guillaume Apollinaire in France; Henry James and Conrad in England – followed by Virginia Woolf and D. H. Lawrence; Mann and Rilke in Germany; Chekhov in Russia; Strindberg in Sweden; Ibsen in Norway; as well as exiles such as the profoundly influential Ezra Pound, Gertrude Stein and T. S. Eliot from the USA.

With such a catalogue of diverse talents, a generalization of all their aims and characteristics, as if they were all pursuing the same ends, would be clearly unsatisfactory and probably impossible. Yet, although Modernism is not a school, many of its artists have shared attitudes and approaches, by chance as often as by design. For example, Modernist writers share among other things a deep concern with form and the problematics of language, but approach them not as obstacles but rather as an opportunity to be explored, through the use of irony, paradox and similar related tropes together with silence and obscurity, to express fragmentation and discord, absurdity and fear in the face of the contemporary predicament. Though not a progenitor of Modernism, W. B. Yeats's 'The Second Coming' (1919) catches the tension and unease of the period:

> Turning and turning in the widening gyre
> The falcon cannot hear the falconer;
> Things fall apart; the centre cannot hold;
> Mere anarchy is loosed upon the world . . .

Among the achievements of Modernism two works stand out as its monuments, T. S. Eliot's *The Waste Land* and Joyce's *Ulysses*. *The Waste Land* (1922), the most significant verse work of Modernism, brilliantly evokes the crises of the age: spiritual collapse and death, cultural aberrancy, the crisis in communication, and the disintegration of traditional social values. Yet through all its broken and perfidious images roams the solitary figure of the blind seer Tiresias, 'the most important personage in the poem, uniting all the rest'. Based on a mythological Greek figure of renowned percipience who existed as both man and woman, Tiresias is perfectly equipped from his unique point of view outside contemporary time to observe and comment objectively upon it. It is through him that *The Waste Land* confronts and comes to terms with the theme of chaos, chaos on the scale of both the private individual and the shared cultural stock of the community. Yet the poem does not make order of chaos. Though it clearly achieves an internal formal sort of order, it only dramatizes chaos, representing it through Eliot's pervasive tone of resignation and, through the poem's polemical ironies, attempts to fix or formulate it while at the same time acknowledging the helpless plight of the individual before the gathering tide of degeneration and nihilism.

Like *The Waste Land*, *Ulysses* is an attempt to come to terms with the dislocated individual in the Human Age and, like Eliot, Joyce exploits past cultural models and myth both for internal order and for theme itself, through a submerged commentary on the contemporary world. Both also come to terms with chaos by at first creating their own chaos, a chaos more easy to manage and to make sense of. In each, form and content achieve a fine coalescence so that each work accomplishes an internal life of its own. There is too in *Ulysses* the figure of the blind stripling, drifting Tiresias-like in and out of view across Joyce's Dublin, though without either the formal or the moral force of Eliot's figure.

As we have seen, many of these formal and thematic features are prefigured in *A Portrait*; we can also see prefigured there the area in which Joyce and Eliot differ most: in their attitudes to the revolution against nineteenth-century values – Eliot despondently regarding it as one of cultural despair and Joyce finding in it a qualified hope, an opportunity to redefine man's relationship in the world by an assertion of enlightened humanistic values and working through a sort of new social contract rooted in fellowship and transcendent mythic values.

Because Modernism is in large part a reaction to nineteenth-century Romanticism it is tempting to see it as a revival of Classicism, whereas it is in fact an intense form of Romanticism which attempts to disguise its acute subjectivism by overlaying itself with obscurity – the obscurity itself a symptom of the age, a parallel and an acknowledgement of the positivist model. This is reflected too in an uncertainty about the use and efficiency of language to express anything other than language itself; language and material reality cease to be directly linked in a relationship of simple correspondence.[8]

There is accordingly a dual attitude in Modernism: on the one hand, a sense of confidence in the self as the guarantor of reality (subjective perception as the only reliable source of truth), on the other, a deep anxiety and scepticism about this truth and the ability of language to express it.

Obscurity is thus a recurrent characteristic of Modernism, a sort of 'negative capability', exacerbated by the often esoteric areas of experience which writers began to explore; it is characterized by the frequent use of difficult and otiose cultural models and mythology, and of references from narrow erudite sources in the search for fresh perspectives among ancient ways. Eliot is a good example of this in his apparent use of dead books and etiolate references (side by side with everyday domestic images with which they are held in uneasy tension). In this way the anxiety of the writer is partially submerged since the obscurity of his sources accords him with a superiority in relation to his reader.

The reader's unstable position is often further undermined by the uncertainties which arise from the absence of conventional plot sequence, from narrative silences, and the suppression of conventional pointers and the commentary of the narrator. In addition, other typical Modernist devices and strategies operated to unsettle the reader, often inducing the hostility of early critics: the absence of easily recognizable characters,[9] the focus on narrative methods to create an internal intellectual discourse – writing about writing – and to vary the distances between the reader and the narrator (further obscuring the evasive author).

At heart, Modernism involves hiding, deceiving, dislocation[10] and uncertainty brought about by the intrinsic failure of traditional reality and the rejection of the old methods of conveying it. Indeed the very resistance of the Modernist work to interpretation is often the source of its energy. Moreover, there is an awesome awareness, implicit if not actually articulated until later in the period, of the void lurking at the heart of modern living, a horrifying emptiness reflected in the Modernist author's frequent silences and that, in this situation of absurdity, all that really matters is the relationship between the author and the reader in a sort of literary game.

Two central challenges have preoccupied the Modernist novel: exploration and expression of the subtle potentialities of consciousness, and a coming to terms with the perceived state of chaos and fragmentation of the real world. Although *A Portrait* is not a fully Modernist text, both of these concerns can already be seen in embryo in it: firstly, in the abandonment of the restraints of conventional chronological plot (in favour of expressive form with modulating styles and shifting author–character–reader relationships arranged through Stephen Dedalus's consciousness); and, secondly, in the sense of awe and fear which Stephen feels in the face of the chaos behind received forms of order (that is, the imposed moral order of the adult world and the Church) and the void awaiting him in the uncertain future beyond the novel:

A sense of fear of the unknown moved in the heart of his weariness, a fear of symbols and portents, of the hawklike man whose name he bore soaring out of his captivity on osierwoven wings . . . (p. 229)

At the start of this century it seemed that the novel might have exhausted its potential in terms both of form and of content (having fully explored different forms and narrative styles, inner and outer states, politics, religion, philosophy, sex as well as violence). The novel could confidently embrace any aspect of human affairs which public taste and the circulating libraries would permit, or so it was confidently imagined.

However, in England the three-volume novel's interest in scientific realism had declined into a sterile preoccupation with plot, materialism and the naturalistic fallacy of surface effects – typified in the writings of Wells, Galsworthy and Bennett who, according to Virginia Woolf, could examine every physical aspect about a character and yet overlook its essential soul. To illustrate her criticism she used the analogy of a

179

railway in which a Mrs Brown might be travelling with them, while they observed everything in the background:

... at factories, at Utopias, even at the decoration of the carriage; but never at her, never at life, never at human nature ... For us those conventions are ruin, those tools are death.[11]

One of the immediate consequences of this apparent dead-end was a crisis of confidence, especially in the capacity of language to communicate, but there also followed a collapse of faith in the realist illusion (a scepticism which had been growing even as the novel itself had evolved, at least since the eighteenth century). The crisis emerged most characteristically in a new form of self-awareness, even in self-consciousness, doubt and a failure of confidence. But this was not new. Lawrence Sterne's *Tristram Shandy* (1760–67) brilliantly epitomizes the novelist's doubts about narrative conventions and exploits them through parody for comic effect. It is of course a witty display of authorial virtuosity, though it accepts the traditional authorial role and material content in order to parody them. However, Modernism goes further than authorial virtuosity, especially in first undermining and then positing new author–reader relationships, directly co-opting the reader's active involvement but also, through its subtlety of form-play, examining and qualifying the very nature of the art form itself as the artist creates it, so that ultimately the reader himself is complicit in the form of the novel.

A Portrait focuses precisely on this and further anticipates later Modernist developments by focusing also on the theme of the artist – the growth of the artist becomes the theme of his own creation, and by extension if we grant the special relationship between Stephen Dedalus and James Joyce the novel eventually comes to discuss itself. For example, in Chapter 5 the villanelle and the art theory are the culmination of growing speculation about the nature of the artist's relationship to his art, to his reader and to society in general:

The image, it is clear, must be set between the mind or senses of the artist himself and the mind or senses of others. (p. 218)

Because of this scepticism there also emerged in the early days of Modernism a distinct feeling of angst, a fear that the author of a novel creates nothing in fact but clearly fakes or forges the so-called reality in a work[12] and that his search for form is partly to justify this (a clear symptom of this is the popularity of the detective story in the late nineteenth century especially among prominent writers such as Wilkie Collins, Dickens, Conan Doyle, Henry James and T. S. Eliot), forging a coherent pattern on to the apparent chaos. Stephen Dedalus too talks of forging in this way (p. 257) – imposing meaning on life through art, forging an order different from that in reality but creating a new aesthetic order. But he also uses 'forges' to highlight the sense that the Modernist artist is a confidence trickster, deceiver, con man like Thomas Mann's Felix Krull. But who is fooling whom? Is Stephen deceiving only himself or, through Joyce, the reader too?

Further aspects of the Modernist novel can also be seen beginning to emerge in *A Portrait*. For example, the form of the novel, rather than being a more or less detached vessel into which the subject matter is poured and contained, actually partakes of the subject matter as later, in the mature Modernist work (such as *Ulysses*), the form actually *became* the content, united and radiant in appropriate wholeness and harmony: these words in this order. As Joyce told his friend, the artist Frank Budgen:

I have the words already. What I am seeking is the perfect order of words in the sentence. There is an order in every way appropriate.

It was a concern very much shared by other Modernist writers at this time, anxious to liberate the novel from its close dependence on external material realism (itself based on assumptions of a direct correspondence between words and reality) and to concentrate on probing the unutterable territory of the human consciousness and the soul, instead of finding their creative energy from within the artist's uniquely private vision. Subsequently, the Modernist novel also became very much concerned with disrupting the traditional forward flow of narrative time by sudden leaps forward and backward along 'timeless' moments (or epiphanies), and setting up conflicts with, while also exploiting, the reader's 'real time' progress through the text.

But one of Joyce's profound innovations here is the use of multiple points of view. *A Portrait* has no single perspective: Stephen's consciousness changes as he matures and, through the shifting modulating style, the perspective of the narrator also changes, setting up an implicit dialectic between the two.[13] The idea itself of an implied narrator – a voice not wholly Joyce's, but a surrogate author and Joyce's representative in the work – is a new development evolving through Flaubert, James and Conrad, and arising directly from the avowed aim of keeping the author's moral presence out of the novel. As we have seen, *A Portrait* excludes any direct authorial moral comment but continues to exert control over the reader's response through the technique of the form – juggling the order, emphasis, theme and point of view.

Time is also of crucial importance. In the Modernist novel time dominates, both as one of the key themes as well as one of the key organizing principles of the design. Marcel Proust's *A la recherche du temps perdu* (1913–27) is a paradigm of this preoccupation with time. An enormous undertaking, its scope is equally epic, its central ideal being that in moments of intense illumination it is possible to penetrate and recapture the long-lost past and to relive its emotions. Because of his special skills and sensitivity the artist, unlike the ordinary person, is able to record and prolong such isolated moments into eternity itself through the magic of symbolism and myth vision (stressing the elevated status of the artist).

But to be able to exploit such moments for the central experience of reality, it was necessary for the novelist to concentrate on pattern rather than plot in organizing his work. Both *A la recherche du temps perdu* and *A Portrait* display this emphasis, and Virginia Woolf made her plea for such novels in which, like *A Portrait*, the interplay of the consciousness of the writer and of his people work to create the form:

> If a writer were a free man and not a slave, if he could write what he chose, not what he must, if he could base his work upon his own feelings and not upon convention, there would be no plot, no comedy, no tragedy, no love interest . . . Life is not a series of gig lamps symmetrically arranged; but a luminous halo, a semi-transparent envelope surrounding us from the beginning of the consciousness to the end. Is it not the task of the novelist to convey this varying, unknown and circumscribed spirit, whatever aberration or complexion it may display, with as little mixture of the alien and external as possible?[14]

At the same time the capacity of the language and the novel form are pressed to new limits in attempting to make language approximate to the inner realities of such phenomena as simultaneity (*Ulysses*), sudden illumination or epiphany (*Dubliners* and *A Portrait*), and relative time and the unconsciousness (the techniques of stream-of-consciousness and 'interior monologue').

We have seen above already that this idea of the 'moment' was one which energized the work of so many Modernist writers – Woolf, Eliot, Proust, and others – but especially of Joyce, in his idea of the 'epiphany', the basic unit of the form in both *Dubliners* and *A Portrait*.[15] Its use underlines vividly the fragmentariness of modern existence and its disintegration, at the same time deriving the form of the work from a principle of significant aesthetic pattern rather than from a conventional chronographic history.

The concept of the epiphany dynamically assimilates the Modernist idea of time as the moment to the special notion of truth as discovery. And the writer's use of his own biography works in the same way, fusing the writer's conception of real life with the need for pattern and coherence, as Proust reflected:

the true life, life at last discovered and illuminated, the only true life really lived, is that of the writer.

The theme of the artist's own biography (sometimes attacked as a form of introversion) is encountered again and again in the Modernist novel. Like Proust's masterpiece, *A Portrait* is both the portrait of the novel's creator and the revelation of the life principle on which the novel is written. It represents that reality which the novelist is most familiar with: his own life and his art. Combined with the epiphany as the most logical means of arranging and signifying experience, his own themes of personal exile and alienation parallel the exile and alienation of the age. In the best work of the period, this theme confronts and resolves one of the central crises in the Modernist novel – the struggle to express the new impalpable realities in the wake of the acute failure of confidence in the language. In *A Portrait* Stephen Dedalus is at the same time both the experience of the novel and its author; Joyce adapts his own experience, and his words are both the means of expressing them as well as being the subject of the expression themselves. The text ultimately forges its justification within itself, again perfectly fusing form and content, technique and subject.

In Joyce's time the 'portrait of the artist' theme occurs again and again: in Thomas Mann's *Tonio Kröger*, André Gide's *The Counterfeiters*, D. H. Lawrence's *Sons and Lovers* and in Proust's monumental work, as well as in submerged form in countless works, frequently involving exile or flight into the unknown – a correlative of the Modernist crises themselves – through which the artist confronts the problematics of artistic creation and his own relationship to it.

Joyce's works expose and confront in full the crises of Modernism and so enter fully into the mainstream of the movement, Joyce becoming its *primum mobile*. His works span almost its complete range and parallel its development in microcosm, *Ulysses* representing the culmination and highest achievement of the Modernist phenomenon and its highest creative expression. Like *A Portrait*, it takes its starting point in the immediate reality of Joyce's own life and times but through its intricate processes (including the use of myth, multiple perspective, epiphany, variable planes of ironic meaning and linguistic experiment) he transcends and metamorphoses the here-and-now to embrace all time. From explicit representational biography (and some autobiography) in the early pages of *A Portrait*, Joyce's career is an artistic odyssey progressing by succeeding phases of ironic detachment and displacement until, by *Finnegans Wake*, art itself has become the myth, the final stage of the search for a self-sustaining art image, existing only in and through the multiple uses of language, without reference to any world other than within itself, germinating and proliferating in ever-widening gyres of meaning and response.

But is *Finnegans Wake* the Big Bang or merely a black hole? As an attempted solution to the problems which Modernism tried to confront, *Finnegans Wake* is quite final. However, it is also silence. It is the silence which lies at the core of all Modernist works, perhaps all creation, a sort of taboo: the silence in the face of the realization that it may all have become a game. If Modernism found its ultimate logical expression in *Finnegans Wake* then it did not overcome the incipient scepticism about the relationship between the word and reality, but succeeded in transcending it by making the word itself the ultimate reality and consequently the word is silence, ironically. What need is there of more words? In the beginning is the word, and in the end.

For this reason some disparagers of Modernism claim that *Finnegans Wake* shows the ultimate folly of the movement: it sows the seeds of its own destruction. Others, however, suggest that the *Wake* took Modernism along only one of several available courses which had been open; the rest lie locked in the room of infinite possibilities which it ousted, perhaps. Certainly *Finnegans Wake* was not the end and, though there has been a reaction in literature in its own wake – signs of a return to the traditional materialistic realism – the flow continued after Joyce and, under his considerable shadow, in the novels and plays of Samuel Beckett (for a time Joyce's amanuensis on *Finnegans Wake*), Vladimir Nabokov, Henry Miller, William Faulkner, Flann O'Brien and more widely in the theatre of Bertolt Brecht and Arthur Miller, Harold Pinter and the post-Modern novels of William Burroughs, John Fowles, John Barth, Alain Robbe-Grillet, and the French *nouveau roman*.

9. Joyce's Achievement in A Portrait – an evaluation

And?   INTERROGATION
                                          (*Finnegans Wake*, p. 281)

It is a curious thing that during Joyce's lifetime *A Portrait* received a generally warmer reception among poets than among novelists – Yeats, Pound and Hart Crane are among those who found it an inspiring novel, perhaps because they found an affinity of poetic spirit in the struggles of its hero. However, the wider response to the novel has inevitably been affected, usually adversely, by comparisons with *Ulysses*, which appeared six years after *A Portrait*. The success of *Ulysses* has also tended to divert attention away from *A Portrait* as critics have preferred to concentrate on the former, justly regarded as Joyce's mature triumph and a novel which has had an enormous influence on twentieth-century literature and thinking.

However, *A Portrait* is a landmark in the progress of the novel, both in terms of its anticipation of the techniques of *Ulysses* and *Finnegans Wake*, and in its own right; a useful starting point in evaluating it as such a landmark is to compare it with Joyce's earlier draft for the novel, *Stephen Hero*. Whereas *A Portrait* is unequivocally a novel of this century, especially for its techniques, *Stephen Hero* is fixed firmly in the tradition of the nineteenth-century novel. The narrator is persistently intrusive and frequently intervenes by directly addressing the reader, to comment on the action and on Stephen. In addition, there are long passages of explicit description or comment; conversations are laboured though realistic; epiphanies have become diluted in their effect rather than being, as they are in *A Portrait*, tight and succinct. In general terms, the considerable explicit discussion in *Stephen Hero* of themes and the detailed explanation of attitudes and motives render the total effect ponderous.

One of the clearest differences between the two versions can be seen in the relative silence of the narrator in *A Portrait*. As we have discovered, material is presented more baldly and with greater discipline and economy, and the reader's imagination is aroused to fill the gaps; where *Stephen Hero* attempts to formulate or define, *A Portrait* instead seeks to communicate the actual intensity of experience itself, forcefully inviting the reader to share in it. But a further point which strikes the reader in comparing the two is that in *A Portrait* Stephen's artistic development is made its central theme; everything in the novel – characters, themes, techniques and point of view – is focused through it, unifying all the diverse elements of the novel.

There are fundamental differences between the two versions in the presentation of character – in *A Portrait* we see almost nothing of Stephen's brothers and sisters. In the earlier version his brother, Maurice, prominently fulfils the parts of confidant, confessor, and adviser (occupying the equivalent place in Stephen's life as Stanislaus in Joyce's); he is mentioned only once by name in *A Portrait* as a 'thick-headed ruffian' (p. 74). There is also more direct criticism of Mr Dedalus in *Stephen Hero* as the cause of the family's suffering, while Mrs Dedalus is shown as more vitally sympathetic to Stephen. In this respect she resembles Mrs Morel, mother of the artist in Lawrence's *Sons and Lovers*, trying to share her son's interests and appearing at least open-minded if not actually encouraging, to his radical ideas, (up to a point at least.) However, in *A Portrait*, unlike the mothers in either *Stephen Hero* or *Sons and Lovers*, Mrs Dedalus is realized only incompletely; her suffering is barely hinted at and she appears to exist, like so many of the other characters, simply as a foil to Stephen's character.

Comparing the two versions, the overall effect of these changes in Stephen's relationships is a marked intensification in his isolation. In *Stephen Hero*, Stephen's isolation comes about as a result of his ideas and the hostility of those around him, making him appear to a large extent a victim of his situation, whereas in *A Portrait* his isolation is of his own making, the result of his own withdrawal, a deliberate policy of self-exile making him cold and lacking in human feeling.

On the other hand, it is principally Joyce's technical innovations which stamp the novel as a great leap forward and which established both it and Joyce in the foreground of the Modernist movement. The way of Stephen's mind was something new in literature and the free approach of Joyce's presentation reflects this apparent emancipation. As we have seen, one of the chief among the novel's innovations is the modulation of styles to parallel and reinforce changes in Stephen's life, continually varying the distances and relationships between narrator and character and reader to facilitate both comment and humour, creating a dynamic flux of surfaces and tensions. In this way Joyce essentially fuses together his subject matter and its form, components traditionally treated in isolation, with Stephen Dedalus thus becoming the total experience of the novel (an approach which prepares us for that in *Ulysses* with its even more radical experiments in style and language).

We have seen how the need for such modulation arises, partly as a result of Joyce's avowed approach of employing a *silent* narrator to exclude all direct authorial intrusion into the novel for direct comment. To retain control, Joyce is prompted into adopting a range of alternative techniques. By far the most effective of these is the use of the dual consciousness – Stephen's and the narrator's – to retain the intimacy of the first-person form of narration while at the same time allowing some degree of comment by way of the mature perspective of the narrator. The stream-of-consciousness method of presenting Stephen's develop-ment, together with Joyce's unique use of epiphanies for disposing the story, brilliantly cultivates the novel's structure, issuing organically from within the consciousness of the novel's hero rather than being imposed from outside by an explicit narrator.

These are techniques which find their full maturity in *Ulysses* though there is no sense in which *A Portrait* is less accomplished in what it sets out to achieve. Indeed, in comparing *A Portrait* and *Ulysses*, the earlier novel usually appears less rigorously organized by its techniques which are less foregrounded, making it also appear lyrical and naturalistic. However, it is through comparison with the rich universe of *Ulysses* that the weaknesses of *A Portrait* also become most apparent.

Essentially, the problems of the novel are the problems of its central figure. Next to *Ulysses* and even to *Dubliners*, *A Portrait* comes through as a sombre, earnest production but lacking most in humour and almost completely in human warmth, a direct consequence of the mani-fest limitations of its main character. There is none of the vigorous wit and philosophical irony of the genial *Dubliners* and of *Ulysses*, while Joyce's own waggish satire is only hinted at – for instance, in the visit to Cork, and briefly in the Christmas dinner scene.

Another source of dissatisfaction with *A Portrait* is, ironically, the novel's point of view and the consciousness itself of its central character. We have already considered how the strict discipline of the novel's viewpoint through Stephen's eyes helps to create intimacy and at the same time to emphasize his solitude. Yet it also engineers an intense claustrophobia which in Chapter 3 helps to consolidate the themes of guilt and entrapment, but by Chapter 5 becomes oppressive and weary-ing. More important is the effect of Stephen's own limitations on that viewpoint. One of the novel's chief drawbacks is the character of Ste-phen himself, especially aspects like his callous pride, lack of humanity and obsessively dogmatic attitude to life. These inevitably contribute to the narrowness of the novel's vision – not only do we see a shrinking of his capacity and willingness to embrace life, but we also see this brought about through the flawed mentality of Stephen. Joyce himself, when considering a central character for *Ulysses*, dismissed the possibility of using Stephen, describing him as an 'immature persona', having a shape that cannot easily be changed, after it appears to be hardened in that posture at the end of *A Portrait*. Because of these limitations, Stephen is unable to reflect positively – as we see him begin to do in the 'Proteus' chapter of *Ulysses* – except in terms of arrogance and egoism. Consequently, there is no genuine sense of sustained inner conflict and thus neither the creative tension nor the humanity which would otherwise have been generated. Any possibility of true self-realization within the range of the novel is excluded, and it concludes unsympathetically with Stephen not so much blind as wilful. While the need for self-realization is highlighted in the closing pages with the insistence of Cranly and Mrs Dedalus on the requirement for ordinary humanity, Stephen himself coldly records on the final page:

She prays now, she says, that I may learn in my own life and away from home and friends what the heart is and what it feels. Amen.   (p. 257)

But it is not treated seriously by Stephen until the early chapters of *Ulysses*, and is not made real until his momentous encounter with Leopold Bloom in that novel.

Just as Joyce's relationship with Stephen Dedalus is something new in the novel, so the novel itself was never the same again after *A Portrait*; its enduring significance is as a major landmark in the development of Modernism, issuing principally from the crisis of confidence in the efficacy of the word. It is typified here in the instability of the text and of the moral stances; the undermining of established author–reader relationships, and their replacement with confrontational authorial silences; the primacy of myth and the new psychological realities, expressed through archetype, symbol, epiphany, and the stream of consciousness. If Stephen's closing words express the anxiety and doubt for his future, they also perfectly express the same doubt and uncertainty of the Modernist predicament. This is the achievement of *A Portrait*; the trick, as someone said, is living with it.

Notes

Full details of books referred to in shortened form will be found in the Selective Bibliography, p. 195.

1. James Joyce and Ireland: Background to *A Portrait*

1. The substance of this section is indebted, as any biography of Joyce must be, to Richard Ellmann's monumental *James Joyce*.

2. Compare with Stephen Dedalus's list of his father's attributes and occupations on p. 245.

3. See especially pp. 25–6 where Stephen feels sorry for his father because he is not, like the other boys' fathers, a magistrate.

4. See *Letters* II, 238.

5. 'Ibsen's New Drama' (1 April 1900). See *Letters* I, 51 and Ellmann, pp. 71–4.

6. See Ellmann, p. 156.

7. See *Letters* II, 165.

8. See *The Workshop of Daedalus* edited by Robert Scholes and Richard M. Kain.

9. In *Ulysses* (p. 173) Stephen reflects: 'Where is your brother? Apothecaries' hall. My whetstone. Him, then Cranly, Mulligan: now these.'

10. Joyce's reply, in a letter to Pound (9 April 1917), is typically jocular.

> There once was a lounger named Stephen
> Whose youth was most odd and uneven.
> > He throve on the smell
> > Of a horrible hell
> That a Hottentot wouldn't believe in.

> (*Letters* I, 102)

For a collection of early criticism of *A Portrait*, see *James Joyce: The Critical Heritage*.

2. A Commentary on the Novel and Joyce's Themes

1. Compare the scene with that Christmas dinner in 'The Dead' (*Dubliners*, pp. 177–8).

2. Compare with Little Chandler in 'A Little Cloud' (*Dubliners*, p. 76).

3. Pp. 69–70.

4. See the motto to the novel on the title page.

5. See Acts 7:58.

6. As the corks do in 'Ivy Day in the Committee Room' (*Dubliners*, pp. 121–3).

7. In spite of his comment about Lessing and statues it is clear from Stephen's definition that he has literature foremost in his mind (see pp. 218–19).

8. Stanislaus Joyce records that his brother destroyed all but five of his early poems, among which was this villanelle which he regarded as worthy enough to preserve (*My Brother's Keeper*, p. 158).

3. Icarus Allsorts: Characterization

1. *My Brother's Keeper*, pp. 39 and 67.

2. Compare the foot of p. 179 with p. 250.

3. This theme of injustice is characteristic of Joyce's work as a whole, especially in *Dubliners* (see 'A Mother' and 'The Boarding House').

4. For the significance of Tim Healy, see Chapter 1, p. 18.

5. See p. 190 and Joyce's short story 'Grace' (*Dubliners*).

6. In his diary for 8 June 1904, the architect Joseph Holloway recorded a visit to a friend that evening, after a music competition, where he met a 'Mr J. Joyce, a strangely aloof, silent youth, with weird, penetrating, large eyes, which he frequently shaded with his hand and with a half-bashful, faraway expression on his face. Later he sat in a corner and gazed at us all from under his brows in an uncomfortable way and said little or nothing all evening. He is a strange boy. I cannot forget him.'

7. Throughout *Ulysses* Stephen is racked by remorse ('agenbite of inwit') at having refused his mother's dying plea to him to make his Easter duty. He prays to her memory to reveal to him the secret of love's bitter mystery, 'Tell me the word, mother, if you know now. The word known to all men.' (*Ulysses*, p. 474; see also *Ulysses*, p. 41).

8. He experiences his first separation from his mother and it is (at this moment) without regret, 'noiseless'.

9. For example, see Joyce's short story 'A Little Cloud' in which Chandler aspires to the courage and enterprise of his hero Gallaher but gets no further than wishing.

10. For a more extreme version compare Farrington in the short story 'Counterparts' (*Dubliners*).

11. See also *Ulysses*, pp. 195–6.

12. The theme of the absent father is developed in full in *Ulysses* in which Stephen–Telemachus, a fatherless son, meets Leopold Bloom, a sonless father.

13. In *Ulysses*, Father Conmee reappears as the patronizing rather than paternal representative of the Church against the State (*Ulysses*, p. 180; see also *Ulysses*, p. 458).

14. In *My Brother's Keeper* Stanislaus, a more virulent anti-Catholic than his brother, claims that the Church deliberately kept the faithful in ignorance of the Bible (p. 114).

15. Ironically, the Tsar's pacifism was probably a gesture aimed at stalling for time while Russia built up its own weapons before the war with Japan (1904–5).

16. Dublin's racecourse.

17. Byrne helped Joyce consolidate his love for Nora Barnacle against the machinations of another friend, Vincent Cosgrave (used as the basis for the character of Lynch in *A Portrait*). However, Joyce appears to have given Cranly faintly homosexual tendencies on account of Byrne's jealousy over Cosgrave's friendship with Joyce. See Chapter 2, p. 68.

18. See Ellmann, p. 629.

4. 'the spell of arms and voices': Joyce, Dedalus and the Idea of the Artist

1. Dublin was at this time in the grip of the commercial theatre, especially of the English touring companies, specializing in spectacle and melodramas on popular subjects, with no interest in the intellectual movements stirring in the theatres of Scandinavia, Paris and London.

2. See *The Critical Writings of James Joyce*, p. 71. Edward Martyn was a close friend of George Moore and a fervent nationalist who founded the Irish Literary Theatre which staged Yeats's *The Countess Cathleen*.

3. *Critical Writings of James Joyce*, p. 71.

4. Another reason for Joyce's animosity towards Moore was that he had been snubbed by him; see Ellmann, pp. 135 and 529 and *Ulysses*, p. 158.

5. See Ibsen's *Ghosts and Other Plays*, translated by Peter Watts, Penguin Books, 1964. (In this edition, the title has been translated as 'A Public Enemy'.)

6. Like Gabriel Conroy in 'The Dead' (*Dubliners*).

7. See also letter by Joyce, 7 February 1905, *Letters* II, 81.

8. See Father Arnall's words extolling the missionary zeal of St Francis Xavier, p. 111.

9. Compare with *Stephen Hero*, p. 36.

10. In *Ulysses* Stephen proclaims that Irish art can be summed up as 'The cracked lookingglass of a servant.' (*Ulysses*, p. 6).

11. Compare with Stephen's diary entry for 6 April (p. 255).

12. 'Remember your epiphanies written on green oval leaves, deeply deep, copies to be sent if you died to all the great libraries of the world, including Alexandria?' (*Ulysses*, p. 34; see also *Stephen Hero*, p. 188).

13. In *Stephen Hero* when Stephen Dedalus defines 'epiphany', he shows

that even a clock is capable of spiritual realization (*Stephen Hero*, p. 189; see also Chapter 7 of this book).

14. In 'A Little Cloud', Chandler strives vainly amid the fury of home life to capture the right inspirational mood: 'He wondered whether he could write a poem . . .' (*Dubliners*, p. 67).

15. See p. 107, 'On Sunday mornings . . .'

16. Joyce twice tried to take legal action over these dealings, and eventually resorted to an open letter to the press (17 August 1911) in an attempt to embarrass Grant Richards (see *Letters* II, 291–3).

5. The Method in His Madness: the Narrator

1. At least one critic has noted another possibility – of not just one but two narrators (in addition to Stephen's point of view), because after Chapter 4 the style changes; the narrator of Chapters 1–4 is more sympathetic to the younger Stephen than the narrator of Chapter 5 which has a more distant relationship with the subject.

2. Frank Budgen, *James Joyce and the Making of* Ulysses, 1972, p. 94.

3. Édouard Dujardin, *Le Monologue intérieur* (1931).

4. Blake too (one of Joyce's favourite poets) may have been a source for this idea: 'Without Contraries is no progression.' (*The Marriage of Heaven and Hell*, Penguin Books, 1958, p. 94).

6. Language and Style in *A Portrait*

1. Compare with the 'Aeolus' section (pp. 96–123) of *Ulysses* where Joyce makes a more systematic parody of formal rhetoric.

2. See p. 141, 'Creatures were in the field . . .'

3. See *Letters* I, 365 (1 May 1935). In the same breath Joyce called him a 'tiresome footling little Anglican parson'.

4. A journey which anticipates that greater odyssey of style in *Ulysses*.

5. These fragments resemble Joyce's own epiphanies jotted down by himself and Stanislaus in youth, and from which *A Portrait* eventually grew (see *The Workshop of Daedalus* by Scholes and Kain).

7. Content and Significant Form: Joyce's concept of 'Epiphany'

1. Although both the stream of consciousness and the epiphany appear to originate in the psychological theories of the early years of this century, chiefly those of Freud, Jung, and William James (see Chapter 8 below on Modernism), Joyce always denied any knowledge of these until much later when he began work on *Finnegans Wake*.

2. The Impressionists also saw their work as recording 'delicate and evanescent moments'. Monet described an attempt to record a series of epiphanies:

'I am working terribly hard, struggling with a series of effects, but ... the sun sets so fast that I cannot follow it ... but the more I continue, the more I see that a great deal of work is necessary in order to succeed in rendering that which I seek: "instantaneity" especially the "envelope" the same light spreading everywhere ...'

3. Hopkins recorded in his journal: 'I saw the inscape though freshly, as if my eye were still growing, though with a companion the eye and the ear are for the most part shut and instress cannot come' (12 December 1872); and 'All the world is full of inscape and chance left free to act falls into an order as well as purpose: looking out of my window I caught it in the random clods and broken heaps of snow made by the cast of a broom' (24 February 1873), both in *Poems and Prose of Gerard Manley Hopkins*, ed. W. H. Gardner, Penguin Books, 1953, pp. 127 and 128 respectively.

4. Virginia Woolf, 'Modern Fiction', in *Collected Essays*, Vol. II, Hogarth Press, 1987.

5. Virginia Woolf, *Moments of Being*, Triad Panther, 1978, p. 92.

6. ibid., p. 142.

8. the word made fresh: Modernism and the Revolution of the Word

1. Joyce once told his brother Stanislaus: 'Don't talk to me about politics. I'm only interested in style.' *My Brother's Keeper*, p. 23.

2. Virginia Woolf, 'Modern Fiction', in *Collected Essays*, Vol. II, Hogarth Press, 1987.

3. In his essay 'Inside the Whale' George Orwell thought that this pessimism was the central trait uniting the Modernist writers – Joyce, Eliot, Pound and others – a pessimism that grew out of the failure of the public values in language and manners which had sustained the world of the Edwardian novelists.

4. Joyce's short story 'Counterparts' gives a grim unromantic picture of one character's response to office routines (*Dubliners*; see also 'A Little Cloud').

5. Joyce also claimed that the German version of his name was 'Freud'.

6. 'Ulysses: A Monologue', 1932, reprinted in *James Joyce: The Critical Heritage*, Vol. II, p. 583.

7. For a discussion of Joyce's stream-of-consciousness technique see Chapter 5.

8. Mallarmé's typographical experiments in *Un coup de dès jamais n'abolira le hasard* (1897) and Apollinaire's poetic ideograms tried to some extent to make typography endorse meaning, and painters such as Duchamp and the early Dadaists employed word games and puns in paintings and their titles for ironic comment on the relationship between language and reality.

9. For example, Virginia Woolf's *The Waves*, William Faulkner's *The Sound and the Fury*, and *Finnegans Wake*.

10. Compare with Stephen Dedalus's principle of 'silence, exile, and cunning' (p. 251).

11. Virginia Woolf, 'Mr Bennett and Mrs Brown', in *Collected Essays*, Vol. I, (in the same essay she complained of the 'indecency' of *Ulysses* and T. S. Eliot's 'obscurity').

12. Compare with André Gide's *The Counterfeiters* in which his central figure, Édouard, a novelist, is also writing a novel called *The Counterfeiters*.

13. This anticipates the decentred universe of *Ulysses* in which the experience of the novel is synthesized through its numerous consciousnesses, in contrast to the single viewpoint of the traditional novel.

14. Virginia Woolf, 'Modern Fiction', in *Collected Essays*, Vol. II, Hogarth Press, 1987.

15. For Joyce's use of epiphany in *A Portrait*, see Chapter 7.

Selective Bibliography

Works by Joyce:

Dubliners, Jonathan Cape/Grafton Books, first published 1914
Exiles, Jonathan Cape/Grafton Books, first published 1918
Finnegans Wake, Faber & Faber, first published 1939
The Critical Writings of James Joyce, (edited by Elsworth Mason and Richard Ellmann), Faber & Faber, 1959

Biographical:

Chester G. Anderson, *James Joyce*, Thames and Hudson, 1986
C. P. Curran, *James Joyce Remembered*, Oxford University Press, 1968
Richard Ellmann, *James Joyce*, Oxford University Press, 1982 (revised edition)
Stuart Gilbert and Richard Ellmann (eds.), *Letters of James Joyce*, Vols. I, II, III, Faber & Faber, 1957 and 1966
Stanislaus Joyce, *My Brother's Keeper*, Faber & Faber, 1982
Kevin Sullivan, *Joyce Among the Jesuits*, Columbia University Press, 1958

Critical:

Morris Beja, *Epiphany in the Modern Novel*, Peter Owen, 1971
Morris Beja (ed.), *James Joyce:* Dubliners *and* A Portrait*: a Casebook*, Macmillan, 1973
Sydney Bolt, *A Preface to James Joyce*, Longman, 1981
Malcolm Bradbury and James McFarlane (eds.), *Modernism: 1890–1930*, Penguin Books, 1976
Frank Budgen, *James Joyce and the Making of* Ulysses, Oxford University Press, 1972
Anthony Burgess, *Here Comes Everybody: An Introduction to James Joyce for the Ordinary Reader*, Faber & Faber, 1965
James Connolly, *Joyce's Portrait: Criticisms and Critiques*, Peter Owen, 1964
Robert H. Deming, *James Joyce: The Critical Heritage*, 2 vols., RKP, 1970

Critical Studies: A Portrait of the Artist as a Young Man

Don Gifford, *Joyce Annotated: Notes for* Dubliners *and* A Portrait, University of California Press, 1982

John Gross, *Joyce*, Fontana, 1971

Hugh Kenner, *Dublin's Joyce*, Chatto and Windus, 1955

Harry Levin, *James Joyce: A Critical Introduction*, Faber & Faber, 1960

Marvin Magalaner and Richard M. Kain, *Joyce: The Man, The Work, The Reputation*, Greenwood, 1979

William T. Noon, *Joyce and Aquinas*, Yale University Press, 1957

Patrick Parrinder, *James Joyce*, Cambridge University Press, 1984

C. H. Peake, *James Joyce: The Citizen and the Artist*, Edward Arnold, 1977

Robert Scholes and Richard M. Kain (eds.), *The Workshop of Daedalus: James Joyce and the Raw Materials for* A Portrait, Northwestern University Press, 1965

Thomas F. Staley and Bernard Benstock (eds.), *Approaches to Joyce's* Portrait: *Ten Essays*, University of Pittsburgh, 1976

William York Tindall, *A Reader's Guide to James Joyce*, Thames and Hudson, 1960

FOR THE BEST IN PAPERBACKS, LOOK FOR THE 🐧

In every corner of the world, on every subject under the sun, Penguin represents quality and variety – the very best in publishing today.

For complete information about books available from Penguin – including Puffins, Penguin Classics and Arkana – and how to order them, write to us at the appropriate address below. Please note that for copyright reasons the selection of books varies from country to country.

In the United Kingdom: Please write to *Dept E.P., Penguin Books Ltd, Harmondsworth, Middlesex, UB7 0DA.*

If you have any difficulty in obtaining a title, please send your order with the correct money, plus ten per cent for postage and packaging, to *PO Box No 11, West Drayton, Middlesex*

In the United States: Please write to *Dept BA, Penguin, 299 Murray Hill Parkway, East Rutherford, New Jersey 07073*

In Canada: Please write to *Penguin Books Canada Ltd, 2801 John Street, Markham, Ontario L3R 1B4*

In Australia: Please write to the *Marketing Department, Penguin Books Australia Ltd, P.O. Box 257, Ringwood, Victoria 3134*

In New Zealand: Please write to the *Marketing Department, Penguin Books (NZ) Ltd, Private Bag, Takapuna, Auckland 9*

In India: Please write to *Penguin Overseas Ltd, 706 Eros Apartments, 56 Nehru Place, New Delhi, 110019*

In the Netherlands: Please write to *Penguin Books Netherlands B.V., Postbus 195, NL–1380AD Weesp*

In West Germany: Please write to *Penguin Books Ltd, Friedrichstrasse 10–12, D–6000 Frankfurt/Main 1*

In Spain: Please write to *Longman Penguin España, Calle San Nicolas 15, E–28013 Madrid*

In Italy: Please write to *Penguin Italia s.r.l., Via Como 4, I-20096 Pioltello (Milano)*

In France: Please write to *Penguin Books Ltd, 39 Rue de Montmorency, F-75003 Paris*

In Japan: Please write to *Longman Penguin Japan Co Ltd, Yamaguchi Building, 2–12–9 Kanda Jimbocho, Chiyoda-Ku, Tokyo 101*